# Guilty Pleasures:
*William Wordsworth's*
*Poetry of Psychoanalysis*

by
Richard D. McGhee

The Whitston Publishing Company
Troy, New York
1993

## ACKNOWLEDGMENTS

A portion of the chapter entitled "A Sober Coloring" appeared earlier in an essay published in *Literature and Psychology*, Vol. 31, No. 1 (1986); for permission to reprint this portion, I am grateful to Mr. Morton Kaplan, Editor in Chief, *Literature and Psychology*.

I am also grateful to Robert F. Kruh and the Kansas State University Bureau of General Research for several grants supporting my research. I am particularly grateful to Rob Grindell, my department head, for relief from teaching duties to make some extensive revision of the manuscript. For her special encouragement and interest in this book, Naomi Ossar, my student, colleague, and friend, has put me in her debt more times than she can know. My wife Marie keeps me always in her debt, as she must know better than anyone. My daughter Beth and my sister Bonnie Sue will understand, better than most, the special appropriateness of the dedication, although my mother, Golda Lucille, will see the point of it as she was the beginning of it.

# PREFACE

*Guilty Pleasures* is an essay in understanding Wordsworth's poetry as a whole writing of the man. It is aimed at recognizing continuities from the earliest to the latest work. Its method is based upon a simple premise that Wordsworth is a poet of psycho-analysis, that his poetry is a record of an unending analysis. He knew he was this kind of poet, which is one of the reasons we still read his writings with great interest. This essay postulates a common identity of purpose between Wordsworth's kind of poetry and Freud's kind of psycho-analogy—a deep analysis of self as a construct of language, expanding to become a deep analysis of history and society. Because Freud is now so permanently established in our ways of approaching matters of psyche, his terms are used frequently here as figures of understanding what Wordsworth's poetic structures and strategies accomplish, or fail to accomplish.

Many readings of Wordsworth's poetry have taken the psychological, sometimes the psycho-analytical, route into their understandings of his work. My bibliographies acknowledge my debt to these readings, as well as to others which have taken different routes. My book differs from most studies by predecessors in these ways: (1) it assumes a common identity between Wordsworth as poet and Wordsworth as psycho-analyst; (2) it unabashedly accepts the Freudian metaphors and models as useful to reading; (3) it is not interested in a reductive analysis of Freudian limitations, but rather in an enriched appreciation of Wordsworthian texts; (4) it is a sustained reading of the Wordsworthian canon as a logical process of the psyche in volution, discovering itself as it makes itself in artifacts of writing; (5) it offers focused readings of major poems in the context of the psychoanalytical milieu of Wordsworth's canon; (6) it proposes the thesis that Wordsworth's "decline" is a paradoxical consequence of his successful identification with the ego-ideal of his long-dead father: this identification came only after long resistance and deep screening by the poet. This last point is an important difference, since most psycho-analytical readings have emphasized, understandably, Wordsworth's more conscious working over of his memories of his mother's death, screening *those* memories in various defensive ways. I suggest that even his mother's death was remembered as a kind of screening defense against feelings the poet associated with his father's death.

# CONTENTS

## DEDICATION

*For Marie, as always,
and for our sons,
Bill and Dave.*

*In memory of my father,
Wai-da-Sut-te
(1920-1987)*

William Wordsworth at Age 28
by W. Shuter

*from* The Wordsworth Collection, Department of Rare Books,
Cornell University Library
by permission

# GUILTY PLEASURES:
# WILLIAM WORDSWORTH'S
# POETRY OF PSYCHOANALYSIS

## CHAPTER ONE:

## My Father's House

*WORDSWORTH* makes poetry of recognition—that dignity and spiritual health are results of mobile adjustments to changing demands of environment: psychic, natural, social, political, and religious. His poetry is a making of the self that is a construct of an earlier self. His making is, therefore, both a synthesis of present power of consciousness and past power of the un-conscious (he called it, variously, an under-power, an under-agent of the mind). But his making is also an analysis of past by present, of unconscious by conscious power, of the fatal by the free. Wordsworth's poetry is an analysis in the service of synthesis, forcing into the light of consciousness as much of the dis-easeful unconscious fantasy as it possibly can. Because the adult mind must contend with its own childish origins, even as it draws upon those origins, its struggle is paradoxically a rebirth of the very parent against whom the child had first to rebel. As we shall see, Wordsworth had eventually to become the father he imagined himself to be when he was a child, and his continuing career as a poet is a continuing creation of that identity.

*ALTHOUGH* the main principle of the leading ideas in

his Preface to the *Lyrical Ballads* of 1800 is a principle of pleasure, Wordsworth's argument is generally a protest against an art which merely offers pleasure as a retreat from reality, as a relaxation from tension. Since the current taste seemed to him in a generally diseased condition, art such as his poems offer should aim to excite and stimulate mental activity. They aim to cure the disease of the time, "a state of almost savage torpor." The mere pursuit of pleasure will lead invariably to mental flaccidity and spiritual depression, consequent to a persistent dependence upon external stimulants for gratification of the senses. Thus Wordsworth must tread a delicate line of moral and aesthetic interests; he wishes to excite imagination, and he wishes to appeal to what in the 1850 text he would call "the grand elementary principle of pleasure," but he wishes also to accomplish his ends "without the application of gross and violent stimulants."

Insofar as he may reach his audience, then, Wordsworth must appeal to man's need for pleasure, the gratification of the senses and the relaxation of psychological tensions. But since the most obvious disease of the age is a torpor of spirit and taste, the poet must seek to counteract the leading tendency to which his poems must appeal. He must, in other words, go beyond the pleasure principle, although not quite in the same sense as Freud has described it. Wordsworth aims not to go behind pleasure to find a more primitive instinct that uses pleasure to serve *its* ends, as Freud believed death to do; Wordsworth aims to heighten the mind's activity with such stimuli of reality that it will keep in continuous process the rhythms of tension followed by relaxation of tension. His poems would "follow the fluxes and refluxes of the mind when agitated by the great and simple affections of our nature." Wordsworth maintains as a general principle that "the end of Poetry is to produce excitement in coexistence with an overbalance of pleasure."

Reality as "excitement" can cause pain, as Wordsworth readily observes: if "the images and feelings have an undue proportion of pain connected with them, there is some danger that the excitement may be carried beyond its proper bounds." To discipline that excitement is an important function of the artist, and so he adds "something regular, something to which the mind has been accustomed when in an unexcited or a less excited state." He goes on to explain how "the music of harmonious metrical language" with its "blind association of pleasure" can provide the discipline necessary for the art of poetry. While discussing the function of meter, Wordsworth takes extraordinary care to emphasize the *secondary* importance of pleasure, as the restraint and boundary to mental excitement.

If his poems are successful, they will excite and calm the mind in a manner consistent with the process of life itself, meeting reality with all its pains and tensions, but aiming for the ultimate gratifications and relaxations from tensions that life aims for. There is no mystery, therefore, in the reasons Wordsworth chose to make most of the new poems which he published in 1800 out of the subject matter of death, the final if not the primary instinct for relaxation, and the relationship of death with love. If his poetry can deal adequately with these subjects, balancing reality and tension with pleasure and relaxation, then his poems will indeed go beyond pleasure to find "a complex feeling of delight." "Delight," then, rather than "pleasure," is what the great artist aims for, "tempering the painful feeling which will always be found intermingled with powerful descriptions of the deeper passions." In several of his new poems in 1800, Wordsworth succeeded in creating this "complex feeling of delight."

In one of these, "Nutting," he describes the pleasure of destruction, emphasizing through imagery and tone how natural is this behavior, despite the ordinary attitude that

it is a perversion. Wordsworth takes care to explain that
the boy's behavior is a symptom of sexual desire that has
not been satisfied in a sexual manner. The poem elaborates the related insights that culture resists the aggressiveness of sexuality, and that nature encourages regression to
submissiveness. In the published version of 1800, "Nutting" opens in a tone of eagerness and excitement as the
boy anticipates his great adventure of the day. He sets
forth in the manner of an epic hero, and he overcomes the
obstacles of resistance by an adversary nature. Then he
comes upon a sacred spot, a place nature has tried to protect, "A virgin scene." Here begins the special Wordsworthian transaction, in a spot of time, where mind and nature come together even as they stand apart. In this gap is
a wound of nature through which healing and creativity
can occur. The boy's adventure has been until this point a
socially acceptable way of expending otherwise destructive
passions. Pausing before the object of his quest, the boy
engages in a foreplay of erotic excitement: "breathing with
such suppression of the heart / As joy delights in," "with
wise restraint voluptuous."

He dallies awhile "in that sweet mood when pleasure
loves to pay / Tribute to ease." This fore-play, however, is
unlike the pleasure of genital excitement, raising tensions
that will drive the self for release. It is rather the pleasure
of infantile sexuality, before genital organization, when
tension is immediately released by an environment organized to gratify every need of the infant. From that state
of dependence upon the mother, or upon Nature as
Mother, the young soul will strive to separate itself in its
drive for life and love, as does the young hero of Wordsworth's poem, when he rises to assault the very environment from which he has drawn such passive pleasure. He
enacts the important psychological truth that "erotic mastery" requires an element of destruction.

What pleasure the young hero gets from his assault is

immediately mixed with a certain, peculiar, kind of pain: "I felt a sense of pain when I beheld / The silent trees, and saw the intruding sky." At some cost, he has successfully separated himself from the efforts by nature to keep him submissive, to keep him dependent in a passive way on nature's secure gratifications. This separation from nature is crucial for healthy mental growth if the individual is ever to find his own identity. But since the primal experience of life is infant dependence on the mother, individuals are always tempted into constant regressions of this kind when they search for a loved one to substitute for mother.

On the other hand, culture insists on separation of the child from the authority of its parents, however much nature might resist that separation. Wordsworth has glimpses of the differential, the overflow of love not satisfied by culturally approved objects of love. This differential is an instance of romantic irony, the abyss or wound of nature, out of which can come the creative pain of guilt. Simply put, the excess is love intended for mother and not deceived by her substitute. Culture dooms a person to the restless pursuit of sexual satisfaction that cannot be approved. The pain felt by Wordsworth's young hero in "Nutting" is a punishment dealt quite as much by his culturally acquired conscience as it is by nature itself. In fact, the pain is a complex function of nature in conflict with culture, of mother in conflict with father as they compete in the mind of the child for the love of the child. This pain is still another sign that Wordsworth knows how it is finally "impossible to adjust the claims of the sexual instinct to the demands of civilization." It does not much matter in Wordsworth's poems whether such pain as this young hero feels comes from a successful separation from nature (through "assault"—a form of egoism) or as a successful reunion with nature (a form of infantile regression), because either form of behavior will put the self in conflict

with the other. The intruder is the boy who has let the
sky into an enclosed space, and while he may feel that he
has violated a taboo when he forced nature to give up its
"quiet being," he has brought himself closer to his own
life's aim in doing so.

*WORDSWORTH'S* subject would be increasingly social
and historical as he directed his analysis outwards from the
individual to the culture which is fashioned by the repressed and sublimated desires of individuals. Even when
his poetry becomes colored by religious language, it is always secular in its main emphasis, and even when his subject is social or political, his method is psychological. The
new poems he published in 1807 show that Wordsworth
has a confidence of style and clarity of purpose that are
lacking in much of his earlier poetry. Some of these new
poems are among the finest in our language, in part because Wordsworth has successfully realized the goal of psychoanalysis for himself as man and poet: to strengthen the
ego, to make it more independent of the super-ego so
that it can draw more forcefully upon its own reserves of
psychic energy and widen its field of perception to do the
work of culture. He made himself the subject of his greatest poem, brought to completion during the period of
writing the new poems for the 1807 volume, and thereby
he learned how art can strengthen the ego by bringing
about a reconciliation of the pleasure-principle with the re-
ality-principle. The artist can make truth out of fiction, because he takes the individual's experience of dejection or
dissatisfaction that comes from renunciation and incorporates it with reality: he makes the dissatisfaction itself into
a new reality.

Many of the new poems published in 1807 are the analytical exercises of a healthy ego widening its field of perception while strengthening its own organization. They
are reviews of the mind as it works to adjust pleasure with

reality, happiness with unhappiness, and relaxation with tension. They take the speakers beyond pleasure without denying the importance of pleasure, and they reach out for a larger embrace of reality without losing contact with the individual and his mental complexities. Among those complexities are the relationships of past, present, and future, the balance of duty (super-ego) with desire (id), the increasingly critical struggle between eros and death, and the pressure to construct and maintain a healthy ego through an existence in a state of permanent crisis.

Wordsworth's poems utilize various metaphors as strategies for keeping the ego strong and healthy, including his famous ones of "natural piety" and "spots of time." These two metaphors are related by their interests in the continuity of time from the past into the present, and by their use Wordsworth emphasizes an important principle of his psycho-analysis: to free the ego from bondage to the past. This freedom is not simple and easy, however; it cannot come from a denial of the authority of the past, for that would merely bury it in the uncontrollable reaches of the unconscious where it could grow "like a fungus in the dark" to become the ghosts of moral and neurotic anxiety. The fantasies of conscience as well as those of the passions must be kept under control by a healthy ego, and to do that it is necessary to keep them in the clear light of consciousness. By this means one comes to terms with life, enduring with dignity the unhappiness that must result when one renounces the pleasures of unreality and accepts the pain of reality.

Wordsworth is increasingly interested in the fantasies of culture, those structures of pleasure that seduce the ego into a flight from everyday, common pains and problems into grandiose schemes of power and social harmony. But in most of his new poems of 1807 he keeps his interest in the struggle to control the fantasies of individual passions. Realizing that "the Child is father of the Man," he frequently examines the child-like sources of adult feelings and desires. Recognizing such feelings for what they are and from whence they come gives the adult speaker a power to command and direct them to realistic ends. Childhood's fantasies of pleasure are a source of energy which will drive even if they are not directed, but they are a reality within the self from which it may not cut itself away without disastrous consequences to its health and identity. In several of the 1807 poems he records brief accounts of the daily battles one fights along the way to ultimate victory, but it is in *The Prelude* that Wordsworth records most fully the battle of the ego to keep its hold on health by keeping control of its childhood.

*IN The Prelude* Wordsworth deliberately divided himself to examine himself, becoming at once audience and actor, analyst and patient, God and creature. The poem has been much praised for its innovative adaptations from conventional aesthetic tradition, but it could never be so highly acclaimed if Wordsworth had not created his own audience or, at least, shaped the mind of his posterity to become receptive to his new form and his new subject matter. We are in a better position than Wordsworth's contemporaries or immediate posterity to appreciate the novelty of his poetic form. Because of Freud and psychoanalysis, we can see more exactly what Wordsworth was up to, and we can honor with applause his heroic accomplishment.

*The Prelude* features a paradoxical combination of strength and weakness, of self-confidence undermined by self-doubt, and affirmation drained by negation. Quickly in the first book, the poet discovers that his powers of assertion are deflected from objects of his consciousness; he suffers from symptoms of manic-depression, enthusiasm disintegrating into paralysis of will. The first book sets forth the exact nature of his problem: freedom without direction, a condition of consciousness that shackles the will and conceals a disease of the spirit. Within himself is a force at work more insidiously than the Adversary of Milton's great epic on which *The Prelude* is a critical commentary, and Wordsworth's task is better recognized by comparing his problem with that of his predecessor poet-analyst. Milton knew already the illness as well as the cure for his patient, mankind, but Wordsworth does not even know that he is ill until he attempts to assert his health. Milton's hero, Adam, had his innocence to protect him from the Adversary, and when Adam surrendered himself he did so with complete consciousness of his deed; Wordsworth's Adversary is the poet's own past experience, with which he must struggle to give it a shape of consciousness, and his innocence is his weakness until the poet makes a synthesis of his past with his present.

*The Prelude* becomes possible as a therapeutic adventure when the poet begins to recognize that he is mentally ill. His recovery becomes possible when he acknowledges the existence in himself of a repressed power at work thwarting his conscious will. Much of the poem is a record of this process of acknowledgment, beginning as negation and concluding as affirmation. The first books are therefore preoccupied with symbols of negation, when the poet's intellect admits through negative constructions that it is keeping a part of the mind in a repressed condition, but at the same time the poet does not accept as an affect what is being repressed. The strange experiences of the early books are consequences of this struggle between acknowledgment and denial, acts of judgment which manifest in the behavior of language how intensely the mind is caught in a struggle between eros and death. Before he can affirm the self as a healthy ego, the poet must pass beyond the negative acknowledgment of his unconscious life to a rediscovery of objects in perception which originally fed his mind and which have been split into realms of the unconscious. He must *re*find what once came naturally from the reality of the external world, then attempt to connect, or reconnect, the affective powers of his unconscious with the intellectual powers of his conscious mind. If he is successful, the poet will integrate himself into a healthy ego that draws upon all its resources, keeping both eros and death in subordinate service. As a poet, he is in a favored position because one of the keys to psycho-analysis is mastery of language: he can connect the unconscious with the conscious mind if he can connect words with memories (articulating the repressed), and memories with perception (recognizing reality).

*DURING* and after his composition of the 1805-6 *Prelude,* Wordsworth wrote many poems which expressed his deepening insights into the psychological development of mankind. His own psychology continued to a be a subject of interest to himself as a poet, but he was increasingly interested in the psychologies of others, whether those who were well known or those utterly unknown. Wordsworth is able during this period of his life, between 1802 and 1816, to develop a disinterested view of human development. This became possible because he was acquiring a masterful control over his instincts and his super-ego, over his imagination, and he was learning how to organize passions and ideals into controlled statement. By his own self-analysis he was able to recognize the importance of transforming the power of instinct into culturally approved activities. He realized the psychological and cultural value of redirecting the aims of primitive instincts, of transmuting infantile objects of desire into ego-ideals that serve to protect the self against the ravages of unconscious powers. Finally, he wrote much in prose and poetry about the importance of heroic standards for individual and national behavior. He knew the crucial importance of a social equivalent for the individual's super-ego, because he knew that civilization, like a healthy ego, must call upon heroes or gods for help against the ravages of undisciplined passion.

Concepts of control, paralleling his insights into his own ego's development, are abundant throughout this period of work. Wordsworth's task as an artist is to control, subdue, and transmute, as he says of "The Happy Warrior." Both the poet and the warrior are skillful in self-knowledge, able to raise "natural instinct" into "moral being" and so find comfort in themselves. When he says that the Happy Warrior succeeds because he "hath wrought / Upon the plan that pleased his boyish thought" even while doing "the tasks of real life," Wordsworth not only emphasizes again the importance of his belief that the child is father of the man, but he is also implementing his notion of true culture as a free play of the imagination. Even the Warrior "plays, in the many games of life, that one / Where what he most doth value must be won." As long as the individual is free to exercise his faculty of play, he will be able not only to survive as a civilized being, but he will also be able to defend himself against the very hero whose help he requires to assist in the process of making a civilization. Art as play is a major defense of civilization against social illness.

Because the health of the national spirit is like the health of the individual mind, Wordsworth frequently mixes the subjects of social and individual psyches. He teaches to others what he is learning from his own self-analysis, the importance of self-control, or ego dominance, the danger of uncontrolled fantasies from the unconscious, whether from below (id) or above (super-ego), and the value of imagination as a power of spiritual therapy and mental health. The artist can do something that not even the psycho-analyst can do—invite and engage the instincts of the audience to participate in a venture of sublimation. The therapist might provide himself as a medium for raising consciousness, through the technique of transference, but the artist can do something even more valuable—the artist can desexualize instincts, inhibit their aim while providing new objects of satisfaction. By emphasizing the importance of the self knowing itself, Wordsworth is often able to provide the utmost in psycho-analytical therapy. At the conclusion of *The Prelude* he celebrates his discovery of imagination as "intellectual love," wherein the power of primitive instinct is transformed into a noble activity of mind. He invites Coleridge to join him as a teacher to others of how they might learn better to raise their passions to higher levels of activity, where "the mind of man becomes / A thousand times more beautiful than the earth / On which he dwells." To achieve that height where love becomes intellectual, readers must so strengthen their egos that "the consciousness / Of whom they are is habitually infused / Through every image, and through every thought, / And all impressions." To make love intellectual is Wordsworth's conscious endeavor to secure civilization through an art of sublimation.

*IN* the lines from "Home at Grasmere" which he published as part of his advertisement for *The Excursion,* Wordsworth not only proclaimed that "the Mind of Man" is his "haunt, and the main region of his song," but he also said that he must sometimes forego this "main region" and "travel near the tribes / And fellowships of men." *The Excursion* emphasizes Wordsworth's secondary interest in the subjects of human society, even as it does not ignore his primary one for the Mind of Man. Indeed, this long poem shows Wordsworth's understanding that the mind, in Freud's words, "can be more easily detected in its behaviour in the cultural community than in the separate individual." Wordsworth's career took him more insistently in the direction of social and religious psychology after an early emphasis upon individual psychology. He began to concentrate his attention on those features of mind which manifested themselves in various social organizations and institutions.

The task of solving the problem of "accommodation between claims of the individual and the cultural claims of the group" is what Wordsworth proposed as a subject of his great poem *The Recluse,* of which *The Excursion* was to be a part. In *The Prelude* "genuine freedom" was found to be a function of the ego's power to renounce and control its instincts as well as to recognize and renounce the tyranny of its super-ego. So in *The Excursion* freedom and mental health are examined as problems for the ego in its constant battles with forces in the external world of nature as well as with those even more subtle forces in the internal world of the mind itself. To find happiness is the goal of *The Excursion,* but finding happiness is not any easier for the poet of *The Excursion* than it was for the author of *Civilization and Its Discontents.* Like Freud after him, Wordsworth championed the value of civilization as a means to educate the mind in the lessons of reality. But Wordsworth, again like Freud, knew that education is sometimes painful and that civilization is a benefit which commands a great cost. While he may not have gone as far as Freud did in condemning religion as an illusion of infancy (one that arrests mental growth), Wordsworth does nevertheless explore the possibilties for illusion in religious faith. In *The Excursion* he subjects not only religions but all ideas and ideals of civilization to an analysis which produces not much comfort and a great deal of discomfiting pain, but as an analysis of civilization *The Excursion* is still an education in reality.

THROUGHOUT the fifteen-or-so years that followed publication of *The Excursion* Wordsworth's faith in the therapeutic value of his art did not fade. During this period he composed and published three major poems, or col-

lections of poetry: *Memorials of a Tour on the Continent,*
in 1820; *The River Duddon: A Series of Sonnets,* also in
1820; and the *Ecclesiastical Sonnets, In Series,* in 1822 (as
*Ecclesiastical Sketches*). In addition, he published two important prose pieces, the "Preface to the Edition of
1815," with its "Essay, Supplementary to the Preface,"
and a political campaign pamphlet, *Two Addresses to the
Freeholders of Westmoreland,* in 1818. In these, the longer
and more ambitious pieces of his writing during the period, Wordsworth continued his life's work of spiritual healing through the art of language. He wrote a great many
short pieces (indeed, even long works are "series" of short
pieces), often occasional and sometimes insignificant, but
for the most part his poetry of this time continued to be
important as a sustained analysis of culture and mind.

Because he was sharply aware that many of his readers
approach poetry for values of religion, Wordsworth took
much care in the "Essay, Supplementary to the Preface" to
define both the affinities and the distinctions between religion and poetry. While his poetry approaches the confines of religious interests, he insisted upon keeping it centered in the mind. If he wished merely to please his
audience, to gratify its instincts and palliate its conscience,
Wordsworth felt that he might easily do so by reducing
his ambition and compromising his aesthetic principles. Instead, he chose the smaller audience made capable of spiritual tranquillity and mental health by virtue of the imaginative therapy which his poetry could provide. Thus he
wrote that

> in everything which is to send the soul into her-
> self, to be admonished of her weakness, or to be
> made conscious of her power;—wherever life and
> nature are described as operated upon by the crea-
> tive or abstracting virtue of the imagination; wher-
> ever the instinctive wisdom of antiquity and her

heroic passions uniting, in the heart of the poet, with the meditative wisdom of later ages, have produced that accord of sublimated humanity, which is at once a history of the remote past and a prophetic enunciation of the remotest future, there, the poet must reconcile himself for a season to a few and scattered hearers.

When he says that poetry should seek "to send the soul into herself" where it is "made conscious of her power," he insists that such poetry is produced from a heart where "the instinctive wisdom of antiquity" is united with "heroic passions" and "the meditative wisdom of later ages." The product is a therapeutic model for the reader, organizing his own mind into a harmony of individuality but also bringing him into what Wordsworth grandly calls "that accord of sublimated humanity." To achieve this accord is to participate in civilization, but to reach his achievement is no easy task for either the poet as analyst or for his reader as patient. Wordsworth sees the make-up of the soul in terms roughly analogous with Freud's dynamically conceived model of the mind. The idea of sublimated humanity which inspires Wordsworth's model is an idea that incorporates what Freud called "power of the present": life and nature are "operated upon by the creative or abstracting virtue of the imagination." This power is a function of the healthy ego, whose meditative wisdom is an accomplishment of union and balance between the "heroic passions" of the id and the "instinctive wisdom of antiquity" embodied in the super-ego. "Sublime consciousness of the soul" is achieved through this union and balance, and when enough members of the community achieve this consciousness, then that community might well be described as "sublimated humanity." Wordsworth then, like Freud after him, looked to his audience for the cooperation that would make for a healthier community, a cooperation which is a "relationship based on a love of truth—that is, on a recognition of reality."

In the period between 1814 and 1829 he wrote a poetry that collectively aims for producing a "sublime consciousness of the soul," calling upon his audience to share with him the analyst's responsibility for loving truth above all things, however complex and difficult it might be, but insisting that truth is above all a function of the mind in the act of knowing itself. While no one poem of this period exhausts the many themes, subjects, and symbols that Wordsworth employed, taken as a group with regard for their chronological relationships, these poems are a cross-section of main themes which preoccupy him as an analyst of the soul in the individual and in the community. In one group, he explored the way the mind becomes conscious of its "mighty and almost divine powers" generated by a tension of desire for home and duty to heaven; in this same group, he examined the tension of the mind torn between mundane preoccupations of passing time and aspirations for timeless beauty. Art is a sublimation of the instincts here as elsewhere, but it is most clearly perceived as a product of tension, though a balance, between love and death, between the id and the super-ego.

In another group, which includes some of his most notorious odes, Wordsworth examined the uses of military power for evil and for good. In these poems he attempted to provide an outlet for the instinct of destruction but also to set a limit on its power as a "heroic passion" of the id. In 1819 he set about to translate the first four books of Virgil's *Aeneid* (completing three), in which he practiced his art to set in balance again the instincts for love and destruction as they had been narrated in that great poem of classical antiquity. In yet another group, he wrote some of his loveliest lyrics devoted to eros, though not to say lust, for certainly sexual love remained a constant value to him, though it must be distinguished from what he called "rebellious passion." And, in a final group, he admitted for closer examination the affinities between religion and poetry when he devoted himself to the exquisite analysis of cultural history he called the *Ecclesiastical Sonnets*.

*THERE* is something of a settled quality about the poetry of Wordsworth's last two decades. Although there underlies this at the same time a continuing anxiety of loss and separations, the dominant note of his writing and in his life is one of achievement and integration: in himself, in his relations with others, and in his relationship with God. His appointment in 1813 as Distributor of Stamps was not only a mark of his need for a more secure income, but that appointment was of enormous psychological importance for him. This was so because the appointment was largely the work of Lord Lonsdale, heir to the same Lord who had been served by Wordsworth's father. By accepting the patronage of Lord Lonsdale, Wordsworth was putting himself into a place comparable with the one held by his father many years before. He "became" his father by this appointment, in this public form achieving for his identity a goal of mental development universally understood. Becoming his father not only put to rest an unsettled mental need, but it also restored the reputation of the man who had died so inconsiderately when his children had such desperate need for him. Because, as Wordsworth well understood through his continuing self-analysis in *The Prelude,* he desired his father's death (however unconsciously), he needed to restore his father and make reparation for the debt incurred through his guilt.

Another feature of his being settled is Wordsworth's famous repose among the women of his household, because he had around him not only his wife Mary and his sister Dorothy, but also his sister-in-law Sara Hutchinson and his daughter Dora. All of these women were devoted to him, and he reciprocated with his constant love and affection for them. Three of them, by their deaths and failing health, test his strength of heart and life during the years between 1835 and 1847, but even those years of emotional stress and hardship served to prove, rather than to question, the integrity of his life and work. Dora's death effectively marked the end of Wordsworth's creative life, although he survived with dignity even that terrible episode. Dora died 9 July 1847; during her illness her husband Edward Quillinan helped Wordsworth finish his last poem, the "Installation Ode." Wordsworth himself died 23 April 1850. Despite the shocks of mortality, which had been with him at least from the time of his mother's death in 1778, he persevered in his art as a therapy of mind and soul. Indeed, the maintenance of his family was of paramount importance to this man who had so early been deprived of his family. He not only "became" his father in public life, but he assumed his father's identity by fathering children of his own. By naming his daughter after his sister, one of his sons after his dead brother John, and one after himself, Wordsworth in effect rebuilt the family his father had lost so many years before. When, in 1842, he resigned his post as Distributor in favor of his son William, he insured the continuity of an identity which had been nearly lost many years before.

# CHAPTER TWO:

## A Guilty Thing Surprised

Stories of vagrant women, deserted mothers, discharged soldiers, and destitute fathers are so frequent in Wordsworth's poetry they suggest an obsessive interest, as if he were trying to give shape to a truth he found difficult to accept. The difficulty is caused by something in himself that he is reluctant to accept even as he feels compelled to say it. To deal with this truth he displaces it as narrative fiction. He tells stories, sometimes stories within stories, and he dramatizes actions by characters whose lives carry the meaning he wishes to analyze.

The way Wordsworth keeps returning, for example, to the story of a chance meeting between a man and a woman on Salisbury Plain, retelling it in three "complete" versions in 1793-94, 1795-99, and 1841-42, is a poet's version of the psyche's compulsion to repeat traumatic experience. He seems with each retelling to be getting closer to some truth of his tale, from what he described at first as merely "A Night on Salisbury Plain" to what he uncovers at last as "Guilt and Sorrow." The mature Wordsworth dealt more easily with these materials in 1841-42 not only because he had a greater command of his artist's tools, but also because he had successfully renounced the pleasure principle.

He made interesting changes in his text for the 1841-42 version, most notably the conclusion, which retreats from the sadism of public execution. At issue is not whether the poem in 1841-42 avoids reality because it tempers the barbarism of the second version's conclusion, but rather the way the poem represses and sublimates the death instinct on behalf of a stable and healthy social psyche. Much occurs, however, in Wordsworth's poetry between 1793 and 1842 before he can successfully deal with the death instinct in a manner favorable to social order and culture. Indeed, in the first version of this story, *A Night on Salisbury Plain,* he does not even attempt to deal directly with the issue of murder and death. He surrounds it with darkness, buries it by making murder the local explanation for the name of the hut where the two main characters meet. But that murder, done some time in the past and discovered only when a horse pawed at the ground of the "decayed retreat," is the buried (repressed) motive for all three versions of the Salisbury Plain narrative.

Repression gives way in the next version, *Adventures on Salisbury Plain,* where the Sailor's story of murder and guilt is the only main interest of the poem. Here Wordsworth shows that "there exists in the mind a compulsion to repeat," and that this compulsion is more demanding even than the pursuit of pleasure. This second version is a sophisticated analysis of the mind discovering in itself the source of social evil and the fate of individual identity. Finally, in the version of 1841-42, *Guilt and Sorrow,* the poem subordinates the fate of the individual to the order of a stable civilization, sublimating the death instinct while acknowledging that it is finally impossible to balance the erotic and death instincts with "the demands of civilization." The result is that "suffering cannot be avoided."

THE peculiar opening of *A Night on Salisbury Plain* is

Wordsworth's statement on the fate of pleasure. Modern man has been successful enough in his pursuits of pleasure through external reality that he *must* be unhappy in a way that the primitive never knew: "The thoughts which bow the kindly spirits down / And break the springs of joy, their deadly weight / Derive from memory of pleasures flown." Because the hungry savage spent his life in a state of tension with little sustained relief, he was better adjusted to external reality than his modern descendants. The savage was not alone in his state of struggle, because the entire human community partook of the same hard lot of "repose in the same fear." The price for this repose was a terrible one, as later stanzas show.

When the Soldier hears the voice from beneath warn him away from "that powerful circle" of Stonehenge, he is being prohibited from violating a sacred place of human sacrifice where primitive guilt was repeatedly expiated by totem rituals. The nature of those rituals is clarified by the Female Vagrant's story, where "the sacrificial altar is fed / With living men" in darkness, and then magicians restore order on the mystic plain when "clear moons spread their pleasing light." This is the way the hungry savage dealt with reality, acting out his savage instincts through totems and taboos that freed him to individual drives that were otherwise damaging to social order.

The modern person has a special pleasure denied the savage, a pleasure of greater social order with a security that keeps tension at a minimum. When, however, that order is broken by external forces (political, economic, agricultural, and military in the poem), individuals are exposed to assaults of fear and anxiety that arise from within as well as from without. This first version concentrates on the Female Vagrant's story of how she attempted to deal with a world whose reality of unpleasure overwhelmed her customary social defenses. The Female Vagrant is able to handle her new reality because she is able to articulate it, as in this story she tells to the Sailor. To put into words the worries and fears of her life is to exercise a measure of control over instincts which must be repressed if she is to survive.

Wordsworth makes an artful transition from stanza twenty-two, describing how the ancient magicians charmed the desert into smiles, to stanza twenty-three, describing how the Female Vagrant's fears are diminished while she talks with the Sailor whose sudden arrival has startled her peace:

> While thus they talk the churlish storms relent;
> And round those broken walls the dying wind
> In feeble murmurs told his rage was spent.
> With sober sympathy and tranquil mind
> Gently the Woman can her wounds unbind.

This juxtaposition with the charm of the ancient magicians at Stonehenge suggests a similarity of purpose between the ancient magic and the modern confessional: both bring peace and calm to troubled nature, within and without. That her troubles have been essentially repressed, unsatisfied, sexual instincts is something the narrator hints when he describes with such detail the Female Vagrant's breasts, using imagery (of swans) which Wordsworth often employs in other poems with highly erotic subjects.

Describing her breasts as twin swans is characteristic of Wordsworth's imagination at this time when he frequently associates sex and death with animals. Birds express erotic desires in *An Evening Walk* and *Home at Grasmere,* a wolf and an eagle express death instincts in *Descriptive Sketches,* and horses express sexual passion restrained in *An Evening Walk.* The abandoned hut of *A Night on Salisbury Plain* has acquired its local reputation as a result of a horse uncovering a corpse beneath its floor. Again Wordsworth seems to have in mind a connection between sex and death. The importance of this connection, however, is not made clear until he rewrites the story for the Sailor in *Adventures on Salisbury Plain*. In the meantime, erotic desire is faintly in evidence as a motivation for the Female Vagrant's unhappiness.

It is not, though, the firmly examined motive in the story she tells. The only hints for its importance come from the passages on her breasts and later in *Adventures* when the narrator says that she loved the Sailor more when "the more he griev'd," and when her place is ultimately taken by the Sailor's dying wife. The Female Vagrant's life story is one of erotic frustration, when her sexual instincts are continually interrupted by counter forces of society and nature until her only happiness lies in escape from reality altogether. Thus she admits that she did not want to return to her homeland after the deaths of all her family. Her desire to remain aboard the ship was, she now realizes, essentially her wish to die. It was her wish to restore the pleasures from which her life had been driven by "cruel chance and wilful wrong." Her story is a recreation of her shocks of separation: from her childhood happiness, father, husband, and children. The final separation, for which she has been prepared, is the ultimate one of death, with its promise of peace from tension. However, the very telling of her story becomes a means of repressing desire for death, leaving her mind open to explore new pleasures of eros through new connections with the Sailor and the world around them. She and the Sailor leave the hut and travel together toward a cottage where the linnets sing their "amorous lays."

Wordsworth leaves the couple as they prepare to enter the cottage with its friendly hospitality, as though they may have recovered their instincts for life and love. But his narrator reenforces a thought uttered earlier by the Female Vagrant when she exclaimed, "Oh! tell me whither, for no earthly friend / Have I, no house in prospect but the tomb." He bids them farewell as a "friendless hope-forsaken pair" that must take their different roads. And he says that their roads will be lined with terrors of nature and society. Modern terrors are more painful than primitive ones, as the poem has already proposed, but repeats the message again at the end, where the point is reenforced that the modern mind has terrors unknown to the primitive in his world of supernatural forces.

Neither the social nor the mental order of the modern world is healthy. When "reason's ray" penetrates the darkness of external reality, it finds only a civilization that feeds upon the energies and lives of people without returning any of its benefits. When it penetrates the darkness of internal reality, if finds an even more desperate condition. Nations, like people, strain for empire at the same time they are crushed by their own fetters. Political tyranny and aggressiveness are symptoms of a sick civilization, externalized signs of a collective psychic illness. The Female Vagrant seems only a victim of this social disease, but her frustrated instinct for love has surely contributed to the larger social illness, feeding upon itself when it is not turned outward to others.

The poet may hope that by "gentle words" all suffering humanity can find some relief from "self-consuming rage," but he offers little hope for a permanent cure. Only one thing seems helpful, that a full recognition of reality might better free society to construct monuments to truth rather than to sickness. Thus he asks if it is necessary for Law always to be an "iron scourge" that creates the very crimes it enjoys to punish? If civilization must be sick that it expresses death rather than life, turning eros into fantasies of self-punishment? It is not for Law to shortcut the way to death without allowing individuals the dignity of choosing their own ways. "Heroes of Truth" are needed to drive back the symptoms of social and mental illness, using "the herculean mace / Of Reason" to clear the troubled region until "not a trace / Be left on earth of Superstition's reign, / Save the eternal pile which frowns on Sarum's plain."

These concluding lines may sound a little odd as the end of the story, but they strike an appropriate stance if the poet himself is one of the heroes of truth. Wordsworth looks at life as a battle for mental health in which all the ills of individuals and society alike are symptoms of spiritual illness. The reign of Superstition is a fantasy of flight from the reality of death and necessary renunciation of pleasure. Freeing minds from the reign of superstition is not only a young political radical's way of protesting against social conditions in England or affirming his support for the aims of the Revolution in France. Such a mission signals the intent of the poetry to become, even more radically, a healer of mental illness as the underlying cause of human misery. Stonehenge, "that eternal pile which frowns on Sarum's plain," should be left as a monument to show that progress in human civilization is possible, so that we not forget in our fantasies what the savage saw in the world around him: it has not disappeared from reality, it has merely been concealed with our buried selves.

*WHEN* Wordsworth turned again to the story of Salisbury Plain, he seems to have taken his earlier conclusion to heart, because he is more truly a hero of truth. He does not waste time moralizing either in the opening or at the closing of the poem. He does not give a story to the Female Vagrant, letting her become instead more of a voiceless sign of the Sailor's conscience, because it is truly the Sailor's story that must be told if we are going to learn the truth of the human condition. We discover the reason for the Sailor's misery, that it is not completely the fault of a repressive society, that he had murdered a man without much cause, and that he has consequently abandoned his family as a refugee from the law. His potential for constructive living, for affection and sympathy, is the first thing we know about him in these *Adventures of Salisbury Plain,* because we first meet him when he helps an old man wearing a ragged coat of "Soldier's faded red."

This incident, which anticipates much in Wordsworth's later poetry, as in "Resolution and Independence" and the boy's meeting with the Discharged Soldier in *The Prelude,* not only tells us something overtly about the Sailor but it hints something more as well, something we can guess at only after we have finished the poem. The Soldier's life of service has not ended even in his old age, since he is trying to find his daughter now to help her whose destitution is greater than his own. Because the Sailor feels self-satisfied after helping the Soldier, he seems to have drawn some spiritual strength of resolution from the example of this old man's fortitude of mind. But his self-satisfaction does not last for long, as the exterior scene with all its desolation reflects the Sailor's unalterable state of mind: lonesome, blank, dreary and wasted, becoming more wild, forlorn and vacant as he moves on. He begins, then, to think of his dreadful deed.

The Sailor has twice attempted to return to his home, with its rich rewards of a wife's love, but each time he has been frustrated by some strange obstacle. The second time he murdered a man, planning to take his "bloody prize" home where he might have laid it, with himself, in her "full lap." Not only are we to see that he has been conditioned to be a murderer by war, but we are to see how closely connected his instinct for love and his instinct for death have become. It is possible that Wordsworth wants to show how the Sailor murdered *because* he does not really want to return to his family. Certainly the Sailor makes no real attempt to reach them, with the goods of his robbery, and pretend it was merely his due compensation. His instinct for death has emerged as a sadistic aggressiveness, and it has occurred in an erotic context. His capacity for love has been diminished, or frustrated, by his discovery of the death instinct in himself. It is his wish to kill that haunts him most, constantly reminded as he is by its presence in various forms around him.

The old Soldier was a reminder of the traveller he had earlier murdered, of the part in himself that was twisted by being a soldier, and so his assistance for the old man was a compensation to himself, to his own conscience, quite as much as it was for the sake of the old man alone. But that turns out not to be a sufficient repayment for his violation of one of society's most important taboos. He is mocked by a swinging corpse on a bare gibbet for thinking he has any right to be self-satisfied, and then he is instructed by Stonehenge in the primitive source of the taboo he has violated. When lightning briefly reveals "a naked guidepost's double head," the poem utters a symbol of the Soldier's ambivalent state of mind quite as much as the appearance of a light gives him "some glimpse of pleasure."

His encounter with the Female Vagrant further heightens his tension, preparing him for yet more traumatic reminders of his guilt that will culminate in a full expression of his wish for death. The Female Vagrant tells him about her own meeting with an old man, strangely "beckoning from the chalky steep," descending to meet her on the road and telling her stories about "the wonders of that boundless heath." His was mainly a story of vision seen connected with Stonehenge, of gigantic beings haunting the area, but the old man was himself a strange creature, emerging as he did from the hills. Like the old Soldier who encountered the Sailor, this old man seems a naturalistic expression of psychological values, guarding the land and warning the soul.

When the Sailor falls into a paralytic trance while listening to the Female Vagrant's story, he repeats what happened to him when he saw the corpse hanging from the gibbet. Not only does his psychic condition of guilt manifest itself in a physical symptom, as a form of hysteria, but his symptom is brought on by this story quite as easily as it was by the hanging corpse. What her story is we do not know for sure, since the manuscript of *Adventures on Salisbury Plain* does not give her story, but if it is the same as it is in *A Night* and in *Guilt and Sorrow,* then we can understand how its content of broken families, as well as her own example of a destitute wife and mother, could bring on the Sailor's second attack. Because she is able to articulate her sorrow and he unable to confess his guilt, she grows more healthy and he more depressed. She is more alive to the possibilities for being in the real world because she has confronted and overcome the fact of death in her life. He is a victim of his fantasy of persecution because of his guilt for violating a social taboo, and so he is becoming more like the corpse he wishes to be.

They depart the hut, and while on the road they hear a sudden scream whose "bursting shrill did all remark prevent." This announces a new and significant episode for the poems' development, when the Sailor observes yet another family in distress of violence. A child has been struck by his father because the boy took his place ("his place / The infant took"). Wordsworth observes here, as he had in *Descriptive Sketches,* the psychological importance of competition between son and father, even at the young age of five years. When the Sailor bends to console the child, he groans with recognition: "The head with streaming blood had dy'd the ground, / Flow'd from the spot where he that deadly wound / Had fix'd on him he murder'd." We are brought closer to a recognition that exceeds even the Sailor's own: he had, in killing the traveller, reenacted the primal scene of murdering his father. His failure to go forward to his family, then, is a punishment that denies him the fruit of his victory over his father—access to his wife, as mother-substitute. This is not as fantastic as it may at first seem, if we remember the roles of the persons he has previously encountered: the old Soldier was throughout presented mainly as a father, the Female Vagrant a daughter, wife, and mother. Even though the poet has transposed the act of violence from son to father in the episode of the five-year-old, he has nevertheless made clear the consequences of competition between the generations.

If society is to survive as a healthy culture, it must find ways of diverting the instinct for aggression from acts of destruction that are examined in the Salisbury Plain poems. The form which that diversion takes is to accept the consequences of internalizing aggression, in guilt and sorrow. Wordsworth ends his poem on a note of sorrow common to both the Female Vagrant and the Sailor. After their repast, "He had resolved to turn toward the seas / Since he that tale had heard," thinking perhaps he might find there the peace of death which she had said she wished for upon returning home. She, meanwhile, "struggled with tears, nor could her heart its sorrow ease," as she left to go her own way. It is she who then comes upon the Sailor's dying wife and returns her to the cottage where he remained behind. We hear nothing more of the Female Vagrant.

But the Sailor must suffer more than unhappiness of heart. When he sees his wife again, now dying, he can no longer conceal his guilt from the witnesses to her death. He is visibly condemned by his countenance as the murderer she has described. He goes to his punishment "not without pleasure." Becoming the corpse swinging from a gibbet that he had seen on Salisbury Plain, the executed Sailor becomes an example to "women and children who were by fathers brought." The hope is that society has not only purged itself of a symptom of its own disease by executing the Sailor, but also that it has thereby discouraged others from also violating its taboos. Two facts, however, suggest that Wordsworth is not so sanguine: hanging in his "iron case," the Sailor by his death repeats in modern form the ritual sacrifices of the savages at Stonehenge, and left to swing on the gibbet he repeats the cycle of murderer condemning murderers: "And now some kindred sufferer driven, perchance, That way may glance And drop, as he once dropp'd, in miserable trance."

*THE BORDERERS* is Wordsworth's earliest completed attempt to make a detailed analysis of a mind driven by its instinct for death. His several versions of the story may date from as early as 1791, when he probably composed what DeSelincourt called a "Fragment of a 'Gothic' Tale." This poem, composed in Spenserian stanzas, has several points in common with the Salisbury Plain poems, including the journey together between an Old Sailor and a young man. Indeed, this fragment may bring us closer to the unconscious workings of the young man's mind. In *Adventures on Salisbury Plain* the young man's hostility is hidden not only from the Old Soldier but even from himself. In the "Fragment of a 'Gothic' Tale," that hostility is a strangely insistent force pressing against the youth's consciousness. When the Old Sailor tells the young man he would like for him to become the child the Old Sailor never had, the youth reacts with these thoughts:

> His hopes the youth to fatal dreams had lent
> And from that hour had laboured with the curse
> Of evil thoughts, nor had the least event
> Not owned a meaning monstrous and perverse;
> And now these latter words were words of blood
> And all the man had said but served to nurse
> Purpose most foul with most unnatural food.

The youth sees all about him "lessons of death," and he feels within himself a struggle as "with impulse horrible his heart had striven."

When he is about to kill the sleeping old man, the youth hears a rumbling noise and a sound of "uncouth terror" which awakens the sleeping Sailor and so aborts the murder. Throughout the fragment the youth moves beneath a burden of feelings which he as well as the poet knows to be "monstrous," "perverse," and "unnatural." This horrible impulse to kill the old man is presented as something quite inexplicable in rational language, unless it is recognized as a psychologically true impulse, common to the unconscious of all men: an urge to kill the father. Wordsworth's fragment and several completed poems of this period early in his career show that he is intent upon exploring this horrible impulse in the development of the masculine identity.

When Marmaduke declares his intention at the conclusion of *The Borderers* to renounce his place in human society, he hopes to find some expiation for his guilt. He says that his only companion will be "the Spectre of that innocent Man, my guide," the accusing conscience that has taken the place of the murdered victim in the hero's mind. These lines occur in the published version of the drama (1842), but not in an earlier one of 1797. When Wordsworth revised the early text for its publication in 1842, he gave it a direction more consistent with his later understanding of human psychology: he shows in the new conclusion that the social taboo can be atoned for by a renunciation, because renunciation is the foundation for obedience to taboo. The murdered father becomes the Super-Ego in the published (public) version.

The intended victim of the "Fragment" drives his young companion into strange thought of murder when he expresses his wish to make him his "child." Blind Herbert in *The Borderers* is always kept before us as, above all things, a Father, and to kill him is to commit "Parricide," as Oswald correctly identifies the deed in Act II. For the purposes of the drama, exploring the strange spectacle of "the mind of man, upturned," it does not matter that the killer is not the actual son of his victim. It is sufficient for the effect produced that Marmaduke discover his victim *is* the father of the woman he loves, and that his motive for killing Herbert is ostensibly his belief that Herbert is merely a "mock Father." "Ostensibly," because Marmaduke wishes to kill Herbert for a complex of reasons, only one of which he can admit to his conscious mind. He has been rebuffed from satisfying erotic desire for Idonea, and so he wishes to eliminate the woman's father to be free for that. He is driven to desperation by Oswald's story that Herbert plans to sell his mock daughter to the infamous Lord Clifford, who in turn plans to deflower the girl in a ceremony that would involve some of his henchmen. Eros is to be served by death in Marmaduke's elimination of the father who seems to stand in the way of erotic satisfaction. The drama enacts the ritual of the primal deed that underlies the structure of social psychology. Sons must remove father-obstacles to their craving for power and sex, take the place of fathers, and then come to terms somehow with the remorse that must follow. Thus Marmaduke *"must,"* as Wordsworth in 1842 saw clearly, go "a wanderer" who is accompanied only by "the Spectre of that innocent man, my guide."

The killing of Oswald is psychologically necessary, as well as a conventional enactment of social justice. Before Marmaduke can enact the process of renunciation that will expiate his violation of taboo, he must repress that in himself which broke free to drive him to his dark deed. The killing of Oswald is tantamount to Marmaduke's self-renunciation and repression of his instinct for death and violence: the dramatic metaphor turns violence against itself. Wordsworth presents the relationship of Oswald with Marmaduke as a strangely close one that troubles Marmaduke's men in a scene added for the published version. When they try to warn Marmaduke that he is falling into Oswald's power, Marmaduke scoffs at their fear and, while admitting that he does not love Oswald, he does honor him for his strong feelings and for his "power to teach."

This relationship between Oswald and Marmaduke is, oddly, the focus of the poet's main interest in the drama (as he makes clear in his Preface of 1796-97). Indeed, his interest may be in Oswald alone. This interest ties together much of Wordsworth's poetry from this period. Wordsworth himself describes his interest thus: in "power that is much more easily manifested in destroying than in creating," and in Rivers (Oswald) as a man whose "energies are most impressively manifested in works of devastation." When Wordsworth says of his character that "all his pleasures are prospective, he is perpetually chasing a phantom, he commits new crimes to drive away the memory of the past," Wordsworth is describing something beyond the pleasure principle: something very like the death instinct, a secret at the heart of every man's darkness.

When Marmaduke discovers within himself a capacity for murder, he feels that he is losing his identity. At first he would rather die himself than to believe that an old man could have evil designs on a young girl:

> the firm foundation of my life
> Is going from me; these strange discoveries—
> Looked at from every point of fear or hope,
> Duty, or love—involve, I feel, my ruin.

This sudden change in his perception of himself makes him recognize that "there is something / Which looks like a transition in my soul, / And yet it is not." When he and Oswald take Herbert out into the darkness of the barren moor with its shattered castle, they are entering into the darkness of the soul itself. Marmaduke exclaims that

> in plumbing the abyss for judgment,
> Something I strike upon which turns my mind
> Back on herself, I think, again—my breast
> Concentres all the terrors of the Universe:
> I look at him and tremble like a child.

Regressing to his primitive instincts for violence, Marmaduke is reverting to childish behavior of a kind that
Wordsworth in his Preface describes thus: "A child, Rous-
seau has observed, will tear in pieces fifty toys before he
will think of making one."

In the end, when Marmaduke renounces society as his
expiation, he will exemplify Wordsworth's solution to the
problems of aggression and the death instinct, putting behind the forces of destruction represented by Oswald. But
before that can happen, Marmaduke must further plumb
the abyss of his mind, where he is increasingly perplexed
by what he finds within himself. He quickly passes beyond
the bounds of his ordinary mental habits and reaches into
a region of amoral calm where he knows no fear and feels
no guilt. Oswald, mockingly, declares that Marmaduke has
left even Oswald behind in this regression to primitive instincts. But Marmaduke remains in his calm:

> Deep, deep and vast, vast beyond human thought,
> Yet calm.—I could believe that there was here
> The only quiet heart on earth. In terror,
> Remembered terror, there is peace and rest.

He thus shows signs of that compulsion to repeat the
traumatic experience that Freud would see as the main evidence for the operation of the death instinct. The "remembered terror" keeps alive for him the reality of his instinct for violence, and his recognition of that truth within
himself is sufficient for his mental "peace and rest" at this
point of the drama. He has submitted to something that

had always been before well repressed. This phase of peace testifies to a sense of self-satisfaction when instincts are gratified—even at the cost of other human lives (egos). For this kind of satisfaction, the self must be sacrificed to the welfare of society, as the conclusion of the drama will show.

Remorse does not exist for Marmaduke at this phase, because he has lifted the restraint of conscious ego. Marmaduke makes reason into an instrument of his passion, which supplies the motive for abolishing remorse. This passion is an expression of Marmaduke's psychic energies (libido) allied with death. But Wordsworth's drama is not designed to celebrate the anarchy of individuals satisfying their repressed instincts for love and death at the expense of social order, however imperfect that order may be. Instead, when Oswald begins to torment Marmaduke with the truth of Herbert's innocence, Wordsworth shows further his sophistication in matters of psychology. Oswald tries to take utter control of Marmaduke just as an instinct will when it has not been subjected to repression, to the constraints of reality. The pleasure of release from tension is renounced when Marmaduke passes once again into a disorientation akin to madness, repeating the scene of his guilt and its accompanying pains, as described by the Forester in Act V. Because Marmaduke is close to becoming a shadow of Oswald, made by Oswald's power, he can escape only by renouncing all pleasures, even those held out by Oswald as by the world: Oswald offers him pleasure with greatness that comes when the self rises above society to a freedom of continuing self-gratification; the world might satisfy his death instinct more absolutely with its socially directed punishment of death for death, but both of these avenues of release are rejected by Marmaduke. Nor will he be able to gratify his erotic desire for Idonea, not even to the extent of calling her "Beloved"; he exclaims that "if I dared, so would I call thee—Conflict must cease, and, in thy frozen heart, / The extremes of suffering meet in absolute peace."

By rejecting all immediate avenues of self-gratification, Marmaduke is recovering his sense of reality, a reality of mental struggle that puts the ego first in the drama of mind. Marmaduke can say at the end that he is raised above, or sunk below, all further sense of provocation because he knows himself better than any other person alive. The ambivalence he admits about his posture is simply evidence of his superior sanity. His only way left is to endure, "That is my destiny." At this point, he has freed himself from the tyranny of his dark passions, represented by Idonea as well as by Oswald, but he has not repudiated his conscience—perhaps he has found it only for the first time.

That is the way Wordsworth left things in the published version of 1842. The original version did not leave room for the erection of conscience in the mind of the self-exiled hero: "I will wander on / Living by mere intensity of thought / A being by pain and thought compelled to live." This is a posture of frank and courageous encounter with reality, both physical and mental. This passage from the conclusion of MS. B. ends with what was surely Wordsworth's clear acknowledgment that his protagonist's mental freedom had been purchased with the knowledge that, while "the aim of all life is death," nevertheless the ego "wishes to die only in its own fashion." When Wordsworth in 1842 elaborated the nature of that "pain and thought" which compels Marmaduke to live, he identified it as "the Spectre of that innocent Man" and so he constructed the phantom of the parent in the mind of the child, the most important voice of society in the individual psyche. In 1796-97, however, he was not fully prepared to admit the grave importance of the super-ego for the maintenance of civilization.

# CHAPTER THREE:

## Those First Affections

"An Evening Walk" describes what its title announces, a conventional form with a conventional subject of topical interest. But this poem works against itself to tame its subject and to retain its conventionality. Either it says something more than it means to say, or it cannot say as much as it needs to say. It is an enclosing restraint upon the imagination as vision. A gate, closing even as the poem opens, closes fast to bring the poem to an end. This closing gate, a kind of oxymoron, portends troubled desire as victimized subject. It is not only the deer in the poem who are troubled, and it is not only the horses in the poem who are in distress.

The closure never completely closed makes "An Evening Walk" into a problematic statement by the young Wordsworth. It strives for the form of a circle, as if the speaker were walking around the lake which itself is encircled by mountains, with their enclosing heights that gradually merge with the darkening day. It comes into focus on a point at the center, a sundial with a moral: time is known by its moving, deepening shadow. The speaker searches for bits of light that can still be found, and he sees some horses still in the sun, as well as a circling kite, a stalking cock, and a swimming swan. In the shadows he imagines a desperate mother holding her dead infants coffined by her embrace. The poet-speaker is baffled by the events of his perception in the darkness, and he eagerly welcomes the relief of light from a rising moon.

This moonlight beckons the poet into an alliance for distancing, removal from painful consequences. The resulting effect is, disastrous in form and tone, self-divisive. We may, however, be grateful that Wordsworth came upon aesthetic disaster in this poem, because the division here is the beginning of a process which opens the gap between what Wordsworth thought he was and what he really was destined to become. Through this gap his "under-powers" will rise to confront him and his posterity with their claims to understanding. The poetic occasion for this fracture of poem and self is an attempt by the poet to convert the power of the moonlight into a magic talisman of childhood fairytales: it can make good out of evil, or at least carry on its magic rug whoever wishes to be transported away from the real world.

At the heart of the Wordsworthian darkness is an abandoned woman. "An Evening Walk" leads to a mother, abandoned with her dying children. Their homelessness strikes a sympathetic chord in the poet, whose own yearning is for a distant cottage illuminated by moonlight at the end of the poem. Sounds of thunder and barking dogs, scenes of fearful cliffs and tumbling rills, prepare the way for his vision of the dying children. He makes deliberate efforts to keep his mind on happier things, but he cannot keep out the sorrow from "sad tides of joy." He must confront the vision of evil that lies at the center of his journey, and yet he exerts the utmost of his energy in an effort to deny that vision. When he can no longer avoid describing this scene of pathetic motherhood, he resigns himself to it and elaborates it with convincing care.

Like the animals earlier and often noticed, this mother

is, in a significant metaphorical detail, *"beat* by summer's
breathless ray" as she drags her children along their weary
path. Like the later, similar figure of Margaret in "The
Ruined Cottage," this woman has left behind her a deserted well, a choked pathway, and a broken pitcher. These
are objects of pain, interferences with her progress because
they are fragments of an unrecoverable past. In his notice
of the mother's backward gaze, the poet is admonished
(admonishing himself) from his own tendency earlier to
look back with "memory at his side." While the mother's
physical pain is sharp, even stinging, as nature's summer
heat makes it worse for her, her mental pain is even greater: she has been deserted not only by her husband but by
all mankind as well. She becomes a kind of mother-nature
for her children and for the poet who imagines her. She
teaches her children to bear their load of burdens with
some measure of independence, but she is also poor human flesh, numb with its own burden of responsibility for
others. The consolations she offers her children are not to
last, because the darkness increases into the cold of winter,
and the pain of separation intensifies into the final trauma
of death. The mother bends to kiss her children, discovers
that they are dead, and then she breaks out with an angry
shriek and despairing moan. Her final gesture is a submission to the reality of her situation with a dying heart. The
anger and despair of the mother, killing the heart of her
being, are surely the anger and despair of the poet as well?

But, no, they seem not to be, if we are to accept the
terms of the poem as a closing structure, fencing off and
securing a peaceful mind from a wild and threatening
world of pain and death. We have every right to ask how
the poet can turn from this morbid scene of unrelieved
suffering to notice how "sweet are the sounds that mingle
from afar." He seems to enjoy the morbidity of the scene
whose pathos has elicited such sympathy; he had early in
the poem rejected the temptation to tell idle tales of idle

pain. At least we have a right to demand of the maker of the poem, if not of the speaker in the poem, that he justify such a trauma of perception.

Looking at the events of this scene in "An Evening Walk" as events made by the man Wordsworth, we may more justifiably draw some conclusions that would not be fair if limited to observation of his speaker in his poem. We will notice, then, how the scene serves to condemn both society, with its culture of military aggression, *and* nature, with its unsympathetic hostility to helpless human beings. Both society and nature, as if in alliance, force suffering upon people whose only escape of repose is death.

This is an early sign of Wordsworth's discontents with civilization and of his ambivalent attitude toward nature. But in "An Evening Walk" he does not confront any of those discontents, and his ambivalence is detrimental to his art. He turns away from the scene of pain and misery, displacing it with a scene of natural harmony and tranquillity. This substitute scene, a kind of consolation, contains the mildest of disturbances that describe the activity of animals feeding around or upon the calm lake water. The poet thus effectively stifles the speaker's passion of sympathy. The poet turns the speaker aside with figures of imagination, with tropes of language, and so produces a fissure of poem and consciousness. The mirror of the surface is chosen at the end, reflecting away from the deeps of the reality only barely explored.

This mirror in the poem re-flects also, and primarily, the speaker's own erotic longing. The deep of the poem remains unexplored as a darkness to which the poet yields his speaker's excursive vision at the end. We can see, from our distance, that this is a darkness of the speaker's own ego, casting its long shadow over the entire poetic transaction. Whether it is Wordsworth's own darkness or not, he represents it for consideration even as he retreats from its implications. Wordsworth does not explore this darkness deeply in most of his early poetry. Instead, he lets it remain as a confusion of ego with natural landscape. And because he will not yet explore his own ego instincts, he cannot acknowledge yet his own aggressiveness, his sympathy with the destructive forces present in "An Evening Walk." More importantly, he does not allow his speaker to recognize fully the primary (real) motive for his evening stroll: erotic desire. Like the animals restrained by closing gates, the speaker's passion of affection is diverted from its natural channel of expression to make itself in various modes throughout the poem. It is in this sense that Wordsworth's poem divides itself between pleasure and pain, showing "a strong tendency toward the pleasure principle."

*WORDSWORTH'S* early poems are thus aesthetically impotent. They show how the poet failed to keep command of his fantasy. A part of him is not awake to the reality of his art. The poems show that Wordsworth lacked courage at the outset of his career: he refused to engage in full encounters with evil, even though he gave notice to the circumstances which produced those evil consequences. The poems are structures of division, openings between opposing states of mind. They are a series of ghostly illusions running after pleasure rather than being the artifacts of reality which the later, greater Wordsworth would create. They are ghostly, as they are impotent, because the reality which he avoids is the reality of eros. These poems are structures of displacement for the love from which the poet has turned. Ironically, then, the evil he notices, without engagement, is a construction made by Wordsworth's own unsatisfied erotic desire. This "evil" is a product of the mysterious alliances between love and death.

*WORDSWORTH* cannot affirm hope in "An Evening Walk," neither in his own voice nor in that of the destitute family. So long as his vision is bifurcated, his mind divided between his report of the facts and his feeling for them, he will not be able to recognize, as he does in Book VI of *The Prelude,* that "our being's heart and home" is with "hope that can never die." Hope as a confidence in one's own being is given away to muse on the being of others, bathed in the rosy glow of erotic longing. The objects of the speaker's musing are mainly animals or shadows of men. It is the animal being that benefits most from his impassioned description, whether in the lighthearted passage on the stalking "monarch" of the barnyard or in the more elaborate picture of the family of swans with which the destitute family is contrasted. The rooster's proud sovereignty over his "sister-wives" is applauded by the speaker's words: the cock is "sweetly ferocious," firm of tread upon his "spur-clad" and "nervous feet" as he struts through his ritual of courtship. Obviously the poet is sympathetic with the erotic power of this stately creature. Just as obvious is his enchantment with the regal grace of the male swan who leads his family in domestic contentment over the lakes' dimpling deeps.

The barnyard harem of the proud cock is safely at a distance from threatening sounds, and the swan family is hidden in a secret bay. This protection by secrecy is favorable to erotic display, something not possible to the speaker. He can express his longing only while alone, at a distance from his dearest friend whose "soft affection" is limited to her hearing these verses. His hope, which he earlier denied, is raised by the appearance of the moonlight at the end of the poem. But the passage which expresses this hope is interrupted frequently with parentheses that qualify the hope as perhaps little more than moonlight illusion. Reality intrudes through parenthetical forms, and the force of the pleasure in hope is proportionately mitigated.

The poet-speaker wanders and roams his darksome rounds, fundamentally because he cannot unite his ego with his desires. He displaces the objects of unconscious wishes with objects allowable to his consciousness, and the result is a kind of neurotic behavior in the speaker and an aesthetic impotence in the poem. Wordsworth presents the neurotic behavior of the speaker in terms that suggest he knows what he is doing, not only by the troping descriptions of penned-up horses, enclosed barnyard love, the secret bay of swan amours, and the destitute mother, but also by his choice of words and formation of phrases to describe the "fair scenes" of the evening. He opens the poem in a mood of ambivalence, even in otherwise innocent descriptions of the landscape: "Where silver rocks the savage prospect chear / Or giant yews that frown on Rydale's mere." Such a couplet can seem innocent because it is conventional, and it is conventional because it can pass as a mask for someone who is searching for pleasures as if they were either departed or contained by the landscape itself. When he recalls how, as a child, "hope itself was all he knew of pain," the speaker is recalling his existence of infinite desire, when there was no division between his ego and erotic longing. But now, being "the sport of some malignant Pow'r," he knows only the pain of hope, because he has denied the identity of those instincts which once were united in his soul.

"An Evening Walk" ends with a series of phrases and images that suggest a relaxation of tension after pained attention to the unhappy mother. This is the mind's tendency toward the pleasure principle, which prompts one to keep tension constant or, better, to lower the tension which has been built up by erotic instincts. At the close of Wordsworth's poem, the scene of relaxed tension dominates as the mood of the speaker's mind, but something in it is not happy with the triumph of the pleasure principle: the complaining owl and the howling mill-dog are virtually a chorus of libidinal demons whose protest finally is compressed into the "yell in the deep woods of a lonely hound."

THE escapist tendency of "An Evening Walk" continues into Wordsworth's next early poem, "Descriptive Sketches." This opens with a misleading hope for finding "a spot of holy ground," as if it were to be a quest for paradise. But it is more obviously going to be a flight from pain, from all the "sad family" of pain. Such a flight smacks of denying reality, even denying life itself. As long as the speaker is allowed to think that his flight is really a quest, then this speaker is a fantasy in flight from the critical intelligence of the poet who makes the poem.

The diction of "Descriptive Sketches" is chosen to suggest a lowering of tension, akin to the ending of "An Evening Walk." Although there is an occasional murmur of resistance, the predominant direction is toward the quiescent rather than for the active life. The murmuring resistance is a signal, however, that the poet has not entirely resigned himself or his speaker to a life of pleasure only. This murmur is an opposing force of his erotic instinct, and it is this that he is attempting to flee. This is Eros, the god of creative power within himself. It will not be totally denied, and so it forces itself into disguised expression just as it had to do in "An Evening Walk." The opposition of this denied power of creativity to the poem's conscious design is the interesting principle of the poem's structure, not its compromising surface of resolutions made through rhyming couplets.

"Descriptive Sketches" provides evidence that the young poet is, as a man, aware that life spent in pursuit of pleasure is basically a life in decline, that pleasure serves death more surely than it does life, because pleasure is an experience of relaxation from tension or, at most, a refusal to increase tension. On the other hand, as the poem suggests for the man Wordsworth though not for his poem's speaker, tension is taken as a clear sign of life in process of becoming, of dealing with reality on behalf of the psyche. Insofar as the poem is the record of a flight from tension, it is also a flight from reality and it is a repression of erotic instincts. What remains to be sorted out by the maker— Wordsworth in the trials of his masculinity—is the need to distinguish pleasure from eros, to recognize that pleasure can be a false steward to life instincts. But Wordsworth does not, perhaps cannot, make that distinction in such an early poem, even though it underlies some of the problems of obscurity and divided feelings in the poem.

Unless certain otherwise obscured details are isolated for attention, this poem seems tame enough. But it is spoken by a person with a wounded heart, someone searching for the healing powers of nature. He is dejected and burdened with a heart "that could not much itself approve." Among the oddities of the poem is the kind of healing the speaker searches for in nature. He fixes on two kinds of therapeutic scenes: the erotic and the destructive. He begins with the scene of Chartreuse's doom, and then he lingers over an erotic scene at Lake Como, where "amorous music on the water dies." Continuing in this dialectical fashion, he comes to focus on the painful scene of "Viamala's chasms," where the Grison gipsy seeks shelter with her baby during a frightful storm while "nearer howls the famish'd wolf." This scene of desolation gives place then to a softer prospect that is later called a "romantic dream" from which the speaker must awaken his soul.

First however, the speaker is made to approach nearer Viamala's chasm. He is made to bend over the abyss to view a figure who is herself bending "o'er the smoke that curls beneath the rocks." This richly ironic *topos* is almost a fixture in the Wordsworth canon: looking at a figure looking at a figure, *ad infinitum,* one might guess. It anticipates the opening of "Tintern Abbey," for instance, where the poet speculates that the smoke he sees may be coming from the campfire of "vagrant dwellers" or "some

Hermit's cave." It anticipates the great moment of insight gained while composing *The Prelude* in 1805, when Wordsworth recognizes his own imagination in the unfathered vapor that rises from deep in the abyss. As in those later poems, the Grison gipsy suggests the mind of the poet forcing itself to look at itself as it is bent over an abyss. She is an aspect of himself that the poet-speaker has sought to repress or deny, and in her condition he observes the consequences of psychological and social repression: "condemn'd, without reprieve, to go / O'er life's long deserts with its charge of woe."

The last word on her plight is that she hears the howl of the famished wolf as it draws nearer to her, drawn by her baby's cry. Wordsworth saves this last bit of horror to cap his gothic scene (which includes a pile of white bones in a bear's cave), but what surprises is the absence of any expression of supernatural evil in the scene. The animate and inanimate forces of nature provide all the evil poor humanity requires. Desolation stalks its way through several more lines until the speaker is allowed to discover a "softer prospect."

The motif of erotic pleasure which dominated the first third of "Descriptive Sketches" gives way to an opposing motif of painful reality in the passage on the Grison gipsy mother and child. The connection between this episode and the equally painful one of the dying father is emphasized by shared images of stalking nature. As the infant's cries draw the howling wolf closer to the terrified gipsy, the struggles of the chamois hunter attract the hungry eye of an Alpine eagle. This is a cruel irony of looking to heaven for help from the raven, only to discover himself the intended food of an eagle flying there. Wordsworth's youthful naturalism is here expressed with bitterness and some cynicism. It makes some psychological sense when it is connected, not with the poet's religious skepticism or his inclination to literary rebellion, but rather with his

analysis of social psychology. He makes his speaker attracted by virginal eyes and panting breasts as one of the terms
in a threefold analogy with the howling wolf by infant
cries, and a wheeling eagle by struggling man. The implications of these structural analogies are deeply significant
for understanding the trials of Wordsworth's masculinity
and self-definition. Lust is a desire for others as objects,
whether for sexual pleasure or for satisfaction of hunger.
Lust is a desire whose energy is shared by all animate being, both human and animal.

Reduction of human identity to the plain of animal
struggle is forced even more cruelly by the scene that follows the death of the chamois hunter, as his wife and
child fearfully await his return, "with cruel hope." Wordsworth compounds this cynical irony with a suggestion that
the hunter's child may one day pass by his father's bones
and start at the remains of "that very thigh, / On which
so oft he prattled when a boy." This should be recalled
later in the poem when families are said to drive away sons
in order for everyone to have a chance to survive in the
struggle for existence. This is such a terrible truth of reality that Wordsworth is unable to express it even in the
voice of his persona, the speaker of the poem. He gives it
to the speech of some mountain swain with "venerable
head." To deal with this pain of forced separation between
sons and fathers ("to pay the filial debt"), the poet turns
willfully away from both the howling wolf and the hungry
eagle, to put his imaginative faith in a "gay lark of hope"
rising with the sun to summon back a "lost fragrance of
the heart." Wordsworth's attention is surely divided, split
off, between the wolf/eagle and the lark. His ambivalence
seems a consequence of his inability to acknowledge the
kinship of his erotic longing and its thrust toward destruction and death.

*HOME AT GRASMERE* is yet another instance of refusal to embrace reality in its totality. It also insists on retreating to forms of pleasure that reduce the tensions of life in its struggles with reality. Later than both "An Evening Walk" and "Descriptive Sketches," *Home at Grasmere* displays Wordsworth's more mature insight into at least one dimension of his being: it is the most sustained love poem that Wordsworth ever attempted, celebrating the bliss of eros as worth all the cost of pain and patience. The erotic quality of the poem is a luxury of sensuous imagination that revels in a recovery of paradise, in the company of a beloved "Eve." It is very nearly the epithalamium which the poet declares he will sing at the end: "the spousal verse / Of a great consummation."

Celebrating the valley's overflowing love, the poet repeatedly tries to lose himself in the immediacy of sensuous pleasures, as he was able to do when he was a child: filled with "one bright pleasing thought" of unrestrained liberty, "to flit from field to rock, from rock to field." Grasmere thus becomes a place of regression, a state of mind in which the poet can find again "all that luxurious nature could desire." It is an impossible state, where "perpetual pleasure of the sense" can make "a termination and a last retreat happy in itself."

Wordsworth knows himself better than his speaker knows *him*self. This speaker may be forgiven his ecstasy of joy in the satisfaction of a great desire (coming back home), but he cannot so easily be forgiven his willingness to make it a last retreat. It is impossible to *retreat* into the *present,* as Wordsworth's greater poetry will show and even as this poem must finally admit. If the speaker could only recognize that in the "calm revelry" he sees in Grasmere ravens is the clue to his own real identity and psychic health, he would be able to bring the vision of his experience into an aesthetic and psychic whole. But he chooses to emphasize the *calm* at the expense of the *revelry* rather than to see them as different modes of the same being, and so he leaves them to their separate identities with his gesture of passing them by: "I leave them to their pleasure, and I pass."

This determination to pass by the pleasure of animals in revelry is the main weakness of the speaker's character. It is a specific feature of his general tendency to retreat to the warm luxury of maternal security (calling for Nature to embrace him, and "close him in"). Here is an extension of his satisfaction of erotic desire in the company of his Emma, the "Eve" of his return to paradise—a place of "surpassing grace." Her presence is necessary to wake his erotic instincts for loveliness and luxury of sensation: "Her Voice was like a hidden Bird that sang; / The thought of her was like a flash of light." Such passages have the ring of Solomon's "Song of Songs" and cannot deny the power of eros that gives it such persuasive charm, even if Emma later will be identified as the poet's sister Dorothy. To know this simply confirms, by anticipation, the point that Wordsworth often relates his experience of pleasure with what he calls the "tranquil pleasure" of socially respectable love, whether for a sister, a mother, or a wife.

The phrase of "tranquil pleasure" occurs during the story of the "generous and easy-minded," though careless, man who seduced a "blooming Girl" while she worked as a servant in his house. This is the first of three stories about people who lived, or still live, in Grasmere, intended to illustrate the virtues (and vices) of the "happy Valley." These stories are a significant part of MS. B, although the first two are removed from MS. D. They set up contrasting images of erotic love as the main drive for pleasure: "tranquil pleasure" and "troubled pleasure."

The focus is to be upon the "unhappy Man," not the unhappy Maiden. We are to see how he pays for his carelessness—with guilt that cannot be relieved: "he died of his own grief, / He could not bear the weight of his own shame." All his restless wandering through the mountains can bring him no relief. He left his family increasingly destitute. "Troubled pleasure" is almost a contradiction in terms. The speaker telling the story does not recognize or admit in the man of his story enough of his own problems to educate his soul as Wordsworth will do for himself in *The Prelude*. Instead of recognizing in the restlessness of this adulterous husband an essential instinct for making and becoming (an instinct denied by the "neatness" and "showy trim" of his unsatisfactory wife), the speaker, in effect, "passes him by" just as he had passed by the ravens in their "calm revelry."

He passes by the adulterous husband as many of Wordsworth's speakers pass by the graves of the dead, especially in *The Excursion* (whose method of interior narration is anticipated in *Home at Grasmere*). Given the contrasting peace and contentment, if not utter happiness, pictured in the next two stories, the story of the adulterous husband suggests that it is better to die than to live on in marriages where form (as neatness and trim) prevails over the energies of desire. By killing off the protagonist of the first story, the poet shows how the valley regulates its energy of desire with a fearful authority that originates in powerful guilt feelings and terminates with absolute elimination.

In the next story a widower with many children is content, even happy, to live as a father of six daughters who have taken the place of his dead wife in his affections. This love, also erotic, is socially acceptable, though the family is strangely happy, even to the speaker, who expected a tale of sorrow. Instead, he discovers that "the whole House is filled with gaiety." A similar pleasure abides in the heart of the widow who is the main character of the third story, although her pleasure is her memories of the love she had with her husband. While these three stories may disguise certain obsessive themes from Wordsworth's own biography, they are most important as illustrations of the ways erotic love is tamed into calm and peace, "tranquil pleasure," in Grasmere. Marriage is the first, basic, social way to insure the stability of civilization, but, as these stories show, marriage can tame eros at too high a cost.

That cost is something, however, which the speaker of *Home at Grasmere* does not emphasize. His interests continue to be in the pleasures of tranquillity, however often they may be threatened by the disruptions of suppressed desires. He compares himself to a Traveller passing through a strange Valley where mists begin to recede, as an "inward frame, / Though slowly opening, opens every day." His simile is a strange one that describes what *is* quite as much as it compares with what *might* be. It is "alternate progress and impediment, / And yet a growing prospect in the main." Whether the speaker knows as much reality in the end as his simile suggests he should is questionable, but at least the poet is allowing us to see the course events should take in the development of his speaker's vision. The distressing thing about this enlarging vision is that it denies what it discovers, selecting the tranquil pleasures and discarding the troubled ones. The speaker goes on after the simile to say that even if he is "sometimes forced to cast a painful look / Upon unwelcome things," he is not only not depressed, he is "enriched at every glance," and the more he sees "the more is my delight." These assertions are evidence that the speaker has subordinated all energy to a deadening force of calm. He has stepped ashore from his stream of forgetfulness only occasionally, but that has done little more than to heighten his pleasures in the stream itself. This is dangerously close to making a choice of illusion over truth, complacently accepting the entertainment of deceit and the pleasure of "placid sleep."

ENTERTAINMENT is what the animals of Grasmere provide in this poem. The speaker delights in a small grey horse, while he chooses to ignore the implications of the paralytic man; he enjoys his acquaintance with the ass rather than with the cripple who rides upon it. The facts of paralysis and human wreck are presented (and the list is longer), but they are subordinated to the main interest of "quietness" which endears the speaker to "this sublime retirement." Wordsworth will not always be so complacent about his ability to discover calm amidst so much wreck, as *The Prelude* and *The Excursion* will attest, just as works like *The Borderers* prove that he has not ignored the darknesses in the human psyche. But when the goal of life seems to be present pleasure, with its relaxations, then such poems as *Home at Grasmere,* though more skillfully done than "Descriptive Sketches," no less than that poem keep divided the two poles of human experience.

These poles of pleasure and reality are brought into meaningful relationships by other poems, because Wordsworth successfully analyzes his own psyche in *The Prelude,* and he frankly admits that his ego is the primary ground of his identity. Even in *Home at Grasmere* there is a beginning of this admission when the pronoun referent is shifted from the "we" that includes the speaker and his companion Emma, to the "I" that increasingly dominates the latter half of the poem, until the speaker makes this reluctant confession:

> Possessions have I, wholly, solely mine,
> Something within, which yet is shared by none—
> Not even the nearest to me and most dear—
> Something which power and effort may impart.

This discovery of self as unique, unable to share fully its pleasures even with the beloved Emma, is an important psychological achievement of *Home at Grasmere.* Coming "home" to himself, the speaker has ceased to stop running from reality. It is important because of the *way* the speaker makes his discovery, as indicated by the passage just quoted; he finds that pleasure is an experience of relaxing tension that cannot be shared, because it is a denial of the very energy which establishes the bonds of life and community. Pleasure, then, cannot be the end of being unless it is the death of becoming. However, pleasure can serve as a means to becoming, as the servant of love whose end *is* sharing and creating. This insight is borne by the lines which open the passage of discovery: "But 'tis not to enjoy, for this alone, / That we exist; no, something must be done."

To realize that "something must be *done*" or that one cannot any longer "walk in unreproved delight" without a "duty that looks further" is to begin to encounter reality. *Home at Grasmere* cannot ignore reality because the poet will not let the speaker (even *as* himself) ignore himself. He begins the poem with a joyful recognition that he has acquired a possession he has long wished for, a home. But in the course of accumulating all the pleasures that should come from that possession, the speaker has finally to admit that his most important possession is something he cannot share, even with his Emma. What it is he cannot fully explain, except to say that it is a kind of "power." Throughout the poem, as well as in "An Evening Walk" and most of "Descriptive Sketches," Wordsworth has analyzed the frustrated attempts to contain this "power," to arrest its surge and sometimes even to deny its reality in the protagonists' searches for "calm abodes" and "tranquil pleasure."

As long as the speaker tries to identify his present occupation of a home in Grasmere with his boyhood "thought" of one day owning such a home, he is bound to a falsehood, because reality is not a simple realization of past and present. When the speaker admonishes himself, or any "sage Man," for his prudence, experience, desires, and apprehensions, he is deluding himself into thinking that childhood wishes can be identical with adult reality. "Something must be done," as the educated soul recognizes at the end, before the desires of the past can become the realities of the present. More than that, there can be no reality of the present which does not take care for the future, the very preoccupations of the sage Man with his prudence and apprehensions. Consequently, the speaker concludes *Home at Grasmere* with a desire to fulfill some "office" of his Being.

The speaker has, after all, something in common with the adulterous husband—a man with troubled pleasure: he has retained something of his boyish days filled with "motions of savage instinct." He can say, "Yea, to this day I swell with like desire." The great difference, though, is that the speaker's present instinct of desire is an act of imagination, excited by the art of fiction. The artifacts of civilization are acts of sublimation, as Wordsworth here allows his ego-speaker to discover. To survive as an individual without suppressing or denying all its powers of instinct, the ego must channel them into socially approved forms of expression. Both the poet and his speaker know that they must make concessions of desire in order to exist as members even of the small society inhabiting Grasmere valley. Among men anywhere there may not be "love, perfect love" even "in midst of so much loveliness." The speaker has had his pleasures interrupted by "an awful voice" of a Shepherd shouting through the gloom, a voice "of ribaldry and blasphemy and wrath."

That kind of energy may express a "savage instinct" untamed by civilization, and so it is a threat to the order, the decorum, of society. Wordsworth would be especially sensitive to the violence of language which reaches the ear "debased and under prophanation." His own making of poems, it turns out, is a process of taming his own "savage instinct" for the sake of society. The power within him that "yet is shared by none" he will use to tame such violence of language, making poetry whose pleasure will serve the end, not of death and chaos, but rather of life and love. His art must learn how to use pleasure for an end greater than itself, to "bind together by passion and knowledge the vast empire of human society," as he put it in his Preface to the 1800 *Lyrical Ballads.*

BOTH editions of *Lyrical Ballads* are, as the poet says in his famous Preface, "experiments." Not the least of his experimental aims is Wordsworth's attempt to use the pleasure of language to civilize, and by civilization he means a society of men who live by discipline and love. Art, therefore, should aim for a delicate balance between the discipline and the love. For the poet as technician, this balance occurs between the order of meter and the content of feeling and thought. Equally important is the balance the art strives for as an effect in the lives of its audience, to enlarge the mind's capability "of being excited without the application of gross and violent stimulants." Too much emphasis upon discipline will produce merely dead formalities of language and feeling, and too much emphasis upon sentiment will produce the very same "savage torpor" which art should be designed to remove by a general awakening of mind. Throughout the Preface an intent to serve the ends of civilization is strong and clear, from the opening emphasis to the concluding summary, that his poetry may be "important in the multiplicity and quality of its moral relations."

The *Lyrical Ballads* of 1798 contain the beginnings of Wordsworth's social psychology, analyzing the psychological relationships of neighbors (as enemies) in "Goody Blake and Harry Gill," of neighbors (as friends) in "Simon Lee," of a father with his son in "Anecdote for Fathers," and of a father with his family in "The Last of the Flock." In "The Idiot Boy," the poet is quite as interested in the relationships of a mother with her son and with her needy neighbor as with the abnormal psychology of an idiot child. This poem, along with "Her Eyes are Wild," "The Complaint," and "The Thorn," are all focused upon Wordsworth's interest in mothers made desperate for their children, and so they indeed turn upon those "elementary feelings" and "essential passions" which Wordsworth in the 1800 Preface says he was looking for when he chose "humble and rustic life" for the subject matter of his poems. The most elementary of human feelings is to be found in the child's relationships with its mother. All of these relationships, from neighbors to fathers to mothers, are to be understood as modes and degrees of pleasure.

When Wordsworth explained the purpose and method of the *Lyrical Ballads* in his 1800 Preface, he repeatedly emphasized the importance of pleasure not only as a benefit for his readers but as the single most important of the elementary feelings and essential passions. His poems were an experiment to discover how far a poet may go to impart "that sort of pleasure and that quantity of pleasure" which his art can provide. He hopes "they who should be pleased with them would read them with more than common pleasure." He feared that mankind has lost its sensitivity to beauty and that the edge of life has been dulled by circumstances peculiar to modern society: "great national events which are daily taking place, and the increasing accumulation of men in cities." His explanation is a social account of a "general evil" whose manifest symptoms are boredom and anaesthesia. To counter this evil, the poet must write "under one restriction only, namely, the necessity of giving immediate pleasure to a human being possessed of that information which may be expected of him as a Man." This necessity of producing immediate pleasure is simply "homage paid to the native and naked dignity of man, to the grand elementary principle of pleasure, by which he knows, and feels, and lives, and moves."

Wordsworth could hardly be clearer when he explains that his poetry has both a social and a psychological purpose which must be understood in terms of pleasure. It is not his manner merely to please with measured language or sweet sounds and soothing images; nor does he limit his subject matter to incidents of happy tranquillity. Pleasure is a complex notion for the mature poet, whose poems no longer insist upon achieving relaxation of tension at the cost of denying reality. Pleasure now is that sentiment of being which affirms the "indestructible qualities of the human mind." These qualities vary from the innocent tenacity of the little girl in "We Are Seven" to the guilt-ridden despair of the father in "The Last of the Flock." Between these extremes of spirit, pleasure is a motive to explain the workings of the mind that still pursues the advantages of pleasure because that is "the grand elementary principle" of human being. To this extent, then, Wordsworth's poems in the 1798 *Lyrical Ballads* are no less in pursuit of pleasure than were "An Evening Walk" or "Descriptive Sketches," but the artistry of these later poems is more successful. In the *Lyrical Ballads* of 1798 the voice of the narrator or the poet himself establishes a norm of reality from which the poem, or the protagonist in the poem, cannot escape and lose himself in quest of pleasure. The aesthetic success is a function here of a psychic victory for the reality principle.

This voice for reality can best be heard in the richly complex poem which concluded Wordsworth's contribution to the first edition of *Lyrical Ballads,* "Tintern Abbey." It stands in the end as a strategically placed comment on all that has gone before and as a portal into the world beyond the book. It is a successfully rendered analysis of pleasure in all its modes, as Wordsworth understood them in 1798. As a poem of connections, "Tintern Abbey" brings together in its loveliness all those various qualities of mind which have been explored in the several lyrical ballads which precede it. It is an explanatory poem of self-analysis, but the poet cannot understand himself without some external reference points that include the landscape before him and the sister who stands beside him. While most emphasis in criticism of Wordsworth's poetry has fallen upon his relationship with nature (which is understandable), more emphasis upon his social relationships can help to understand the development his poetry undergoes in the later years of his life. This development is increasingly a sophistication of Wordsworth's social psychology.

His relationship with his sister in this poem echoes the relationships of the speakers with their various loved ones in "An Evening Walk," "Descriptive Sketches," and *Home at Grasmere.* The brother-sister relationship should be added to the list of categories to describe the concerns of the 1798 *Lyrical Ballads,* including "We Are Seven," "Lines Written at a small distance from my House," and "Lines Written in Early Spring." These relationships are all bonds of strength, emphasizing the pleasures of identity with another human soul, but also illustrating how the power of eros can drive the soul to hunger for sexual attachment, as much for a sister as for the mother or a stranger. In "Tintern Abbey" Wordsworth saves for a later turning of the poem the surprise that his sister stands with him to view the prospect which has been earlier described. She emerges, as it were, from that landscape—her wild eyes in harmony with the wild secluded scene and the sportive wood run wild.

His sister's emergence into the poet's consciousness is a sign of his psychological/aesthetic accomplishment, because she is himself with all his former pleasures kept near him as he enjoys a present pleasure. The poet adds to his manifold of pleasures one even more to be valued, what he calls "a sober pleasure" that comes with maturity. In the poem, then, are several degrees of pleasure, modified by the passing of time and by the accumulation of experience, but they are continuous to bind together the developing identity of the speaker: from feelings of "unremembered pleasure" to the "sober pleasure" of after years.

Of all the kinds of pleasure Wordsworth analyzes in

"Tintern Abbey," present pleasure is the most psychologically dangerous, because it threatens to arrest development
of the reality principle, as in "We Are Seven" or in such
earlier poems as "An Evening Walk." To possess a present
pleasure rather than to be possessed by it is the aim of the
mature ego. In "Tintern Abbey" the present pleasure gives
way to "pleasing thoughts," thus replacing sensation of effect with consciousness of cause. Pleasure cannot be an
end in itself unless it is unremembered, and so it should
be replaced by the reality of mind or be conditioned by
mind in some important way. This is what occurs in
"Lines Written in Early Spring," and, to a lesser degree, in
"Her Eyes are Wild," a poem about reconciliation with reality.

"Her Eyes are wild" has an important connection with
"Tintern Abbey" in a shared imagery of wild eyes. It
makes the eyes a sign of madness, while "Tintern Abbey"
makes them a sign of mental health. The wild eyes are,
then, signs both of a destitute mother and a happy sister.
When the mother urges her infant to "suck, little babe, oh
suck again!" she is enjoying an erotic pleasure as well as
providing a maternal service: "It cools my blood; it cools
my brain." This sensuous experience (though crudely expressed) makes her life meaningful in the present pleasure:
"Thy lips I feel them, baby! They / Draw from my heart
the pain away." Then, surprisingly, Wordsworth lets us
see that this is a substitute for the lover who is absent:
"Thy father cares not for my breast, / 'Tis thine, sweet
baby, there to rest; / 'Tis all thine own!" The mother
vows, however, not to let present pleasure drive out the
rest of reality for her and the baby. She will do what is
necessary to care for her child, and so in the end she rises
above immediate pleasure to make of it a means, not an
end in itself.

"Lines Written in Early Spring" delivers a similar message, though with quite a different emphasis and in a very

different mode. Here the speaker imagines a pleasure that surrounds him and in which he participates as a creature of nature. But when he says, "And I must think," he gives himself away, because it is his thought that carries the pleasure to be shared by all around him. Whatever feelings occur in the poem are delivered by this "thought," the source of both pleasure and pain. The poem is a commitment to reality because it subordinates pleasure to thought. By the end, the poet-speaker like the destitute mother of "Her Eyes are Wild," rises above immediate pleasure to recognize himself as the source of both pleasure and reflective pain. He discovers himself as a creature of mind who has the power to mix pain with pleasure. He is saddened to observe that nature, without thought in itself, can enjoy its being without the burden of consciousness, while man with all his advantages and all his power, suffers too much to be able fully to enjoy his being.

Thought therefore modifies pleasure and gives it a human shape—"pleasing thought," as Wordsworth puts it in "Tintern Abbey." Both pleasing thought and present pleasure suggest a degree of consciousness that is not present in the "coarser pleasures" with their "glad animal movements." Those coarser pleasures are all gone by, except for the glimpses the poet catches in the wild eyes of his sister, who still knows the delight of glad animal movements. To recapture that boyish experience is the aim of the speaker in "Lines written at a small distance from my House." These coarser pleasures bring their own special instruction in the humorous banterings of "Expostulation and Reply" and "The Tables Turned." And "The Idiot Boy" makes an ambitious attempt to imagine "glad animal movements" in a mind unburdened by consciousness.

*MIND* must advance from coarser pleasures to sober ones by a slow process of experience and reflection, a pro-

cess of coming to terms with a reality that requires modifi-
cations in the principle of pleasure: from neighbors to sis-
ters ("Simon Lee" to "We are Seven"), from mothers
("Her Eyes are Wild") to fathers ("Anecdote for Fathers"). But the single poem in the 1798 *Lyrical Ballads*
which most elaborates this truth is "Tintern Abbey,"
where all the degrees and modes of pleasure are examined
in the life of the speaker, with the help of his sister's presence. Present pleasure yields to the past with its gradation
of unremembered pleasure, coarser pleasures, and former
pleasures. This yielding occurs as a process of pressure
from thought, which takes the place of pleasure as an end
in itself, becoming "pleasing thoughts." This in turn generates a new energy in the mind as a power of recognition
in which the pleasure is subordinated in an activity of
knowing: the self is recognized at its various stages of being prior to full consciousness. Pleasure comes from the
harmonious overlay, identification, of thought with matter
in which the image of the present fits the image of the
past. Finally, the harmony is completed by addition of yet
another image of self in a state of "sober pleasure," a state
for the future. The process is a dialectical one, of interchange between pleasure and thought, until the two are
one—united by "a motion and a spirit, that impels / All
thinking things, all objects of all thought." This testament
of harmony and unity is, however, a problematic experience that Wordsworth only rarely achieved and infrequent-
ly maintained, as even "Tintern Abbey" admits by its coun-
terflowing through "gleams of half-extinguished thought."

# CHAPTER FOUR:

## Indisputable Shapes

*Peter Bell* is one of Wordsworth's more subtle analyses of the unconscious becoming conscious. Here he strikes a note of such ambivalence that readers sometimes resist the appeal of the poem. Although *Peter Bell* was an ambitious project for the poet, he obviously felt uncertain about it for a number of years before he could publish it. Like so many of the poems of this period, between 1793 and 1800, *Peter Bell* was kept from publication and rewritten several times. However, it has the additional complexity of a perplexed tone, mixing high seriousness with humor and even mockery. It could be read as a mock-heroic, but it must also be read as Wordsworth's serious attempt to analyze the soul of a hardened man.

Peter Bell is such a hardened creature, existing on the mental and moral frontier that separates the savage from the civilized man. Like the savage, he has no interior censor against his willful pursuit of pleasure; to this trait is added what the poem calls "whatever vice / The cruel city breeds." Although no specific vice is named to explain this trait, Peter Bell's character is twisted in one particular way that might relate it to the cruel city. He is sadistic, mixing aggression with erotic desire. The poem is an examination of such a man discovering a truth about himself that he has hidden far away from his consciousness until he has the experience narrated here. Peter Bell is a "Hero in a trance" who deserves the mockery of the poet until the trance is broken and the Hero renounces his life of willful pleasure to acknowledge a greater world of reality. This greater world is "a world of death," which Peter Bell has never acknowledged as a matter of concern to himself.

Although he is middle-aged he is no more mature than the hero of "The Idiot Boy," with which this poem has some important affinities. The narrator says that Peter might as well have been fast bound in the Fleet, for all the good his years of wandering experience have done him. Indeed, Peter *has* been a kind of prisoner because of his unconscious refusal to admit certain painful facts about himself. The poem is a record of the therapy that will free him from that mental prison to live a sadder, but a wiser and socially responsible life: he "forsook his crimes, renounced his folly, / And, after ten months' melancholy, / Became a good and honest man."

The "good" here is in the act of renunciation that confirms a reality greater than the pleasures of self-gratification; the "honesty" here is in the recognition of truth within himself quite as much as in his dealings with others; and the "ten months' melancholy" is necessary as a period of mourning that purges him of the guilt he has confessed. What exactly that guilt is and how Peter Bell discovers it buried within himself are the main interests of the poem. What seems an innocent enough departure from the beaten track becomes a nightmare of guilt and terror for the hero. As usual he was travelling alone, along a winding river, "led / By pleasure running in his head," when Peter "chanced" to see "a path / That promised to cut short the way." That nothing is truly left to chance in the development of a person's character is something that Wordsworth knew long before Freud wrote his *Psychopathology of Everyday Life*. The pain that afflicts Peter Bell in the form of guilt and terror is a punishment required by his own soul. Deep within him there is a furious raging, disguised as an apparent "chance" of his leaving the main road to follow a side path into darkness.

Turning aside to cut short his way, Peter weaves through a thick wood where his whistling is "buried like a bird / Darkling." His patience gives way to downright fury and wrath as his path grows dim. He pauses before "shadows of strange shape, / Massy and black," before pressing his way "through the yawning fissures old" of a quarry. Suddenly he breaks into a strangely quiet clearing which the poet emphasizes for its anonymity: "field or meadow name it not." It is a place where there is "no one dwelling," "no little cottage"; it is a "green spot, so calm and green," a "deep and quiet spot." It has all the features of mystery, where discoveries are possible and transformations likely. It is a Wordsworthian dis-location, a spot of time. Like the abysses of "Descriptive Sketches" and *The Prelude*, "Nutting" and "Tintern Abbey," this is a gap of discovery.

At the center of the spot is an Ass, a comic version of Peter's own essential character, and a parody of the animal symbols Wordsworth has employed so frequently in his early poetry. While the Ass and Peter Bell have much in common, there are some features of the animal that Peter cannot boast, such as the beast's stubborn loyalty. When Peter attempts to move the Ass from its station, he jerks as if he were pulling up an iron ring "from a dungeon-floor." Peter is opening up regions usually concealed beneath ordinary consciousness. His growing fear that "'there is some plot against me laid'" is well founded, because unconscious forces are pressing to be unleashed through his behavior in this strange place.

These forces express themselves in the violence of Peter's attack on the stubborn Ass. There is no rational motive for the ferocity of Peter's hostility. Wordsworth went out of his way to remove various possible motives which he had first written into his poem, including these:

> Did Peter e'er with club or stake
> Smite some poor traveller on the head,
> Or beat his father in a rage
> And spill the blood of his old age,
> Or kick a child till it was dead?

Unlike the Sailor of the Salisbury Plain poems and unlike Marmaduke of *The Borderers,* Peter Bell is, as a fact, quite innocent of murder. The poem heightens the mystery of Peter's disproportionate ferocity by letting it appear as if the Ass's own helplessness were the cause alone, as if Peter's rage were merely the effect of his frustrated attempt to steal the animal. When the Ass brays out its agony, Peter feels joy knock at his heart, and he turns again to the "blind work" of beating the animal, compelled to do it as if he were chained "by demoniac power." Something is driving him into a frenzy of violence that would eventually kill the animal if suddenly Peter did not see a startling thing in the stream.

Wordsworth's analytical imagination is highly speculative, daringly hypothetical in its search for causes. The poem speculates that Peter has possibly seen a gallows, a coffin, or a shroud. When the poet suggests that what frightens Peter is a sight of Peter himself ("Is Peter of himself afraid?"), he is getting closer to the heart (or heartlessness) of the matter. Wordsworth does not solve the mystery for several stanzas, letting Peter fall into a trance of fear at what he has seen. Peter's imagination, as distinguished from the poet's, has been fired by something within him until the sight takes on terrifying forms, including "a fiend that to a stake / Of fire his desperate self is tethering." When he finally recovers, Peter pulls a corpse from the river. It "uprises like a ghost," but now

Peter has pulled himself together and he feels pity rather than fear. The man whose body he has pulled from the stream is identified mainly as a father, as subsequent events will emphasize. When Peter hears the doleful sound made by a little boy looking for his father, Peter is properly haunted by the boy's cry of pain. The manuscript makes the point even more emphatically that "the boy is seeking his dead Father / His Father dead and drown'd." Here is a scene repeatedly found in varied ways throughout Wordsworth's early poetry, and as he usually does, Wordsworth distances himself from identification with the boy through devices of narrative, metaphor, and symbol.

When Peter hears the little boy cry for his father, Peter hears his own dead child cry for himself, a father who never was. In this narrative episode Wordsworth thus transfers identities, so that a son can kill his father, search for him, and become the father without ever actually doing the deed itself. But the matter is still more complex, necessarily relating sex with death and guilt in fathering identity. For Peter Bell has spent his life in pursuit of erotic pleasures, having been "married" to twelve wives. His life has been a careless satisfaction of sexual desire. But, and we begin to understand the motive behind his aggression, there was one particular wife he cannot now forget. When Peter hears the little boy cry for this father, Peter Bell hears a ghost of the unborn. The Ass carries Peter past an abandoned chapel, a "ruinous" place that reminds him of his marriage with his sixth wife. This reminder is a recognition that makes him feel "a stifling power compress his frame," a return of the feeling he had while beating the Ass. Earlier he asked himself why he should feel so much guilt and fear for having thought of stealing the Ass, and he could only think that "the devil in me wrought." The real reason, the one that supplied the energy of feeling so disproportionate to the earlier event, is a reason kept buried until now in Peter's "forgotten" past. This real reason

is to be found in the death of his sixth wife and their unborn child, for Peter's ways of life had caused that sixteen-
year-old child-bride to die "of a broken heart."

Not until this day has he acknowledged his guilt for
that girl's death. The Ass takes Peter home in a metaphorical and literal sense, for when Peter sees the grief of the
family left by the dead man, he can grieve for his own betrayed family (or families). Peter earlier responded to the
voice of a Methodist Minister with an emotional outburst
of tears: then "each fibre of his frame was weak; / Weak
all the animal within," as Peter identified with the very
creature he was riding—the "trusty guide" and guardian
who kept to its station. When Peter arrives at the home of
the dead man, he is mistaken by a little girl, who joyfully
cries out, "'My father! here's my father!'" Her recognition
is painfully false in one sense, but in another it is absolutely correct. Wordsworth reenforces this identification when
he allows Peter's erotic instinct to rise one more time,
when he tries to console the widowed mother: "He longs
to press her to his heart, / From love that cannot find relief." His love now, however, is conditioned by conscience, and so Peter Bell will not repeat his previous mistakes this time. The woman leaves in her grief, and Peter
turns to walk into a shade of darksome trees. There he
feels "as if his mind were sinking deep / Through years
that have been long asleep! / The trance is passed away—
he wakes."

WORDSWORTH has, then, in Peter Bell described and
analyzed a mind which seems uncommonly hard and cruel,
crossed between the savage and the vicious urbanite,
haunted by a ghost it tries to keep buried away from its
consciousness. But there are several clues that Peter Bell is
not a unique kind of person, that he is in fact a very common man who has undergone a sensational experience
common in the development of every man. First of all, in

the digression that opens Part Third the narrator tells how a "gentle Soul" was once reading when his room darkened to reveal on the page of his book an illuminated "*word*— which to his dying day / Perplexed the good man's gentle soul." If Peter Bell's violent response to seemingly insignificant events can rouse feelings of guilt in strange fashion, then how much more strange when "a gentle Soul" can be thus perplexed:

> The ghostly word, thus plainly seen,
> Did never from his lips depart;
> But he hath said, poor gentle wight!
> It brought full many a sin to light
> Out of the bottom of his heart.

The powers that bring about such events are called, first, "Dread Spirits," then "potent Spirits," but finally "Spirits of the Mind." The narrator himself has felt their presence often "In darkness and the stormy night."

The poet-narrator summons these same Spirits of the Mind to assist him in telling his tale. He is putting before the reader the very "word" that perplexed the good reader's "gentle soul," perhaps even bringing "full many a sin to light / Out of the bottom of his heart." The narrator is, in fact, identified in his function with Peter Bell himself after Peter's transformation. When Peter tries to tell the widow what has happened to her husband,

> He trembles—he is pale as death;
> His voice is weak with perturbation;
> He turns aside his head, he pauses;
> Poor Peter from a thousand causes
> Is crippled sore in his narration.

This repeats the narrator's own experience when he rushed from his flight of imagination to join a group gathered to hear his story:

> I spoke with faltering voice, like one
> Not wholly rescued from the pale
> Of a wild dream, or worse illusion;
> But straight, to cover my confusion,
> Began the promised Tale.

When, in MS material rejected from the published version, the narrator further adds that he is "somewhat out of breath / With lips, no doubt, and visage pale, / And sore too from a slight contusion," he suggests an identity not only with Peter Bell but also with the Ass itself, whose beating is the first scene the narrator wants to describe. The tone of the poem is, then, made ambivalent by the self-mockery of the narrator's identification with the savage hero as well as with the stubborn Ass, but their unified function is clear as a discovery of conscience, the "trusty guide" of father to son on the way to social order and civilization.

IN "Michael" Wordsworth again examined this difficult process of civilizing the instincts, and again he presents it as a matter primarily determined by relationships between fathers and sons. The point here is that the process takes a terrible toll on the paternal affections, even as Luke's own separate identity requires that he must do something to break from the authority of his parents. The father's point of view serves the natural purpose of regression to submissiveness: it contradicts the cultural purpose of the child's separation from the authority of parents.

Michael has a right to be satisfied with his naturalistic identity. His strength is as much in his mental health as in his physical prowess. He is industrious, and he is patient. His erotic instinct, also, has not failed him in his old age: it is "a pleasurable feeling of blind love." This blind love is his animal connection with the nature that surrounds and includes him. Although it is a "pleasure which there is in life itself," this instinct in fact draws Michael closer to the inanimate source of his life, closer to his death. The poem is a picture of patience and stoical forbearance, as Michael endures and then accepts his natural end in death. But the poem is also a picture of dehumanization, as Michael's identity with the land increases until after his death only the land remains.

When Luke was a babe in arms, Michael did "him female service." Michael is both a mother and a father to Luke. Michael is the hold that nature has on a child through the child's dependence on its parents. Insofar as Michael attempts to keep Luke subservient to his or nature's authority, Michael is acting "naturally," but he is nevertheless no friend to his son's own spiritual development and he is no friend to the aims of culture. From Michael's point of view, the cause for his son's loss is evil and vicious, a fact of law and society. But, at the same time, Luke's rescue might also have come from law and society, from the kinsman in the city who could employ Luke for a while. From Luke's point of view, then, the prospect of going to the city is exhilarating, as even Michael is forced to admit: "Heaven bless thee, Boy! / Thy heart these two weeks has been beating fast / With many hopes; it should be so—yes—yes," but Michael cannot accept what he admits: "I knew that thou couldst never have a wish / To leave me, Luke."

In this same talk with Luke, Michael reveals the main hope he has for keeping Luke tied to him and to the land: "thou hast been bound to me / Only by links of love." The link of love fast becomes the chain of duty when news of Luke's delinquency reaches Michael: "Meantime Luke began / To slacken in his duty." The hold that Michael has on Luke has lasted from the cradle to the day of Luke's enforced departure. The very stones that Michael points out to Luke for building the sheepfold are signs of Michael's fundamental intention toward his son, to fix the boy, even enclose his heart, to himself and through himself, to nature. "The strength of love" that allows Michael to survive Luke's betrayal is a psychological irony of profound importance, but it is also a poignant reminder of the unhappiness forced upon a person who succeeds in achieving the separation from parental authority that culture demands.

Most of the other new poems published in 1800 are poems whose main subjects center on death. The Matthew poems elaborate the principle that a person does not willingly abandon a love-object, not even when a substitute is available. The Lucy poems examine a grief that has been so intense that a turning away from reality ensues. And "The Brothers" is an ambitious poem that dramatizes mourning, with hints at the complications of melancholia; it elaborates a theme of *Peter Bell* and anticipates one of *The Excursion*. "The Brothers" also echoes "Michael," for Leonard is a Luke who has come back home after many years of absence, and the Priest is a Michael in his unchanging attachment to the land as well as in his industry for domestic order.

As the Priest reminds Leonard, the older brother had always been seen as the main support for the younger. James at first was sorrow-stricken when Leonard left; he "pined, and pined." James seemed to recover his spirit, but just then occurred the strange accident when he fell over a cliff to his death. Leonard is alarmed that James committed suicide, but the Priest offers the explanation of sleepwalking. Psychologically, Leonard's alarm is well founded, as Wordsworth well knows, and the Priest's explanation (a "conjecture") does not mitigate the force of belief in suicide. James could not sleep because of his "disquietude and grief" at his brother's separation.

James is a sketch of despondency, of melancholia, distinguished by "a profoundly painful dejection," loss of interest in the outside world, and a lowering of self-regard. The poet's insight into the reason for James's death is deeper than the Priest's, and Leonard's understanding is accurate but necessarily repressed in the process of his own mourning. What Leonard must do by his mourning is to repress his feelings of guilt for James's death. That he feels guilt is not only natural to the experience of mourning, but it is ironically suggested by the poem's conclusion, when Leonard leaves without identifying himself to the Priest: he writes a letter in which he adds, "with a hope to be forgiven, / That it was from the weakness of his heart / He had not dared to tell him who he was." To be "forgiven" is what he must accomplish within himself, if Leonard is to free his ego from bondage to the dead. Leaving the valley behind him forever is a good sign that he has successfully repressed his feelings of guilt. Repression, however, does not mean elimination. He has had to give up much pleasure in choosing to leave the valley again. His years of self-imposed exile have left him with a sign of his grief as well as his survival, "grey-headed Mariner" that he has become.

This instance of strengthened ego coming from a successful repression of guilt is particularly well examined in several of the Matthew and Lucy poems of 1800. In the case of Matthew, as in "The Fountain," for example, the old man proves to be strong to resist the impulse to compensate, or sublimate, through friendship and song. These are products of his ability to wear "a face of joy." The strength of his ego is indicated by his hunger for love. When Matthew says "by none / Am I enough beloved," he not only reveals the continuing power of eros in his life, he touches upon a cause for the inescapable sorrow of human existence, a sorrow which Freud explained in this famous way: "A strong egoism is a protection against disease, but in the last resort we must begin to love in order that we may not fall ill, and must fall ill if, in consequence of frustration, we cannot love." Matthew, like his creator Wordsworth, knows better than to think he can abandon either his need to love or his accommodation with death; his life is a healthy achievement of ego, which has constructed a useful mask of happiness as its defense against enemies of stability. Matthew has learned from experience that his identity is a construction from complex forces within and without himself. The mask, which for Matthew is "a face of joy" that he "wears" for the world, *is* Matthew in the sense that it is a sign of his ego's command over his passions and his conscience.

Unlike Matthew and Leonard, the speaker of the Lucy poems does not always have command over his feelings. He has no mask to identify the command of a triumphant ego. The Lucy poems show a tendency by their speaker-lover to regress, to yield to the temptation of nature, and to submit to death—turning away from reality while clinging to the lost love through a kind of hallucinatory wishfulness. "A Slumber did my spirit seal" is the climactic statement of the speaker's urge to identify with the dead. This poem also hauntingly shows how much of love is narcissistic, especially the further the mind regresses to infantile states of being. Matthew is old enough to have carried through the long process of mourning to a healthy conclusion, although it cost him a great deal of pain and unhappiness. The speaker of the Lucy poems is still too close to his loss, either in time or in force of memory, to have ably assumed command over himself and his emotions. In "She dwelt among the untrodden ways" the lover's self-centered emotions draw his mourning back to himself when he ends his poem with, "the difference to me." The lover's loss of Lucy does make a *difference,* but it is a difference to *"me."* This last word of the poem is also the important last word in the process of working through melancholia.

Ego must withdraw from a fixation with the past, with the lost loved one. The mind must call back its erotic energy if it is to be healthy. In the *difference* is the Wordsworthian gap, or abyss, again, out of which will arise the energy of his poem; from the wound of his loss comes the vigor of his creation. This calling back, or return, of the power to love, from the lost object to the losing subject is an important first, though precarious, step in maturation. It must not be the final step or the lover will end up loving only himself as he did when he was an infant. Between the position of Matthew and this of Lucy's lover is a great psychological distance, difficult to cover and dangerous to achieve. Not only is the lover vulnerable to the threat of infantile regression into narcissism, but he is also vulnerable to an equally strong temptation to construct out of his dead beloved a ghostly "ego-ideal." That is merely projecting into the future what has been binding in the past in the "infantile ego," something that considers itself capable of "all perfections." The spectrous ego-ideal is a reconstruction, a defense against loss, of parental authority, what had been the primal love object; this same ego-ideal is, at the same time, a power against which the adult ego must constantly battle to maintain its stability. Wordsworth's later poetry will be increasingly concerned with this bizarre twist to mental development, when the infantile ego of the past gives place to the ego-ideal of the future, promising illusions of pleasure quite as unhealthy as those of childhood.

*KEEPING* in touch with his past, with childhood's pleasures, seems not to be a great problem for the speaker in most of the 1807 poems, such as "To The Daisy," with its "pleasures high and turbulent," or "To The Same Flower" (i.e., the Celandine), with its point that "pleasures newly found are sweet." The apparent ease of rediscovering pleasures of childhood does not mislead the poet into thinking that those pleasures are unimportant. In the popular little poem, "I Wandered Lonely as a Cloud," Wordsworth narrates the important function of recording and recovering pleasure. The ease of statement in this poem is a function of a technical mastery that should not be confused with the psychological process it describes and, by describing it, enacts what it describes. The value of the recovered pleasure is possible only because the speaker has experienced the pain of its loss.

The great poems of 1807 are, however, generally not praises for pleasure discovered or rediscovered. They are dramas of the soul renouncing immediate pleasure as a release from tension, and embracing reality as a mounting tension of sorrow and pain. Because the embrace is a gesture of art, reality acquires a depth of value that transforms pain into greater, paradoxical, pleasure. This is the statement of such poems as "Resolution and Independence," the "Ode to Duty," and the "Ode: Intimations of Immortality." The most dramatic of these is the encounter with the old leech gatherer, reminiscent of encounters described in the Salisbury Plain poems.

In the earlier poems too little is made of the actual encounters, even between the Sailor and the Female Vagrant, where confession is more important than discovery. "Resolution and Independence" has a clarity of self-discovery and a firmness of understanding that are missing from the Salisbury Plain poems. The psychological value of his encounter with the old man is that the youth acquires a strength of ego ("resolution") that frees him from anxieties and fantasies for an open engagement with reality ("independence"). The form of this acquisition has similarities with the form of the phenomenon known in psychoanalysis as "transference." While the poem does not, of course, describe a psycho-analytic session between patient and physician, its emotional dynamics follow a course from strange unhappiness, anxiety, and dejection, to healthy stability of mind that psychoanalysis aims for. Wordsworth's poem achieves the aim of therapy: "to replace what is unconscious by what is conscious," and to force the patient "to transform repetition into memory"—by recognizing "that his feelings do not arise from a present situation," but that they are instead a *repetition* of something that has happened earlier in his life.

The old Leech Gatherer is a catalyst of imagination for Wordsworth's youthful speaker, bringing into focus what troubles the youth and thereby giving the youth power over himself through the knowledge he has won from the experience. The speaker is his own therapist. Not the least of his new self-understanding is his discovery that he can *be* his own therapist. His life of pleasant thought yields to one of blind thoughts, which in turn become images of dead poets who come in the end to "despondency and madness." Then he is startled by his encounter with "the oldest man. . .that ever wore grey hairs." This pattern is a familiar one to readers of Wordsworth's earlier poetry. The energies of the youth's unleashed feeling (libido, imagination) seize upon this new object, endowing it with a strange meaning that expresses a desire of something that has been buried in the unconscious of the young man. The old man is seen "as a huge stone" "couched on the bald top of an eminence," which in turn is "like a sea-beast crawled forth"; these similes manufactured by the self-conscious poet are shapes assumed by the unconscious power of the mind when it finds an object around which it can gather its attention. In themselves these images are highly suggestive of what has suddenly cast the youth into dejection, a mixture of blind ambition and beastly passion. The content, however, is less important than the process of its discovery.

Still absorbed by his imaginative (libidinal) apprehension of the old man, the youth only faintly hears the Leech Gatherer's gentle answer to his question. The poet in him is most impressed with the orderliness of the old man's courteous speech, as his words "in solemn order followed each," "choice word and measured phrase, above the reach / Of ordinary men." While this talk begins the process of therapy, emphasizing as it does the importance of disciplined language for mastering experience, the youth cannot yet attend carefully to what the old man is saying: "nor word from word could I divide." Suddenly the old man seems like someone "met with in a dream," bringing back the former thoughts of fear and pain, images of death. Just as suddenly, the youth recognizes and therefore makes conscious, the source of his fears. He masters them by an identification with the old man, internalizing the old man's authority, and submitting to the discipline of this newly discovered, or manufactured, ideal.

The vague fears of failure and death which have shaken the confidence of the youth are mastered because they are made conscious. The exact mechanism is for the moment a healthy reestablishment of parental authority. What the youth must beware, however, is allowing himself to become as enslaved to this newly internalized authority as he has successfully avoided becoming enslaved to dark forces of unconscious origin. He has conquered the fantasies of his passions by means of a new fantasy, an ideal of culture. This new ideal is one of the most uncanny phenomena of the mind, allowing the ego to free itself from bondage to parents and the past but, at the same time, threatening to establish a new bondage to culture and the future. In the poems of 1807 Wordsworth tends to call this ideal of control "duty."

The "Ode to Duty" skirts one of the new dangers for mental health, addressing Duty as a "stern Daughter of the Voice of God." The danger here is to mistake a construct of mind for an object of authority, to forget what the poet of "Resolution and Independence" realized—that "by our own spirits are we deified." Another danger of submission to an ideal of duty is to fly from the reality of pain and tension, to regress to infantile pleasures, and finally, to abandon the power of eros and life for the repose of death. All these versions of danger the poet realizes, even as he calls upon Duty for "guidance" and "support." The "Ode to Duty" is an exciting poem because it contains Wordsworth's realization that human happiness is a very problematic achievement of delicately balanced powers. Duty is the ego-ideal which has taken the place of the parent in the mind of the speaker, necessary as one of the sources of power for the ego's use to control dangerous instincts—either to repress them from full expression, or to direct them through approved projects of work and love. The poet is no longer a child driven by "chance-desires," which are a weight dragging mature mind back into primal unconsciousness. The key for mature development beyond pleasure is "control," "but in the quietness of thought." Wordsworth recognizes, and emphasizes, the danger of longing "for a repose that ever is the same." He makes it clear that the *longing* is not the same as giving into the longing. The rest of the poem is designed to add to his control a consciousness of the dangers attendant upon submitting to an ideal of duty.

The clearest evidence for this conscious need, to "control" the idea of control ("duty"), is in the stanza which was removed from later versions of the poem:

> Yet not the less would I throughout
> Still act according to the voice
> Of my own wish; and feel past doubt
> That my submissiveness was choice:
> Not seeking in the school of pride
> For "precepts over dignified",
> Denial and restraint I prize
> No farther than they breed a second Will more wise.

His removal of this stanza suggests that the later Wordsworth no longer wanted to control his ideal, but rather to be controlled by it in an increasingly willful way. On the other hand, the rest of the poem (even without this stanza) continues to emphasize the power of the ego itself, which should use all of its resources for control, including its ideals of conscience and duty: "Oh, let my weakness have an end!" and "The confidence of reason give," are not the empty gestures of a helpless ego. They are utterances of an honest soul trying to keep itself balanced between power and weakness as virtues of independence and humility, renouncing pleasure for the larger claims of reality.

Among these larger claims is the fact of death, and its struggle with eros for possession of the ego. It is this struggle between eros and death, as well as the ego's own struggle with both, that lends some of the drama and power all feel in reading the great "Ode: Intimations of Immortality From Recollections of Early Childhood." The further virtue of this poem, its dignity, is a product of its psychological poise and mental strength quite as much as it is a function of its stylistic discipline and successful realization of a traditional genre. Indeed, its style is its poise and strength. It has affinities with both "Resolution and Independence" and the "Ode to Duty," but it stands alone, quite apart from those poems, because it shows the self probing itself without an external prop, and it admits more of the elements of conflict in the process of submitting to a new "control." In a psychological sense, as well as in the literary sense, this poem deserves its fame, because it is an exercise in mental therapy as well as an achievement of imaginative power: in a poem by Wordsworth, the achievement *is* the exercise, and that is a major revelation of this poem as well as others yet to come.

It is not the world around him that counts the most for the speaker of the "Ode: Intimations of Immortality." This is not to say that external reality is unimportant, for the speaker still celebrates its pleasures of beauty and loveliness. The point, however, is in his self-knowledge. The center of the poem is in the ego, the "I" that knows: "Turn wheresoe'er I may," "The things which I have seen I can see no more," "But yet I know, where'er I go," and "I again am strong." He has been acted upon, in the distant past when "every common sight, / To me did seem / Apparelled in celestial light," and in the more recent past when "To me alone there came a thought of grief." He is more actor than acted upon, declared by the force of his statement that, "I again am strong." His strength comes from his egoistic ability to keep control over his ideals of the past and his ideals of the future, balancing erotic instincts with death instincts—and commanding both to do the work of the ego for endurance with dignity.

The source of identity may lie in a realm of mystery and consciousness, whence "our birth is but a sleep and a forgetting," but that identity itself is a matter of coming into consciousness, a phenomenon so primitive in the evolution of an individual mind that it seems never to have existed "in entire forgetfulness." The primal instincts which make for existence were sufficient unto themselves at the earliest stages of individual as well as cultural history; in that sense, at a minimum, "heaven lies about us in our infancy." Instinct as a "light" is a center without circumference and blind to itself. Certainly, to instinct itself, any imposition of limits will seem threatening, but those limits must and will be imposed by the process of maturation, until "at length the Man perceives [the light] die away, / And fade into the light of common day." Both naturalization and domestication, or acculturation, are enemies to the light of instinct, which seeks immediate gratification as its only rationale for being.

Naturalization requires that instincts be made subordinate to the authority of parents for survival and gratification, while acculturation requires separation from parental authority as well as continuous self-control and sublimation of desire. Wordsworth's poem does not condemn these processes of human development, for condemnation would be a foolish denial of reality. It does, however, deplore failures of mind and spirit when they occur as defeats of individuality and victories of death. When a person spends his entire life in "endless imitation" of human life, he will inevitably fall beneath the weight of its "earthly freight." This death of self occurs when "custom" bears down heavy as frost and nearly extinguishes the instincts of self-gratification. Naturalization had made the self aware of "pleasures of her own," "yearnings she hath in her own natural kind," directing one toward realistic, though increasingly complicated, gratifications. But domestication substitutes new, artificial forms of gratification for natural desires, until instincts seem extinguished and self is lost in society.

Recovering those buried instincts, making conscious the sources of childhood energy even as the fantasies of childhood, is the task of the healthy ego, battling as it must to keep its independence from the authority of culture as well as from the authority of nature and parents. Culture wants the energies of life for its "dialogues of business, love, or strife," and so it trains the ego as if its "whole vocation/ Were endless imitation." Nature wants to divert the ego from its independent "glories" to a reliance upon all those pleasures with which she "fills her lap." To keep these claims in balance is the great need for a healthy ego, and this it can do if it will use one claim against the other. Culture keeps the ego busy, raising tension and building things; nature lures the ego into a luxury of relaxation, lowering tension or keeping it steady. The task of the ego is to mix the business of culture with the luxury of nature, and one of the most successful ways to do this is to do the work of art, turning fantasy into reality.

Art gives form to the formless. It is an activity of culture that requires a renunciation of infantile pleasures. However, art preserves what it shapes, keeping within forms those instincts of passion which drive life toward its self-chosen goals. The poet gives thanks, therefore, when he can recover his buried instincts, "those obstinate questionings," those "blank misgivings of a Creature / Moving about in worlds not realized." It is not for the liberties and pleasures of childhood, with its simple creed, that he yearns in his maturity. What his adult ego needs is the self-direction which instincts insist upon. That self-direction includes a self-chosen way to die as well as a self-chosen way to live. Therefore, when he recovers the powers of instinct, he can "look through death" with a "philosophic mind" which does not deny the reality of its instinct for death any more than it does its instinct for love.

# CHAPTER FIVE:

## The Child Is Father

The critical point that turns *The Prelude* (1805-6) in the right direction occurs in Book One just as the poet admits that much is wanting in himself. He says that he feels "like a false Steward who hath much received / And renders nothing back." This alludes to the parable of the talents, but it also prepares for later analyses of guilt that take up much of the poem's energies of self discovery. The poet has hoarded his creativity, his erotic powers, and he feels the internal pressure of an accumulated energy demanding release. The affirmative impulse of eros drives the poet against his negative instinct to deny. The tension between these powers has produced his feelings of guilt.

After he begins his rigorous inquisition of his past to determine whether he has betrayed his character, Wordsworth makes the leap that will allow him to turn his negations into affirmations. His present sense of guilt is a refinding of himself as a child, when his guilt first emerged in contacts with external reality. He will need considerable time and analysis before he can uncover the primal scene of his guilt, but he moves in the right direction toward that discovery when he admits that he "was a fell destroyer" as a child. This admission is playful in one sense, but in another it is deadly serious, as most of the incidents he remembers from his childhood are episodes of intrusion and disobedience—if not outright acts of destruction. His instinct for aggression dominated his childhood, leaving him with memories of "troubled pleasure" and painful (far from the bliss of) solitude.

When in Book Two he exclaims of the baby nursed in its Mother's arms, "No outcast he, bewilder'd and depress'd," Wordsworth is contrasting his own present sense of bewilderment and depression with infant security, once his own but now seemingly disappeared forever. He recalls himself mainly as an "outcast." His present freedom from the confines of "yon City's walls" has become a reenforcement of his feeling that he is an outcast. His fear that he cannot survive as an outcast is the main threat his ego has to deal with. By recalling the many childhood experiences of fear at being an outcast, Wordsworth is exercising therapeutic control over his death instinct—not by mixing it with eros and turning it into sadism, which was his childhood defense, but rather by accepting the guilt and draining the energy from destruction to leave eros in command.

Contemplating himself as a child, he sometimes thinks of himself as "two consciousnesses, conscious of myself / And of some other Being." The past has a "self-presence" that cannot be denied without risking serious mental illness. At first Wordsworth calls up memories from what Freud designated as the "preconscious," experiences available for consciousness, poised on the threshold of attention; to get at those "days / Disown'd by memory" and linked with "no conscious memory," the poet must probe more deeply into the scenes of guilt and troubled pleasures. Hence, the remarkable achievement of *The Prelude:* the conscious mind of the poet not only admits the existence of an unconscious realm, but it actually consents to join in exploration and revelation of those very experiences which it had itself repressed and earlier denied.

*THE FIRST* four books of *The Prelude* explore the unconscious workings of Wordsworth's "other Being." The poet traces the flow of desire from underground sources until they emerge into a full sunshine of healthy consciousness. He discovers in the process that some of the tools of maturation, forces of separation from dependence upon nature and mother, have become ends in themselves. Books Five through Ten explore the unconscious workings of conscience (consciously akin to "duty") through such social institutions as education and politics. Finally, in Books Eleven through Thirteen, Wordsworth synthesizes the products of his analysis and achieves the balance of mind which he celebrates as "genuine Liberty." This balance brings him the amplitude of mind that Keats called the egotistical sublime.

The "wantonness" Wordsworth enjoyed as a naked boy of five is remembered as "a strong desire" which "o'erpowered [his] better reason" when he plundered the bird-traps of others. When he "heard among the solitary hills / Low breathings coming after" him, he was projecting an internal fantasy as an external reality. Such experience was a part of his passage through the crisis of his sexual development, with which Wordsworth identifies the origins of his creative powers as a poet. When he borrowed a boat to row out upon a lake, he repeated his earlier action of swimming in the river, with the rising and falling motion of rowing or swimming. He also experienced fears of guilt that possessed his conscious mind after he plundered the bird-traps. Again he associates his activity with a bird: "as I rose upon the stroke, my Boat / Went heaving through the water, like a Swan" (a simile he used in "An Evening Walk"). More clearly than before, he here describes his memory in erotic language. Later the boy's mind is haunted by "huge and mighty Forms that do not live / Like living men." In such instances as this, Wordsworth recovers through memory his instinct for love combined with his instinct for aggression; therefore, he required as a child the same discipline that he seeks to exercise over himself as an adult: "sanctifying, by such discipline, / Both pain and fear, until we recognize / A grandeur in the beatings of the heart."

The ideal of his quest, to identify discipline with desire, provides a major motive for Book Second, wishing to give "to duty and to truth / The eagerness of infantine desire." Immediately Wordsworth translates this wish into an experience of repression: "A tranquillizing spirit presses now / On my corporeal frame." The wish followed by resistance, paradoxically in this instance, causes *not* union and synthesis (as objects of the wish) but rather a division of consciousness: "I seem / Two consciousnesses, conscious of myself / And of some other Being." The poet is not yet ready for the fulfillment of his wish; indeed, the wish itself is divisive. This "other being" is akin to the "vague longing," "strong desire," "troubled pleasure," and troubling forms like the huge cliff with its "voluntary power instinct" of Book First. All those feelings seemed to rise to penetrate the boy's consciousness from a realm below the threshold of his conscious mind, from where "there was a darkness, call it solitude, / Or blank desertion." His childhood memories, as fantasies, carried for Wordsworth a combination of "danger or desire."

Book Second tries to discover something more about the nature of that "other Being" which childhood had such trouble repressing. Throughout, the poet has had to deal with all kinds of resistances that thwart and perplex his efforts. He submits himself to a kind of trance, or hypnosis, in order to approach the primal scene of desire:

> Oh! then the calm
> And dead still water lay upon my mind
> Even with a weight of pleasure, and the sky
> Never before so beautiful, sank down

Into my heart, and held me like a dream.

Just as his present need is to recover his capacity to feel
and to give affective direction to his new-found freedom,
his earliest childhood needs were to "gather passion from
his Mother's eye," to hold "mute dialogues with his
Mother's heart" while "Nurs'd in his Mother's arms." By
way of his mother he had a "filial bond" with the world.
It is no surprise, then, to discover that Wordsworth's adult
anxiety of lacking direction in his life derives from his
childhood anxiety of losing connection with the world
that was his mother. He describes how strange it felt to be
"left alone, / Seeking the visible world, nor knowing
why": he "would walk alone" and "among the hills he
sate / Alone." He is not quite prepared, however, to confront this issue directly in his present analysis. Wordsworth
interrupts the course of memory associations with his
mother to describe his separation from the Lake District
(with all its associations of nature and family) when he
went down to Cambridge. This separation he deals with in
Books Three and Four, but he deals with it as an external
rather than an internal problem. When he returned to his
home for his first summer vacation, his joy of release from
captivity quickly gave way to "an inner falling-off" in a
repetition of the familiar Wordsworthian pattern of psychological experience.

Although he claims that "to the brim / His heart was
full" on that glorious morning when "vows / Were made
for" him, he has to admit that for the most part "something there was about him that perplex'd / Th'authentic
sight of reason, press'd too closely" on his mind during
that summer vacation. When, in Book Five, he summarizes
the value of education, he describes the "natural" education provided by a mother hen to her brood of chicks.
This Wordsworth intends to contrast with "the monster
birth / Engender'd by these too industrious times." But,

as he admits, his "drift hath scarcely . . . been obvious."
To interrupt with such an admission seems like an aesthetic fault in the poem, but it is a psychological symptom of
an ego defending itself from admitting more than it intended.

This interruption is akin to those scenes of division, of
woundings in sacred places where the mind turns round
upon itself. For Wordsworth again regressed to his own
childhood trauma of separation from his mother. It is not
only the picture of modern education he recoils from
showing, and it is not only the perverted product of modern education he calls a monster birth: he admits what he
does not fully accept about himself, that he desired his
mother and he blames her for having left him alone when
she died. The real monster with which he has to contend
is his own guilty self. As before, he associates his mother
with a bird: "Behold the Parent Hen amid her Brood,"
and her relationship to her chicks is "a centre of the circle
which they make." There is more security in the natural
world of the barnyard than there was in his childhood—a
structuring theme to be found in much of Wordsworth's
early writing.

> Early died
> My honour'd Mother; she who was the heart
> And hinge of all our leanings and our loves:
> She left us destitute, and as we might
> Trooping together. Little suits it me
> To break upon the sabbath of her rest
> With any thought that looks at others' blame,
> Nor would I praise her but in perfect love.

There is in the mind of the mature poet a check on his
desire to blame his mother, a check that reveals itself in
the ambivalence of the language itself. He says what he
says he will not say when he protests that it suits him "lit-

tle" "to break upon the sabbath of her rest." Hence is he checked. But the many lines of praise for his mother constitute a defensive reaction of compensation for admitting, even as it is unconscious to the present process, a criticism of his beloved mother.

Wordsworth has in this passage come as close as he can to the source of his originating anxiety. Until he can take control of his unconscious life, he will not be able to give direction to his conscious life. Before he can understand the meaning of his adult independence ("freedom"), he must make conscious his childhood anxieties of separation from his mother, his desire for her, and his aggression toward his father. In other words, he must allow those repressed feelings (unconscious energies of affect) to emerge into his consciousness where his ego can take control. If he can admit that underlying his present fears and uncertainties are feelings toward his parents which he had repressed, he will have mastered his unconscious life. His desire for his mother, from whom he was traumatically separated, must be reworked to overcome pressures from his unconscious life, and his fear of his father, along with his wish to usurp his father's place, must be reworked to overcome the tyranny of his punishing conscience.

*MOST* of *The Prelude* is taken up with Wordsworth's reconstruction of his social conscience, although readers generally applaud and emphasize the early sections with their scenes of early childhood. Of course, Wordsworth realized how important those early experiences of childhood and infancy were for the development of his mind and imagination: "our childhood sits, / Our simple childhood sits upon a throne / That hath more power than all the elements." That throne of power is, psychologically speaking, the reservoir of mental energy that Freud called the id, with its "dumb yearnings, hidden appetites" that "must have their food" (as Wordsworth describes it). The ego is charged with the task of guiding while satisfying those yearnings and appetites, including the child's desire for his mother, for maintaining his bond with his mother and with all the forces of nature which the mother represents to the infant. Wordsworth had to find ways of sublimating his desire for his mother early in his life, because at about the time when most children experience the problems of the Oedipal project, he lost his mother to death. His feelings of barely suppressed anger at this event were complicated by his contemporary need to work out a defense against Oedipal desires, and so his major work of analysis in *The Prelude* is to uncover his struggles against his "conscience" (super-ego), to which he had submitted much of his psychic power as his defensive reaction to the loss of his mother. Most of *The Prelude* is, then, from Book Four, an analysis of the poet's moral anxiety growing out of his relationships with his father and various other authority figures whose images he had incorporated for psychic strength.

After the trauma of losing his mother, the boy's energies were increasingly of a narcissistic kind. In his loneliness, all that he saw "Appear'd like something in himself, a dream / A prospect in his mind." It was at that time he felt "a plastic power / Abode with" him, "a forming hand, at times /Rebellious, acting in a devious mood." When he went to Cambridge, his behavior was so self-centered that some who saw him thought he was mad. He was "a spoil'd Child" in the sense that his life had been turned back to himself after the great betrayal of his mother's death.

While much of the remainder of *The Prelude* explores the poet's ways of redirecting his psychic energies, finding objects for satisfying the aim of his frustrated desires, at the same time the poem analyzes the concurrent pressures of authority figures with which the boy's ego identified—in order to get the strength it needed to control those psychic energies. If the mature Wordsworth can bring into his consciousness the cause for his guilt feelings toward his father, he will free his ego from its bondage to yet another part of his past. But, before he can disclose the causes for his guilt, he has to recognize the guilt itself. By noticing how often the poet uses the word *rise,* or variants of it, we can follow the process by which he gradually is able to identify the force which at first seems to come from below his consciousness but finally reveals itself as a power of repression. In other words, what seemed at first to be an unconscious force breaking through repression (from the unconscious) is discovered to be an unconscious force *of* repression: the "other Being" is not a monster of the id, but rather a tyrant of the super-ego.

At the opening of the poem, following his first impulse of joy in freedom, Wordsworth felt "a longing" in him that "rose / To brace himself to some determin'd aim." He knows that this longing must be satisfied, but he does not know how to bring that about until he can identify it: if he can name it, then he can use it rather than be used by it. It is something like "duty" and "discipline," but those words miss the mark. This longing is not the same as his desire for attachment with nature, or behind nature for attachment with his mother. This longing is something quite different, akin to his need to be punished and his feeling of guilt. When he stole the boat, the cliff "uprear'd its head" as if with "voluntary power instinct" and became a trouble of his dreams. This trouble worked as a "weight," a "pressure," and a "discipline" on his childhood desires described in Books One and Two. When he first approached Cambridge, the Chapel of King's College seemed to "rear / His pinnacles above the dusky groves" while the place "seem'd more and more / To have an eddy's force, and suck'd" him into its power. The sky itself "rear'd above his head." When he recalls his first summer vacation in Book Four, Wordsworth admits that it might have been better had he spent his time in study and thoughtful quietness, "to exalt the mind," as he puts it. Such sublimation of psychic energies would indeed be desirable for the function of his super-ego, but "the memory of one particular hour / Doth here rise up against" him even as he suggests he may have wasted his energies.

What rises on this occasion, however, is not the great represser but an object of repression—or so it seems at first. The memory is one Wordsworth describes as an unconscious dedication during a glorious summer morning after a nighttime of revelry. To have given himself so fully to an evening of "promiscuous rout," "unaim'd prattle," and "young love-liking" might indeed have excited his conscience into an activity of repression, but what that evening gave way to was an experience of almost mystical self-discipline and as such was something much approved by conscience and super-ego. That morning when he felt that he "should be, else sinning greatly, / A dedicated Spirit" was what his conscience allowed him to remember, to rise up as testimony to prove that he had paid a moral price for his summer of licentiousness. Furthermore, he reconstructs an event of haunting power which occurred during the same summer vacation. This event, an encounter with a discharged soldier on a moonlit road, rises to conclude Book Four. It is a very important episode for the poet to remember because it was further reenforcement of his identification with his father. In fact, the episode describes how the boy took into his mind the figure of authority to make it a part of himself, until the tall man and the boy exchange roles between them.

Like the cliff that rose to stride after him during the boating incident, this "uncouth shape" intimidates the young man's mind. But now his ego is strong enough to deal with the episode as an external reality, and so after perusing the man for a long time "with mingled sense / Of fear and sorrow," Wordsworth left his concealment and approached him. The young man became the older man's guide, although the young man was astonished by the "tall / And ghastly figure moving at his side." Even while he has taken on the function of an authority, giving guidance and moral instruction to his elder, the young man is still something of little boy in his feelings—he wishes, as Freud observed in "Family Romances," "to be big like his father."

BY THE END of *The Prelude* it is clearer that underlying the image of the cliff that rises to haunt the boy rowing in a borrowed boat is a complex of feelings associated with the authority of his father. The repeated images of rising and heights carry with them a burden of such feelings, of ambivalent wishes for removing the father and for identifying with the father. When Wordsworth works through to a recognition of the force which has haunted his imagination for most of his life, he ecstatically announces his psychic independence in terms of autonomy for his ego. While composing his lines that describe the Simplon Pass episode, he suddenly recognizes the importance of something in his mind that he calls

> Imagination! lifting up itself
> Before the eye and progress of my Song
> Like an unfather'd vapour.

To be unfathered is precisely what his ego wants, but it cannot fully articulate this desire this early, because his power of creativity remains attached to an image which he has not yet consciously identified. Hence, the poet remains "lost" even while he recognizes the glory in which his consciousness it halted.

Before he can step through and out of the cloud enveloping him, he must consciously detach the "vapour" from his father. By the end of the poem, Wordsworth has done exactly this. In Book Thirteen he explains how he has stepped through the obscuring mist to discover within himself a resourcefulness for life and power that always had been there, but until now lacked the direction of his conscious mind. "Genuine Liberty," then, is "the highest bliss / That can be known," the consciousness of one's own identity as a power that knows itself independently of the world around. Finally, then, figures and forces do not rise within or around the poet. *He* rises of his own volition and power:

> Anon I rose
> As if on wings, and saw beneath me stretch'd
> Vast prospect of the world which I had been
> And was; and hence this Song, which like a lark
> I have protracted, in the unwearied Heavens
> Singing, and often with more plaintive voice
> Attemper'd to the sorrows of the earth;
> Yet centring all in love, and in the end
> All gratulant if rightly understood.

This blissful station is possible to the mind that has learned "to keep / in wholesome separation the two natures, / The one that feels, the other that observes." Wordsworth discovered a way to creative vigor and psychological health because he learned to separate the pressures of id from the restraints of super-ego: the "feeling" nature of his attachments to his father. Before his ego could declare its conscious freedom, it had to put both the id of feeling and the super-ego of observation in their subordinate places. Only then could the poet, as man and artist, "cease to be a child and become a member of the social community."

Wishing to identify with a tall man, whether the tall soldier of Book Four or the dream figure "mounted high" on the camel in Book Five, Wordsworth realizes in his

self-analysis that there is a kind a madness in such wishing:
"I, methinks, / Could share that Maniac's anxiousness,
could go / Upon like errand," referring to the "Arab
Phantom." The fantasy of the child wishing to take his father's place underlies the adult's memory and dream of
identification with tall men; the adult poet's analysis forces
him to recognize the regressive quality of such identifications, hence its "madness." Later in Book Five, after recalling the dream of the Arab phantom with his warning
of the great flood, and after analyzing his ambivalent feelings toward his mother, Wordsworth remembers his childhood experience of watching while a corpse was dragged
from a lake: "At length, the dead Man, 'mid that beau-
teous scene / Of trees, and hills and water, bolt upright /
Rose with his ghastly face; a spectre shape." Within the
context already established by preceding episodes of Book
V, this memory is a striking revelation of the boy's wish
for his father's death (he who had been drowned by the
flood waters of desire about which the Arab phantom
warned the dreamer). The corpse rises, bolts upright to
confront the child with the consequence of such wishing.
But Wordsworth is not yet prepared to accept responsibility for such wishing: he explains that he had no fear on the
occasion of that memory, but he does later confess that
"dumb yearnings, hidden appetites are ours" in childhood.

His need to escape admonishment and restraint from external authority caused the young man Wordsworth to
leave England for his first tour of the Alps, described in
Book Six. Something more, however, than juvenile wan-
derlust drives the young student to leave Cambridge; he
admits, while remembering and writing about the adventure in retrospect, that he "turn'd / From regulations
even of his own, / As from restraints and bonds." He
takes the trip even though he admits it was an "act of disobedience towards them / Who lov'd him." His emotional state was, indeed, "baffling" to him at the time. He as-

pired to that "patriarchal dignity of mind" which he had
observed about him as a child, but he did not recognize at
the time how much emphasis his unconscious mind was
putting on the *patriarchal,* for what he most wished was
to replace his father, to disassociate himself from his father's authority.

His was "an under-thirst / Of vigour" mixed with a dejection of "deep and genuine sadness" which he did not
understand. It was released momentarily to express itself as
a conditioning of his vision, first as a "dull and heavy
slackening" and then as a visionary transport of insight,
which the youth experienced as an objective discovery in
nature. What he saw there was at most a mixture of his
passion with natural forms, or it was at least a reflection of
his own, largely unconscious, feelings. Hence, high woods
decaying, winds bewildered and forlorn, and other features
combined to create a "sick sight / And giddy prospect" of
tumult and peace. To interpret the experience as a vision
of "mind" and "Eternity" was to express his wish for a
power of liberation from natural restraints, at the same
time he felt guilty for entertaining such a wish. Not until
he can write, many years later, in the process of analyzing
his mind's growth, when he recognizes "imagination" in
his feelings at the time of the vision and the dejection,
does Wordsworth also realize that his wish contained, as
well, his desire for separation from his father. He wished
to have all that power of creativity for himself, not shared
with—or even derived from—his father.

In more than one sense, then, did "Man" rise to assume
prominence in Wordsworth's mental development. He explains at the end of Book Eight how his love of nature has
led to his love of man:

> Then rose
> Man, inwardly contemplated, and present
> In my own being, to a loftier height;

As of all visible natures crown; and first
In capability of feeling what
Was to be felt; in being rapt away
By the divine effect of power and love,
As, more than anything we know instinct
With Godhead, and by reason and by will
Acknowledging dependency sublime.

"Man" at this point is an ideal abstracted from the poet's experiences as they have been narrated thus far in *The Prelude*. Wordsworth knows that his affections for "man" have been ambivalent, and much of this section of the poem is an effort to explain to himself how he worked through the ambivalence to a clearer commitment of feeling. The "dependency sublime" which the poet, as a man, acknowledges is a sublimation of his dependency on his own father.

*INDEED,* the image of the father is rising more frequently in the poem from Book Eight to the conclusion. The poet is discovering this for himself as he analyzes his mental growth through some particular episodes recounted in Books Eight through Eleven. After his shock of recognition, in Book Eleven, that he wished for his father's death, Wordsworth exerts much effort to assert his emotional and imaginative independence in Books Twelve and Thirteen. His analysis may be followed, then, as he discovers for himself and in his own terms what Freud discovered and reported in *The Ego and the Id:* "the battle with the obstacle of an unconscious sense of guilt." Like the psychoanalyst, Wordsworth engages in "the slow procedure of unmasking his guilt's unconscious repressed roots, and of thus gradually changing it into a *conscious* sense of guilt." This will give his "ego *freedom*" in the essential sense that he has been searching for since the inception of his self-analysis.

One of the episodes of Book Eight used to illustrate the progress of the poet's affection for mankind occurs in a story he narrates of a shepherd's rescue of his son (who was, in turn, rescuing a lost lamb). Surely this story satisfied a profound yearning in Wordsworth himself for some kind of rescue by his own father when Wordsworth lost his mother? The story is a wish fulfillment of the most forceful kind. It is a double displacement (expressed in the doubling of the rescue motif) because Wordsworth must have felt doubly betrayed after his father's death so soon after his mother's. The image of the shepherd boy "safe within his Father's arms" (taking the place of the earlier image of "the Babe, Nurs'd in his Mother's arms") recurs in a passage near the end of Book Eight.

Here Wordsworth introduces a scene from London to balance the one of the shepherd rescuing his son, as if to allow the rural scene to illuminate the urban one. The health of the shepherds contrasts with the illness of this urban family, but there is no loss of affection in the latter. Indeed, the scene is more tender, if not more sentimental. Wordsworth recalls how he saw a man "sitting in an open Square"

> with a sickly babe
> Upon his knee, whom he had thither brought
> For sunshine, and to breathe the fresher air.
> .   .   .   .   .   .   .   .   .   .   .
> He held the child, and, bending over it,
> As if he were afraid both of the sun
> And of the air which he had come to seek,
> He eyed it with unutterable love.

This is the last such scene in the poet's analysis, as if he has completed the work of reconstructing or discovering his wishes for security from his father. In later images of fathers, he will emphasize instead the hostility and tension, followed by the deaths of fathers, including that of his own father. The function of the father in his poem is to admonish the son for loving attachments to the mother, and then, when that is successful, to take her place within the mind of the son, becoming first an ego-ideal and then a punishing super-ego.

The opening of Book Nine explains how Wordsworth ranged at large, "coasted round and round the line / Of Tavern, Brothel, gaming-house, and Shop," all the while looking "for something that he could not find." Then he finds in Michel Beaupuy a guide for his thoughts and feelings. One of the themes they discussed was that a man's "blind desires and steady faculties" are both needed for individual growth and freedom: blind desires provide the important motivation "to break / Bondage," while steady faculties enable one "to build Liberty / On firm foundations, making social life" possible. Social rebellion was justifiable as analogous with psychological rebellion. The young poet "knew" that he had a need to break from his bondage to images of his father—whose original image has still not come into focus for the older man Wordsworth making his analysis of himself. He says he can still weep to think of certain scenes from his residence in France, but he seems confused about why he is weeping:

> Yet at this very moment do tears start
> Into mine eyes; I do not say I weep,
> I wept not then, but tears have dimm'd my sight,
> In memory of the farewells of that time,
> Domestic severings, . . . .

It is this image of "domestic severings" that strikes almost too deep for tears, because Wordsworth feels the association more personally than his conscious mind can admit. He fantasizes the emotions connected with domestic severings and human separations by way of his narrative about

Vaudracour and Julia.

The story may illustrate the agonies of France in its Revolution, but it also may express Wordsworth's own pain of mind from an ambivalent attitude toward his own father. Repressed hostility toward his father gives to the story a strong psychological point. One of the first thoughts to occur to the young man when he soon afterwards visited Paris was that the deposed King lay in prison "associate with his Children and his Wife / In Bondage." That evening the young man Wordsworth experienced a fear that transcended his concern for bodily safety: greatly agitated, he "kept watch, / Reading at intervals; the fear gone by / Pressed on him almost like a fear to come." This continued until he was forced to put himself on trial for some unknown crime:

> in dreams I pleaded
> Before unjust Tribunals, with a voice
> Labouring, a brain confounded, and a sense
> Of treachery and desertion in the place
> The holiest that I knew of, my own soul.

Wordsworth recognizes while he composes his poem that his essential problem at the time he experienced those ghastly visions of despair and tyranny was a problem of melancholy: "Most melancholy at that time, O Friend! / Were my day-thoughts, my dreams were miserable." The real location of his problem, as he notes, "in the place / The holiest that I knew of, my own soul." The political and social strife of the time lay upon his heart like a weight, it is true, but more immediately for him was his private emotional turmoil, which seemed to him like a "most unnatural strife." Again Wordsworth remembers how painful it was to be "cut off, / And toss'd about in whirlwinds." As he draws now more closely to the screened-off event of his distant childhood, the event whose traumatic effect was to produce a most unnatural strife, Wordsworth protests that "this is a passion over-near ourselves, / Reality too close and too intense." Although he teasingly suggests that something more than a political embarrassment lay behind his feeling of this passion over-near himself, he does not clarify it: it was, he says, "mingled up with something, in my mind, / Or scorn and condemnation personal, / That would profane the sanctity of verse."

A mingling of fear and love for figures of authority lends the memory an aura of ambivalence. The poet does not enjoy his analysis of self and society, but he proceeds with conviction that whatever happiness is possible for him, it must be a product of truth. He has not hesitated to outline the importance of an identification with the cause of freedom, having shown how he identified with Michel Beaupuy. Now, however, he must probe more deeply behind that authority figure. Like a surgeon, he

> took knife in hand
> And stopping not at parts less sensitive,
> Endeavoured with my best of skill to probe
> The living body of society
> Even to the heart; I push'd without remorse
> My speculations forward; yea, set foot
> On Nature's holiest places.

And what more holy a place than the family itself? This Wordsworth earlier described as the source of all society: "household love, / Benevolent in small societies, / And great in large ones." The family, as a figure of speech, is "the very world which is the world / Of all of us, the place in which, in the end, / We find our happiness, or not at all." The poet brings to the bar of judgment, then, not only his society, but also—more profoundly—his family and his own soul. His crime has been to mix two feelings, joy and melancholy, love and hate.

When he dragged "all passions, notions, shapes of faith, / Like culprits to the bar," he undertook an analysis of his mind which cleared away many youthful fictions (themselves screens for infantile fantasies). Psychoanalytically, those fictions were symptoms of neurotic fixations, points where the ego had constructed defenses against undesirable instincts. To clear away those symptoms as fictions of defense was not to be a pleasant task: Wordsworth "lost / All feeling of conviction, and, in fine, / Sick, wearied out with contrarieties, / Yielded up moral questions in despair." What was happening was an event of momentous importance for the man, as it was also for the emergent poet. He had worked through an analysis of his unconscious guilt, a feeling of "despair" and "melancholy" for something he could not quite understand or articulate in himself. He was restoring some balance to his mental apparatus, resisting the pressure of an authority that was punishing his ego with feelings of guilt. He was treating himself for "melancholia," and after analysis, he sought a cure through identification with his sister, who brought him "a saving intercourse / With his true self."

Because Wordsworth is attacking symptoms, as he must, without knowing the disease which those symptoms betray, he is treating himself for melancholia, not for mourning. His long-term uneasiness of spirit, his "sadness," "tremblings of the heart," and especially his "disquietude" reported in early passages of Book Five, were all stirrings of his melancholia that forced itself into his consciousness as a profound dejection—in the famous Simplon Pass episode of later Book Five. When he defined that experience as a comparison with "an unfather'd vapour," Wordsworth came close to uncovering the cause for his melancholy. As Freud explained, "melancholia is in some way related to an unconscious loss of a love-object, in contradistinction to mourning, in which there is nothing unconscious about the loss." The ego mourns the loss of a loved-object through the process of withdrawing its psychic energy, but instead of redirecting it to a new object, it makes itself (in a process of narcissism) its own loved object. Thus Freud's explanation of melancholia: "the shadow of the object fell upon the ego, so that the latter could henceforth be criticized by a special mental faculty like an object, like the forsaken object. . . . The conflict between the ego and the loved person transformed into a cleavage between the criticizing faculty of the ego and the ego as altered by identification." In other words, the super-ego punishes the ego as though it were a beloved person, punishing the lover for having harbored ill feelings toward itself. In terms of Wordsworths' self-analysis, his super-ego has assumed the authority of his dead father and has throughout most of the poet's life been punishing his ego for having harbored feelings of hate for his beloved father. Hence, he must suffer guilt and exhibit the symptoms of endless mourning.

Melancholia is a continuing symptom of mourning, both real and fancied, for the death of the father—an event much desired by the child competing for love of mother, much desired by the boy wishing to punish the father for abandoning him in adolescence, and much needed by the man wishing for emotional and intellectual independence. If we think back to the opening of *The Prelude,* with its strange dejection of spirit ("listlessness in vain perplexity"), compare that with the recurring melancholy of the later books, culminating in the despair of Book Ten and the depression of Book Eleven, we can recognize in Wordsworth's mental history (a past always present in the poem) most of the features which Freud described in "Mourning and Melancholia":

> The distinguishing mental features of melancholia are a profoundly painful dejection, abrogation of interest in the outside world, loss of the capacity of

love, inhibition of all activity, and a lowering of
the self-regarding feelings to a degree that finds utterance in self-reproaches and self-revilings, and
culminates in a delusional expectation of punishment. This picture becomes a little more intelligible when we consider that, with one exception
["the fall in self-esteem"], the same traits are met
with in grief.

"Expectation of punishment" is the strange conclusion to
Wordsworth's most haunting memory, recorded in Book
Eleven: a spot of time that embalms his grief for his fa-
ther's death.

*BY THE TIME* he actually confronts the memories of
his father's death, Wordsworth has worked his way
through several screen images of authority figures, and so
he has acquired a tone of confidence as he begins reconstructing that scene of grief. He asserts that he may find
"a vivifying Virtue" in those spots of time which have
been depressed by "false opinion and contentious thought,
/ Or aught of heavier or more deadly weight." The overlay of "trivial occupations" in the "round / Of ordinary
intercourse" gives way to such moments when the mind
rises to demonstrate its autonomy "as lord and master."
However, in fact, those spots of time are episodes of trauma, when his mind was overwhelmed by emotions. Or,
more accurately, his ego-as-consciousness was flooded by
feelings from deep within itself, from the reservoir of energies in his unconscious. What Wordsworth remembers as
occasions of mental autonomy are, at least from the exam-
ples he cites, episodes of neurotic anxiety caused by his
ego's original feeling of helplessness in the face of an unknown danger. As he composes his poem Wordsworth
brings this danger (which is not known to the ego) into
consciousness. His ability to make depressed images of fear

into conscious memories is not only a sign of his mental autonomy (that his "mind / Is lord and master"), but it is more particularly a sign that his ego has been assisted by his super-ego to establish authority over its environment. Wordsworth's spots of time are memorials of conquest by the ego over the id. They are also warnings to the ego that it may be overwhelmed in turn by the super-ego.

The rich complexity of the two spots of time described in Book Eleven may be sorted into three phases of psychological development. First, the trauma of childhood fear; second, repression of that fear, and a resulting anxiety; and third, conquest over the super-ego, which had assisted in repression, by the ego in the process of bringing the danger situation into consciousness.

Both episodes contain references to horses and both center on fear of death. As we have noticed before in Wordsworth's writings, he sometimes identified his passions with various kinds of animals (including specifically the horses in "An Evening Walk)"). In the episode that occurred when he was six, he explains how he dismounted through fear, and led his horse stumbling on until he came to a place where a murderer had been hung in iron chains. When he was thirteen, he waited impatiently for two horses to be sent to fetch him and his brothers home at Christmas time. His desire for the expected Steeds is parallel with his "anxiety of hope" for which he felt chastised by God, "who thus corrected his desires." These are strong suggestions of (sexual) identification with the horse, so that he had to dismount out of fear of punishment and then waited eagerly for the opportunity to take his father's place after his father's (desired) death.

The episodes are strikingly concerned with death: the one a fantasy, the other a reality (anticipated in retrospect!). The possibility that underlying the child's fear of death was a psychological fear of castration is worth consideration. The place where a man was hung in chains was a place where the boy later took his loved ones when he was grown, as though to reaffirm his masculinity after such a threat to his potency, "the hiding-places of his power." Both this and the later episode occur near or atop a projection of the landscape, suggesting again some association with phallic consciousness. The earlier episode was in a valley, whence the boy looked up for his "lost guide" and saw instead a pool, a woman, and a beacon on the lonely eminence nearby. The later episode occurs on top "a crag, / An Eminence" whence the boy looked down for the arrival of the horses. The complex patterns of imagery for both episodes are strongly suggestive of the boy's desire for creative power (fundamentally sexual, maturely polymorphous). However, that desire is repressed by vague fears of unknown dangers threatening destruction.

The traumas, then, of the two episodes are threats of danger, with the first a threat more realistic than the second, although the second is in some ways a psychological consequence of the first. Freud's definitions of anxiety and trauma may be helpful to sort out the differences and likenesses between Wordsworth's two spots of time:

> A danger-situation is a recognized, remembered, expected situation of helplessness. Anxiety is the original reaction to helplessness in the trauma and is reproduced later on in the danger-situation as a signal for help. The ego, which experienced the trauma passively, now repeats it actively in a weakened version, in the hope of being able itself to direct its course.

His traumatic experience at age six was for Wordsworth a "danger-situation of helplessness" (in fear he dismounted; he saw the "monumental writing," while "faltering and ignorant where he was"; and then he looked without success for his lost guide). The resulting feeling was an anxiety that Wordsworth describes, in his famous phrase, as "visionary dreariness."

In the later episode which occurred when he was thirteen, Wordsworth remembers it as something that repeated the earlier one at age six. At least, the boy waiting for the horses was anxious for something more than the arrival of the horses. He experienced something like an anxiety attack, with the same symptoms of visionary dreariness that had occurred at age six. Although the specific items of the scene have changed, they "were spectacles and sounds to which / He would often repair." Thus he not only repeated his earlier anxiety as a visionary dreariness, but he has since he was thirteen repeated *that* experience as well. In psychoanalaytical terms, his ego "which experienced the trauma passively, now repeats it actively in a weakened version, in the hope of being able itself to direct its course."

The next distinct phase of his mind's working over this material of spots of time is Wordsworth's having successfully repressed the specific fears that were experienced at ages six and thirteen. The main equipment for helping the ego overcome its fear of danger, truly unknown because it is an "instinctual danger" but vaguely associated with images of death, is the super-ego, the authority figure which has been introjected in the process of development. Wordsworth recognized the obvious connection between his childhood fear of separation and helplessness with his later fear of death. He also recognized (though less clearly) the connection between his fear of death and his dependence upon his father, or some other authority figure.

What makes the second episode difficult to sort out is the complexity of perspective in the poem: the poet is remembering with his conscious mind, at a time when his ego is in control, an event of instinctual fear which has been repressed by the authority of his super-ego, whose powers of repression have in turn been overcome by the

very process of analysis which the poem reports. Nevertheless, there are some signs in the text of the second operation that can be isolated for observation. The boy's fear
was specifically a fear of punishment: "The event / With
all the sorrow which it brought appear'd / A chastisement." However, that fear was consciously experienced
only after the death of his father ("the event" to which he
refers). He immediately connected his fear of punishment
with his earlier hope for a quick return home at Christmas
time. Wordsworth in maturity knows that what the boy
feared was a fantasy of punishment, but Wordsworth as
poet and analyst knows how important that fantasy was for
its real consequences in psychological and creative development. His desires were so repulsive to something in his
mind that the boy needed chastisement for them.

What the boy wished for when he was eager to return
home at Christmas vacation was not something for which
he need feel guilty—the occasion for the emotion was far
less than the power of the emotion itself would need to
explain its source. It is this powerful emotion of guilt and
fear of punishment for which the boy confessed a need
that constitutes the "instinctual danger." The guilt for
which he needs to be punished is his desire for the very
death that did occur. Then, when his father dies, "in
deepest passion, he bow'd low / To God, who thus corrected his desires." The voice of God, his conscience, is in
Freudian terms the super-ego itself, which has taken the
place of the father for whose death sons must wish if they
are to become free.

# CHAPTER SIX:

## Desires Corrected

Wordsworth's techniques of narrative anticipated what Freud called "transference," which occurs when "new editions of the old conflict" are created "in the patient's relation to the doctor." The poet's ego needs a collaborator in its work of analysis: to succeed in freeing its mental powers (imagination, libido) from fixation on infantile objects and from being exhausted by efforts of repression. The ego needs a "doctor" upon whom it can concentrate its energies, drawing it away from its symptoms of guilt and suffering, and through whom the poet can recognize what it is within himself that resists discovery. Wordsworth's sister Dorothy gave him a new object of love, a "real object" to displace the image of his mother in his fantasy. Dorothy was restored to Wordsworth "after separation desolate" as if she were "a gift then first bestow'd." Her love brought his soul to "what by Nature it was fram'd."

*The Prelude* records Wordsworth's discovery, or rediscovery, of a real object of love in his sister, but *The Prelude* is also a confession, or narration of memories, dreams, and free-associations, to a particular person whose presence is assumed or imagined by Wordsworth. This person is of course Samuel Taylor Coleridge, the "Friend" addressed in the poem. Coleridge plays a role in the poem that allows Wordsworth to project upon him, or transfer to him, much of the emotion which his ego needs to recognize before it can free itself from subservience to its super-ego. Coleridge, as listener, is the imagined analyst to Wordsworth's ego as the real patient. Coleridge is recognized as the authority figure, the father image, which has been assumed as Wordsworth's super-ego and which has subjected the poet's ego to much pain of guilt. Simply put, though admittedly very reductive, it may be described thus: Dorothy took Wordsworth's mother's place and allowed him to become capable of "enjoyment," Coleridge took his father's place and allowed him to become capable of "efficiency."

At the end of his poem Wordsworth invites Coleridge to join him in a work of human redemption. This is clearly an invitation from an equal, if not a superior. Wordsworth has been able to disengage his dependence on Coleridge because he has consciously recognized in his sympathetic listener an authority which comes more fundamentally from within Wordsworth's own mind. He is a "Power," one of those whose "highest bliss" is "the consciousness / Of whom they are habitually infused / Through every image." Wordsworth has recognized this Power resident in several images recalled throughout his poem, not the least being the image of his father, finally projected as his analyst-friend Coleridge. Knowing this, he can say with confidence to all men: "Here must thou be, O Man! / Strength to thyself; no Helper hast thou here; / Here keepest thou thy individual state."

This euphoria of self-certainty and strength of ego is the dominant tone that concludes *The Prelude*. Wordsworth will later in his life be less assured of his achievement, be more conscious of the price which must be paid for civilization, but when he completes his version of the poem in

1805-6, he is understandably happy in his success at self-analysis. He can confidently project many careers for his newly liberated imagination, because he no longer has to invest portions of it in the process of repressing infantile fears. Nor does he have to worry that his instincts may be repugnant to his conscience, because his ego may dispose of its powers through the important process of sublimation. "Having track'd the main essential Power, / Imagination, up her way sublime, / In turn might Fancy also be pursued / Through all her transfigurations, till she too / Was purified, had learn'd to ply her craft / By judgment steadied." Out of this sublimated imagination and disciplined fancy, Wordsworth proposes "to take a station among Men" and to build "up a work that should endure." His imagination will become more social and his talent dedicated to the tasks of civilization.

*IN HIS* astonishing experience of the adventure on Salisbury Plain, Wordsworth works and reworks material which haunted him for years. Even in *The Prelude* he turns that episode of his recent life again into poetry: he analyzes it now as a projection (an "imagination") of his own suppressed hostilities. He felt as though his consciousness were flooded by a power from deep down within himself. "To such mood, / Once above all, a Traveller at that time / Upon the Plain of Sarum was I raised." At the time of the experience, he was not yet the "free" being he will be by the time he completes his self-analysis, and so his view was ordinarily more limited and bound to objects of perception (or in memory). To be raised to some high mood of release from bondage to objects was not only to transcend space and time, it was also an experience of sublimation—literally, to lift a passion (instinct) from below the threshold of consciousness up into a fullness of consciousness and recognition. In this particular episode Wordsworth sublimates instincts of hostility and aggression in a scene that Freud might have used to illustrate his thesis in *Totem and Taboo.*

Wordsworth's "reverie" of primitive rituals with human sacrifice was a sublimation of his own aggressions. If Freud was right, it is a recognition in fantasy of the poet's desire to kill his father (who is already dead) and to take his father' place. Wordsworth, however, emphasizes the community action of sacrifice, rather than the reason for the sacrifice. Neither does Wordsworth identify the victims as fathers, merely as "living men." Nevertheless, coming so soon after his analysis of memories of fearing death and being chastized for his father's death (in Book Eleven), his recall of this reverie is psychologically significant as a continuing process of working over his suppressed hostilities toward his father.

Wordsworth's emphasis throughout his reverie, of "the sacrificial Altar, fed / With living men," is to recognize the group organization, as though he were identifying with the persons acting out the rituals of sacrifice/ instruction. The entire twelfth book of *The Prelude* records his search to find "in Man, and in the frame of life, Social [as well as] individual" values of whatever is "good or fair." He has discovered himself as an ego with psychic ties to other human beings who are neither mother nor father to him. He found "once more in Man an object of delight / Of pure imagination and love." His need was an instinct of "craving" for "the universal heart," or "the very heart of man." Eros has been working through the poet's imagination, has sublimated his infant desire for his mother and his childhood desire to be and/or have his father. He has become capable of seeing

> into the depth of human souls,
> Souls that appear to have no depth at all
> To vulgar eyes. . . . .
>                         there I found

Hope to my hope, and to my pleasure peace,
And steadiness; and healing and repose
To every angry passion. There I heard,
From mouths of lowly men and of obscure
A tale of honour; sounds in unison
With loftiest promises of good and fair.

His ambition is to become, like the Druid "bearded
Teachers" of his reverie, an instructor in a science even
more mysterious than whatever the Druids taught. His
ambition is to become a poet of psychoanalysis, his instruction to heal the sickness of the heart.

The last book of *The Prelude* is virtually a hymn to
Eros, the power "which holds together everything in the
world." Wordsworth has risen above the struggles within
himself to take command of his instincts and his super-
ego. His achievement of "this freedom in himself," this
"genuine Liberty," is the reward of therapy. It is the recovery of power by a mature ego that is to itself witness
and judge, balanced by "an ennobling interchange / Of
action from within and without." His moods of triumph
and self-satisfaction are signals that his "ego and ego-ideal
have been fused together." Because he is conscious of
what he has achieved, he is not deluded nor is he suffering
from mania. Wordsworth notices something has happened
to him in the process of his self-analysis, a psychic event
explained by Freud as a "transformation of object-libido
into narcissistic libido." This is a process of abandoning
sexual aims, and it is the "road to sublimation" whereby
the ego acts as a mediator changing the direction of sexual
love *via* self-love. Wordsworth's egotism is not only a sign
of intellectual health. It is a necessary stage in the process
of sublimation, essential to the production of culture. He
reviews the stages of growth in his power to love:

> From love, for here
> Do we begin and end, all grandeur comes,
> All truth and beauty, from pervading love,
> That gone, we are as dust. . . .
>           but there is a higher love
> Than this, a love that comes into the heart
> With awe and a diffusive sentiment;
> Thy love is human merely; this proceeds
> More from the brooding Soul, and is divine.

This higher love is "but another name for absolute strength / And clearest insight, amplitude of mind, / And reason in her most exalted mood." These images of heights achieved are metaphors of sublimation, of the sublime: "it rose once more / With strength, reflecting in its solemn breast / The works of man and face of human life."

This power that rises from within the mind has assumed not only the authority of the father, but also of God the Father. It is "the sense of God," a power "from the Deity" that produces "the highest bliss," a presence from which to draw "the feeling of life endless, the great thought / By which we live, Infinity and God." Imagination and intellectual love are no longer divided for Wordsworth; his "soul hath risen / Up to the height of feeling intellect," where he combines in a single ego-ideal the feelings of affection and reverence illustrated by the significant image that has dominated much of the poem: "a nursing Mother's heart." His love for both his mother and his father has been diverted to his love for himself (hence his egoism, his narcissism) as a step toward the genuine liberty he needs for maturity. But he must sublimate that love of self, change the aim as well as the object of infantile sex instincts, or he would merely regress to infancy. Wordsworth uses artistic illusion to reach the remarkable achievement of accomplishing desires "in play, just as though it were something real." Wordsworth is able to fulfill his desire for his mother in the "illusion" of loving nature, and he is able to act out his ambivalent feelings for his father in the "illusion" of God.

From nature Wordsworth received gifts of emotion and calm, an "interchange / Of peace and excitation," both the energy and the stillness of the mind. That he senses, if he does not fully recognize (or have a clinical word for), a libidinal quality underlying these gifts, he indicates by explaining the ways this energy expresses itself in experience: it is that "by which he seeks the truth, / Is roused, aspires, grasps, struggles, wishes, craves." The rhythm of nature's energies is the rhythm of what Freud called the libido in pursuit of the pleasure principle, subjected by the ego to an accommodation with the reality principle. Wordsworth acts out again and again in his poetry this program of accommodation. But he also must act out, sublimate, an accommodation with the super-ego, that "image of right reason" which has assumed such an important place in the growth of his mind. The ego not only learns to control (through the play of art) the instinct of the id as the energies of nature (striving for pleasure, pausing for reality), but it also learns to control the super-ego by gratifying *its* demands for discipline, duty, restraint, punishment, and sacrifice. Wordsworth acts out this accommodation through an art of the sublime (complementing his art of the natural), figuring forth an "amplitude of mind" as "the great thought / By which we live, Infinity and God."

Love for the objects of nature may be the beginning and the end of the mere mortal, but love for Infinity and God is the "higher love" which guarantees absolute strength and clearest insight to the mind. It is very important that Wordsworth emphasize the quality of "infinity" in this identification. He "feeds upon infinity" in his sense of God: religion is an "endless occupation for the soul";

he achieves "the feeling of life endless" from his self-analysis; and he becomes a keen observer of the "infinite varieties and shades / Of individual character." The freedom for which Wordsworth's poem is a search comes to him as an experience of Infinity and God. It is, therefore, especially important that he make it a product of his discovery that all is centered in love, because he needs an ego-ideal that satisfies his need to love his father as well as his need to be free from his father. The key to his notion of freedom is, as his last book in *The Prelude* affirms, his capacity to love without end. He must be able, not only to *have*, but also to *be* his father. This he can accomplish when he acts it out in his art of the sublime.

Love for God is love for his father, and freedom through an art of the infinite is freedom from guilt and punishment by the super-ego: these are the energies of a healthy ego (the egotistical sublime). The poet felt a command to sublimate his sexual energies (transcend the limits of nature) even while he was a child:

> the soul,
> Remembering how she felt, but what she felt
> Remembering not, retains an obscure sense
> Of possible sublimity, to which
> With growing faculties she doth aspire,
> With faculties still growing, feeling still
> That whatsoever point they gain, they still
> Have something to pursue.

The "what" of this feeling is the object of love, the soul seeking to satisfy itself in possession, but the soul cannot remember this "what" because it has had to change its original object (the mother) and even its aim (sexual satisfaction). Therefore, the poet in maturity realizes the profound importance of emphasizing the "how" rather than the "what" of feeling. The power of love is a paradox of frustration. If love is to continue as a growing faculty, it must always be aim-inhibited—hence, sublimated over and over again. In his maturity, after his self-analysis, Wordsworth celebrates this pursuit of love for the unattainable; this is to be his "endless occupation," his "genuine Liberty," and his "great thought / By which we live, Infinity and God."

WORDSWORTH recognized the connections between sexuality and art, although he was not always so clear about it as in this surprising statement of the 1800 Preface:

> From this principle the direction of the sexual appetite, and all the passions connected with it, take their origin: It is the life of our ordinary conversation; and upon the accuracy with which similitude in dissimilitude, and dissimilitude in similitude are perceived, depend our taste and our moral feelings.

The principle is "the pleasure which the mind derives from the perception of similitude in dissimilitude," a principle describing the chief cause for "the pleasure received from metrical language." Wordsworth has in mind the power of rhythm, based in biological processes, for controlling an otherwise irresistable force of passion. Meter brings order and regularity to bear on ideas and feelings that do not "succeed each other in accustomed order." It is important to impose this order on such passions, because "there is some danger that the excitement may be carried beyond its proper bounds." On the other hand, when a poet needs help to revise his language to a higher level of excitement than the words alone will achieve, he may use meter "to impart passion to the words." Rhythm controls, but it also creates, passions, because rhythm in meter carries, by convention, associations of emotional excitement.

Since meter both controls and creates, through implementing the principle of similitude in dissimilitude, it "is
the great spring of the activity of our minds, and their
chief feeder." Without the control, all experience disinte-
grates into a chaos of undifferentiated passion and feeling;
without the creativity, experience falls flat to the level of
unconscious habit usually associated with inanimate existence. The chief tool of the poet is meter. Since the health
of a culture, or civilization, is a norm of behavior that ap-
proximates good poetry, meter is also an important tool of
civilization. Poetry can sublimate instincts and thereby improve not only "the present state of public taste" but also
"society itself." The poet is, for Wordsworth, an important
social therapist because the poet "binds together by passion and knowledge the vast empire of human society, as
it is spread over the whole earth, and over all time."

By his control of meter the poet exercises a control as
well over "the direction of the sexual appetite." Wordsworth hints, then, at understanding what Freud explained
when he defined sublimation as an "abandonment of sexual aims, a desexualization." To inhibit the aims of erotic
impulses from sexual consummation does not prevent "the
main purpose of eros, which is one of uniting and binding." Art is an especially efficient way of sublimating sexual instincts into forms that unite and bind; it creates "symbols and substitutes which are able to provoke real
emotions." Art is thus one of the best ways available for
social man to reconcile himself to the sacrifices he makes
on behalf of civilization. Art is perhaps the best way to
achieve this reconciliation, because it partakes of the nature of children's play: a strategy for bringing together the
pleasures of id and super-ego in fantasy, and the responsibilities of ego in dealing with reality.

The artist can help the adult enjoy fantasy without losing the path back to reality. Wordsworth knew that his audience needed the therapy of play, of exercising powers of

instinct which were being perverted or repressed until all emotional life was in danger of serious illness: "for a multitude of causes unknown to former times are now acting with a combined force to blunt the discriminating powers of the mind, and unfitting it for all voluntary exertion to reduce it to a state of almost savage torpor." If he can recover, by the play of his poetry, the spontaneity of childhood without abandoning the discipline of adulthood, Wordsworth can tap the great reservoir of unexercised imagination that once constituted the mind of the adult as a child, when one "is capable of being excited without the application of gross and violent stimulants." He could hope thereby to rescue his society from its "degrading thirst after outrageous stimulation."

*THE INDIVIDUAL'S* accommodation with fellow creatures in a state of social harmony is a major theme of Wordsworth's middle years. This accommodation is difficult. It requires an active imagination for achieving what the poet calls an "accord of sublimated humanity." He pressed the need for individuals to sublimate their passions in the creation of "a spiritual community" within which "taste, intellectual Power, and morals" are inseparably linked by "magnificent desires." Where people are not a society, they are a herd, and they may not constitute a society if they have no place in their minds for the feeling of being self-governed. The healthy nation is one with governors who understand "the rudiments of nature as studied in the walks of common life," because successful government of a nation is a successful government of the self by all who make it into a society. It is no easy matter to achieve self-government, however important it may be for achievement of "rational public freedom," where "the best culture is that which does most good to the human heart."
Wordsworth repeatedly sounded the warning that in-

stincts, if they are not satisfied or exercised in accord with nature and society, will work against a person (even when the person knows it not) and against a nation (when it suppresses rather than transmutes those instincts). In *The Convention of Cintra* he developed this warning with great elaboration and sophistication: when the "inward passions" have been perverted by "outward arrangements" of neglect, injury, and insult, they produce "alienation and hatred." These emotions have been driven out of sight by the tyrannies currently in Spain and Portugal, but still "they must exist":

> They may be quieted or diverted for a short time; but, though out of sight or seemingly asleep, they must exist; and the life which they have received cannot, but by a long course of justice and kindness, be overcome and destroyed.

Wordsworth's analysis of political order and disorder is an application of his understanding psychological development, believing that "the instincts of natural and social man" are intimately related—perhaps identical. If these rudiments of nature are to produce a society, a spiritual community rather than merely a herd, they must find a "steady and noble object" with which their passions can identify.

A social nature is possible only when people have the intellectual courage to act from motives of selflessness rather than for immediate gratification. Since "courage is a projection from ourselves," we must find a way to make that projection as economically as possible; that way is a strategy of uniting passion and justice until they have "sublimated the objects of outward sense" and substantiated the "beauty of the inner mind . . . in the outward act." For Wordsworth, this strategy is the work of the imagination, raising "an heroic spirit"—by transmuting, exalting, and consecrating passions. The essential knowledge for a free people is self-knowledge, wherein "mind gains consciousness of its strength" and knows that it is greater than the objects of its contemplation: "the passions of men . . . do immeasurably transcend their objects." As with his own self-discovery in *The Prelude,* Wordsworth emphasizes the great value of mind as self-consciousness and of passion as a reservoir of mental power. When "the course and demands of action and of life" so regularly disappoint the expectations of mind and passion, men suffer depression of spirit and loss of self-confidence. Self-dignity, and national honor, cannot suffer while this reservoir is drawn upon for strength and courage, a feat made possible by the sublimating activities encouraged by culture and civilization.

This reservoir of power has some similarities with Freud's hypothesis of the libido, although for Wordsworth it lacks the biological features Freud emphasized (as when he compared it with the amoeba). For Wordsworth it is more like one of his own beloved lakes, increasing in its power through some device of repression comparable to a dam. When it reaches a certain level of intensity, it will overflow its restraint or explode. The dam of repression with which Wordsworth was most often concerned in his writing is political tyranny, and mainly the tyranny of Napoleon in particular. Hence, when the British generals "betrayed" the Spanish and Portuguese patriots with their "Convention of Cintra," Wordsworth was outraged that they lacked intellectual courage to resist tyranny and to assist a great people achieve as fine a society as the British enjoyed.

While every person has it within himself to substantiate the beauty of mind in the grace of an outward act, not everyone can do so unassisted—especially after a history of repression, until he accepts as a part of his own nature what is actually a repression from others. While Wordsworth does not analyze the psychology of self-punishment in subjected citizens, he does recognize the importance of the opposite instinct of aggression toward others, as when he startlingly calls upon his countrymen to imitate their enemies in this passage:

> Leaders and masters. . .often survive when they have become an oppression and a hindrance which cannot be cast off decisively, but by an impulse—rising either from the absolute knowledge of good and great men,—or from the partial insight which is given to superior minds, though of a vitiated moral constitution—or lastly from that blind energy and those habits of daring which are often found in men who, checked by no restraint of morality, suffer their evil passions to gain extraordinary strength in extraordinary circumstances. By any of these forces may the tyranny be broken through. . . .I wish then that we could so far imitate our enemies as, like them, to shake off these bonds; but not, like them, from the worst—but from the worthiest impulses.

In order for these impulses to be of the worthiest, they must be "transmuted" instincts, even if only through "intense moral suffering." This transmutation can occur by identification with persons of heroic spirit, exemplified by "the Boy of Saragossa" who fought with courage and wrestled a banner from the enemy. In that banner, anticipating a similar one of *The White Doe of Rylstone,* Wordsworth sees "an object which the most meditative and most elevated minds may contemplate with absolute delight; . . .an organ by which they may act; a function by which they may be sustained." Or this transmutation can occur by means of identifications achieved through art, in which noble objects are arranged for summoning heroic spirits from the audience—these noble objects are Wordsworth's equivalents for ego-ideals. Even the sword, when it is "in the hands of the good and the virtuous," is an "intelligible symbol of abhorrence."

Artists have the power to render objects into symbols of ideals which summon the heroic spirit, transmuting instincts into "higher" forms of expression. Not only the artists, but also the political leaders can summon this spirit into action. Whatever the efficient or formal cause, the material cause should be a union of "passion and justice" which "sublimate the objects of outward sense." Passion is the instinct, and justice the ego-ideal. When these are united in deed or in design, they invest or incorporate themselves in "objects of the outward sense." This is Wordsworth's closest approximation to Freud's notion of sublimation. However far it falls from the distinctly sexual quality of Freud's notion, it does emphasize the *creative* function at the same time it emphasizes the neutral source of instincts, which can be creative *or* destructive.

*WORDSWORTH* tells his young correspondent in his "Letter to 'Mathetes'" that for those who can penetrate the deepest into their minds (using "the organ of Reason" as a "telescope of Art") "joy and love may be regenerated and restored." All may accomplish for themselves what Wordsworth was able to do for himself in the self-analysis of *The Prelude*, to achieve joy and love, by measuring "back the track of life which he has trod." A healthy culture permits one "to accumulate in genial confidence; its instinct, its safety, its benefit, its glory, is to love, to admire, to feel, and to labour." As an artist Wordsworth takes seriously his responsibility to help his readers achieve these aims of life. He observes that, "though it is impossible that a man can be in a healthy state that is not frequently and strongly moved both by sublimity and beauty, it is more dependent for its daily well-being upon the love & gentleness which accompany the one, than upon the exaltation or awe which are created by the other."

"Love and gentleness" are qualities of experience Wordsworth treasures, but they cannot be enjoyed by minds that have been depressed by tyranny or perverted by bad taste and bad education. France lost her opportunity to enjoy the benefits of "rational public freedom," Spain and Portugal have recently shown signs of discovering them (despite the Convention of Cintra), but Britain must beware that she not endanger (even betray) her heritage of enjoyment. That she might do so is Wordsworth's constant fear; therefore, he attacks, in his "Letter to a Friend of Robert Burns," those "remorseless hunters after matter of fact" as "the blindest of human beings." They would reduce human being to a mere accumulation of material facts with no spiritual connections, reduce ideals into mere instinct (as they have in the instance of Burns's life). If the poet is not allowed his "privilege" "to catch a spirit of pleasure wherever it can be found," then not only art will suffer. So will the society held together by that art.

Certainly during the decade that concluded with the defeat of Napoleon at Waterloo, Wordsworth's faith in the integrity of society and in the health of civilization was often tested. During this period he composed most of the poems he later collected under the title of *Poems Dedicated to National Independence and Liberty,* including many sonnets which carry on the spirit of Milton's great political poems. In one of these, "Composed While the Author was Engaged in Writing a Tract Occasioned by the Convention of Cintra," Wordsworth asserts his fundamental faith in the capacity of human nature to triumph over "the World's vain objects." Such a world, essentially dead, with its threat to "enslave / The free-born Soul," he contrasts with the world of "mighty Nature," where he has set his heart to school, and where he weighs "the hopes and fears of suffering Spain." Society cannot survive as a civilization if it sees the world merely as an array of objects; instead, it must, like the poet, enjoy the living passions of nature which are to be rediscovered after exploring back its way "through the human heart."

"In these usurping times of fear and pain," he feels a special testing of his faith in the values of civilization, especially if they have been perverted as in France, betrayed as in Spain, depressed as in Germany, and threatened even in his own beloved England. The questioning, uncertain tone of the central poems *Dedicated to National Independence and Liberty* expresses Wordsworth's confession of spiritual weakness. Without his basic trust in the power of mind to find within itself the strength it requires to survive, he might have surrendered to despondency rather than continue to write praises of culture and civilization. Everywhere, however, "O'er the wide earth, on mountain and on plain," there dwells what he increasingly liked to call "a Godhead" in "the affections and the soul of man." This image of God, at rest in man himself, is a religious product of Wordsworth's lifelong search for an ideal with which he could identify in a cause common to all humanity. Instincts are the source of divinity—beginning but not ending with "the universal Pan." Civilization requires "arduous strife, "high sacrifice, and labour without pause." People must, therefore, have some compensation, some ideal to organize civilization's expense of passion.

Infants and children are Wordsworthian heroes of imagination. They are, as heroes, symbolic images of an unconscious strength in the adult mind to be autonomous and independent. When the adult's reality is made up of "vain objects" and rigid, heartless formalities, then the adult's great psychological need is to shatter or modify that reality with "tender fictions": these draw upon the energies of instincts which have been repressed or perverted by an overdemanding world of tyrannical reality. When the world has become a rigid projection of the super-ego, a child can come as an heroic agent of unconscious power to assist

128     *Guilty Pleasures*

the poor ego in its struggle to survive. Or, when the world threatens to overwhelm the passive, weakened ego with unregarding and devouring instincts of a primitive nature, then the ego must call upon its childhood dreams of parents as heroic redeemers. Wordsworth's poetry invokes both strategies as subjects of his poetry: the parent as hero, the child as hero.

In a poem he addresses to his "Infant Daughter, Dora" in 1804, he compares his child with the moon, since Dora has just reached her first month of age. This poem echoes Coleridge's "Frost at Midnight" with its hope for the child's happy maturity. It also anticipates Yeats's "A Prayer for My Daughter" with its anxiety for the child's discovery that her life may be a "mournful labour." Wordsworth focuses on the infant as an instance "of infirm humanity" continuously challenged by a reality of natural changes and mutability. When he celebrates the child's birthday of one month, he sees it as an occasion to compare human life with the lunar cycle that must pass through a dark phase of lunar death. The poet-father is relieved that his child has "survived that great decay, / That transformation" of one month's passage. But suddenly he realizes that for an infant the passage of time is an unreal event, since a moment is no more narrow than a month and a month no more capacious than a moment to a child. The child's strength is in its obliviousness, in its narcissism. Wordsworth as adult admires this strength at the same time he wonders at the infirmity of the child's humanity.

This infirmity requires protection from "mother's love" and "father's thoughts," made more valuable by advantages of culture and civilization. The poet contrasts his child's cultural advantages with the harsh conditions of primitive societies, where nature works without assistance of much imagination ("amid wilds / Where fancy hath small liberty to grace, / The affections, to exalt them or refine"). Clearly it is an advantage to the child that it be reared in conditions of imaginative freedom, where fancy has large scope to operate. That is a function of civilization, organized by a sublimating process of imagination: exalting and refining affections. Where this is lacking, Wordsworth speculates, "the maternal instinct itself" is a "joyless tie / Of naked instinct." This father's poem addressed to his infant is itself an example of culture at work, discovering "parallels" and "contrasts" between his helpless infant and the greater helplessness of children without advantages of civilization, finding "resemblances" between his child's transformations and the changes in the moon—but led to a greater triumph over mutability by his imaginative conception of childhood instincts as powers of a living creature. Just as the father begins to worry about the sorrows of death which his infant must experience some day, he corrects his despondency with a notice of the child's smiles. These he calls "feelers of love," a crude metaphor of acute psychological insight.

Childhood is a time of power, with impulses that have yet to be distinguished from an environment of pure instinct and contradictory forces. While Wordsworth might admire such a time, as he does in the opening books of *The Prelude* or in the slight, but charming poem "Characteristics of a Child Three Years Old," he always qualifies his admiration with a concern for the direction these impulses may take. The dangers of an undisciplined instinct pursuing its need for pleasure are responsibly emphasized by the storyteller of "The Blind Highland Boy," where the vigor of that quaint tale is a product of the speaker's sympathy for the boy's dangerous adventure. On the other hand, in one of Wordsworth's greatest poems of childhood, the "Ode: Intimations of Immortality," the dangers of discipline itself are wistfully acknowledged as necessary even while the poet bids farewell to "the glory and the dream" which have been sacrificed to achieve maturity. "The Blind Highland Boy" and the "Ode: Intimations of

Immortality" are not quite poems about children as heroes, just as the "Address to My Infant Daughter" is not quite a poem about parents as heroes, but all three court the idea that the healthy ego must make use of such heroes throughout its great adventure of development.

While "The Blind Highland Boy" celebrates a child's momentary escape from the restraints of civilization, the "Ode" sadly acknowledges the need to accept those restraints, recognizing that civilization may exact too high a price at the same time it offers compensations for lost childhood. Psychologically, the blind Highland Boy would be destroyed as an ego if he were allowed to retreat completely into his dark world of fantasy, and so his adventure on the river could be seen as a retreat from reality quite as much as it is an assertion of independence. This truth Wordsworth is very much aware of in poems such as the "Ode," where the child's world may be bright and alive with instinct, but where also reality suffers a great foreshortening. The adult may be blind to his own heritage from childhood, to the debt he owes his infancy especially as he has been successful in repressing or sublimating instincts, as the speaker of the "Ode" acknowledges with the stanza that opens the poem: "The things which I have seen I now can see no more."

It is precisely this quality of being blind to something that Wordsworth turns into a psychological triumph, taking the reader back into that condition when "the Babe leaps up on his Mother's arm," a condition buried in the psychic primeval past. The poet forces one to regress with him, as though under hypnosis, into that sleep of the mind, before the birth of an ego, where "our birth is but a sleep and a forgetting." One must pass from "the light of common day" and through "shades of the prison-house" before one can recover the "Heaven" of "our infancy." This "Heaven" is a family romance of royal glories and an "imperial palace" that Mother Nature works hard to help the child forget through a kind of brain-washing (from the child's point of view) or adjustment to reality (from the adult's point of view). This conditioning continues through institutions of civilization, particularly the family. To be healthy as well as successful, this conditioning must be wary of accelerating the process of maturation, as Stanza Seven warns. When he is finally able to make his way through the shadows and customs thick as frost (blocking access by consciousness into regions of psychological darkness), Wordsworth as analyst find something not at all dead to anything but reality. In a stunningly conceived appreciation of infancy, Wordsworth celebrates a surprising quality of buried life in the ninth stanza.

Here he puts aside those virtues of childhood that most would consciously look back to with nostalgia, including carelessness and liberty. It is "not for these" he is grateful. In fact, childhood liberty is something of an illusion, certainly not the "genuine liberty" he celebrated at the end of *The Prelude,* where the poet assumes a terrible responsibility for his power of mind. Instead, childhood liberty is a tame projection of a radical irresponsibility that dwells deeply within the psyche of the child, thrusting deeply into the unconscious regions that constitute infancy. In those regions "sense and outward things" are brought into question; there reality falls away and vanishes before the power of "high instincts" that make up the central core of psychic being. In that core is a power without consciousness, without identity—as close to the instincts of rainbows, roses, birds, and lambs as human being can be. It is the source of all that is human, although it may not be in itself distinctly human. It is, paradoxically, "the fountain light of all our day," "a master light of all our seeing," because those first affections are Wordsworth's conception of what Freud called the id. Self-absorption, with its denial of the rest of the world, is a natural psychological fact upon which all the rest of human experience is based. But no healthy, mature human being would be content to remain long in that state.

Instead, as Wordsworth affirms through the last two stanzas, one finds "strength" not only in "what remains behind" from childhood, but one also builds upon that "primal sympathy" until one achieves "the philosophic mind." In two key stanzas of the poem, Six and Seven, the poet observed this building process at work. It is the process of civilization, training the child to care for others as well as for itself and teaching the child to discipline its instincts for love and death. When "earth fills her lap with pleasures" for "her Foster-child," and when she supplies new "yearnings" for the growing child, earth is merely teaching the infant how to survive according to the pleasure principle. However, this principle must be modified by the introduction of a new, crucial principle of reality, introduced with some satire in Stanza Seven, where the poet describes the need for a training which sounds very much like sublimation. "Among his new-born blisses," the child of six years exists "mid work of his own hand," while having to deal with the problems of interfering, erotic, mothers ("Fretted by sallies of his mother's kisses"). The "light" that seems to come "from his father's eyes" and weigh "upon him" as with a force of judgment tells that the light image of the poem has a special meaning in this context. The growth of consciousness and responsibility are functions of identifications with fathers (and super-egos), while reversions to mother's laps and kisses are regressions into irresponsible instincts (of the id). To make a connection between the interior light (which is a darkness to the ego) and the exterior light (a darkness to the id), mother nature and father culture conspire to teach the child how to project, introject, identify and sublimate:

> See, at his feet, some little plan or chart,
> Some fragment from his dream of human life,
> Shaped by himself with newly-learned art.

These plans, charts, and dreams are childish models of love and death: "A wedding or a festival, / A mourning or a funeral"; and, later they are models of work and war as well, "dialogues of business, love, or strife."

Wordsworth may mock, in tones of sarcasm, the business of childhood where one's "whole vocation" seems to be "endless imitation," but he does not blink at the necessity for learning how to shape life's materials in ways that will allow the ego to grow to social responsibility. After all, only those who are sensitive to others' suffering will be able to achieve "the philosophic mind," because it is they who will acquire the great gifts of "soothing thought," which "spring / Out of human suffering." The child may be the source of tenderness, joy, and fear, but without the capacity for "thoughts" (those that sooth, but also those that "do often lie too deep for tears"), there would be no civilization, no poetry, no consciousness of glory. The poet mocks, then, at the process in education which may abort childhood with a rush to responsibility, thus bringing on "the inevitable yoke" with its premature death of the soul, buried beneath the frost of accumulating customs. This abortion of childhood is a threat to society and civilization because it substitutes a darkness of matter for a darkness of spirit, rather than connect a light of ego with a light of civilization. Art, as a tool of civilization, allows "the little Actor" to learn various "parts" for himself in the pageant of life. Art must be constantly exercised, or the ego will be denied opportunities for growth in social awareness through identifications with other persons and other parts. There is a danger even here, however, because if the ego only plays roles, acting as if "his whole vocation / Were endless imitation," it will merely become its own father or mother, become a mere puppet of its super-ego.

To prevent either error of education, abortion of childhood through premature assumption of responsibility (and so loss of playfulness), or endless imitation of prolonged play (indeed, a form of prolonged foreplay without gratification), civilization must keep alive the play in the work, just as it keeps faith in the values of childhood for the healthy life of the adult. Civilization must be something more than the "exterior semblance" that belies the "Soul's immensity." It can do this most successfully as long as it provides means of sublimation for its children. Work without play is merely a "weight," or, worse yet, a "yoke" that kills the spirit; play without work is, at best, an "endless imitation," but at worst it may be a denial of reality, the "blank misgivings of a Creature / Moving about in worlds not realised" and, as such, a life of neurosis—even psychosis. Work and play are obviously necessary to maintain the healthy soul, when the "sway" of habit is governed by "delight" as well as by "human suffering." For Wordsworth the most likely form of human activity that can identify, not merely link, work with play is the art of poetry, where thought and image unite to maintain "primal sympathy" with "the philosophic mind."

# CHAPTER SEVEN:

## Blind Thoughts

"Resolution and Independence" is one of the best of Wordsworth's poems for illustrating his art of therapy through sublimation. The young man of this poem has the uncanny experience of finding in his encounter with an old man a psychological cure. The young man draws upon his narcissism to construct a powerful ego-ideal. The imagery of the poem develops a basic pattern of bringing order out of chaos, turning the "pleasant noise" of the first stanza into the "lofty utterance" of Stanza Fourteen. Consistent with this pattern is the poem's theme of turning the young man's mind from childish fantasies to adult realities, from a preoccupation with immediate pleasure to a regard for future realities. Finally, the young man converts his "dim sadness—and blind thoughts" into a clear image of fortitude and perseverance; he passes thereby from a boy's careless happiness to a man's happy care.

At the very moment the speaker claims he has no remembrances of "the ways of men, so vain and melancholy," he sinks into dejection: "fears and fancies thick upon me came; / Dim sadness—and blind thoughts, I knew not, nor could name." His conscious mind seems helpless before this onslaught of frightening emotions. Unless he gains control through a conscious ability to "name" them, these feelings may drive him into that very "despondency and madness" which seem the legacy of the poets who begin their life "in gladness." Wordsworth's poem narrates the therapy for preventing both the despondency and the madness. Immediately after admitting he could not give a name to his feeling, the speaker begins to analyze his condition: "My whole life I have lived in pleasant thought," a confession which leads him to a self-admonition that one cannot "expect that others should / Build for him, sow for him, and at his call / Love him, who for himself will take no heed at all." Before he can begin to command his environment, he must command himself, and he will do neither unless he learns to work and to love. Paradoxically, the speaker has already begun to achieve some control over his feelings before he encounters the old leech-gatherer, and he has done it through analysis of himself. He takes note of two heroes of poetry, Chatterton and Burns, and he rejects them as ego-ideals, thereby achieving further control over his anxieties.

But still he is startled by the sudden appearance of the old man standing "beside a pool bare to the eye of heaven." It is as though his unconscious mind suddenly took shape before his conscious mind, producing the effect which Freud called "the uncanny," which occurs "when the distinction between imagination and reality is effaced, . . . or when a symbol takes over the full functions of the thing it symbolizes." While Wordsworth's poem does not present this experience as a defense against the fear of castration, it does not contradict much that is implied by Freud's account of how the super-ego is constructed to be such a defense. It may be that behind the young man's "dim sadness—and blind thoughts" is his unconscious fear of castration (for, as Freud suggests in his discussion of "The Uncanny," "the fear of going blind, is often enough a substitute for the dread of being castrated. The self-blinding of the mythical criminal, Oedipus, was simply a mitigated form of the punishment of castration"). However, it is sufficient for Wordsworth's thematic purpose that the speaker's fear is a fear of lost creativity, deteriorating into "despondency and madness." The sudden and startling appearance of the old man is a surprise only to the speaker's consciousness—not to his unconscious needs, which almost immediately bind themselves to the figure of the leech-gatherer. The poet explains how his imagination begins to make sense of the old man, synthesizing his figure through similes with a huge stone and a sea-beast, images which carry to the conscious mind expressions of instinctual needs: security and repressed life crying out for release from below.

It is no wonder, then, that the old man seems to bear "a more than human weight," because indeed he does exactly that for the speaker, whose unconscious needs are being expressed through the person of the leech-gatherer. That the speaker's ego is directing operations is hinted by the synthesizing features of the process, described in Stanza Eleven when the old man is said to be like a cloud that "moveth all together, if it move at all." The speaker reveals his hidden desires when he asks the old man what his "occupation" is, and then hears not the substance of the man's answer, which is lost in an impression of orderly speech: "Choice word and measured phrase, above the reach / Of ordinary men." While listening to these words, the speaker falls into a trance in which he sees the old man as someone "whom he had met with in a dream," as someone sent "to give him human strength, by apt admonishment"—exactly the function of an ego-ideal, particularly one derived from identification with the father. But Wordsworth's poem does not cease with this construction; he takes the process a step beyond to show how the speaker's ego introjects, or takes into itself for total control, this image of the old man as moral instructor. Because he has made an outer experience serve his inner need, the speaker has, in effect, sublimated his instincts of fear and desire. Because he has heard especially the "stately speech" of "admonishment," the speaker has identified his need for expression with the power of language, and in that he becomes the poet his maker.

*THE OLD LEECH-GATHERER* is not the only ego-ideal celebrated by Wordsworth's psychological heroes, although he is one of the most effective for curing the hero of anxiety. Other figures who serve this function in the poetry of Wordsworth's middle years include Toussaint L'Ouverture and Robert Burns. Toussaint evokes the poet's testament of faith in "man's unconquerable mind" that can convert adversity into triumph, even as the power of dejection can be reversed to become a power of joy—or as dark instincts can be tapped to supply the ego with the power to construct ideals. This latter capacity Wordsworth attributes to the art of Robert Burns, which Wordsworth says in his poem "At The Grave of Burns" was a

> light I hailed when first it shone,
> And showed my youth
> How Verse may build a princely throne
> On humble truth.

Standing at the grave of Burns, the poet needs to recall the light to rescue his mind from the shivering fears and pains he feels at the opening of the poem. They are felt as weights pressing upon his consciousness, and he wishes them away: "Off weight—nor press on weight!—away / Dark thoughts!" Burns himself, or rather his poetry, is the poet's rescue from these dark thoughts, lifting the speaker from his dejection just as Burns was lifted by his art from earth to heaven. As in "Resolution and Independence," in this minor poem Wordsworth searches into his own nature to account for his strange dejection, considers the possibilities for rescue (lost to him with Burns's death), and finally asserts an independence that can do without external aids. When he asks, "Why go on?" he refers to his unwillingness to speculate on what might have been, and turns to the reality of what is, by observing not only the grave of Burns but also the smaller grave of Burns's son who only recently had died and was buried next to the poet his father.

In this image of two graves, son and father, Wordsworth can concentrate his symbolic purpose, for by these deaths he is forced to acknowledge the ideal of Burns as a product of his own imagination, constructed to serve his own ego's needs. The death of the son is a sacrifice for the death of the father in a psychological sense that the poem barely hints: in the sense that the ego harbors unconscious desires (and needs) for the death of the father at the same time it must punish itself for harboring such desires (hence, the son as well as the father must die). Wordsworth is moved by the presence of the son's grave alongside the father's as a "Soul-moving sight! / Yet one to which is not denied / Some sad delight." The "sad delight" is a strange, but nice phrase for expressing an ambivalence of feelings between sons and fathers, though Wordsworth's more pedestrian explanation is that the dead are always better off than the living because they no longer have the worries of the living. Still, the poet lives on and draws some strength from this meditation on the two graves, one for his heroic ideal of the poet whose place in Wordsworth's mind is "hallowed" by his poetry. Appropriately, the poem closes with the music of "a ritual hymn" heard at the end of the day: it is heard as a chant of "love that casts out fear," and so it memorializes the therapeutic function of all art, including Wordsworth's as well as Robert Burns's.

This is a theme also of Wordsworth's great ode to psychological sanity, the "Ode to Duty." It is a dedication to the high standard of psycho-analytical therapy: to make the unconscious conscious. Never has Wordsworth been more clear-minded about his goal than in his poem, where he uses the familiar imagery of "light" and "control" to convey his point about the importance of some ideal for achieving mastery. Duty is a "light to guide," but it is also a "rod / To check the erring, and reprove." It is a voice of reality destroying childish illusions of "empty terrors," but it is also a comfort to calm "weary strife" of adult living. Duty has the functions of conscience, and, as such, it is a name for the super-ego, entrusted with the task of watching over the innermost regions of the mind. Although "there are some who ask not if Duty's eye / Be on them," they are persons of childlike innocence who do their work "and know it not." Still, the poet implies that his "eye" is ever on the watch; even those who are conscious of its presence should supplicate for its control.

Wherever minds do the work of Duty "and know it not," they are vulnerable to "chance desires." So, until "love is an unerring light, / And joy its own security," all minds need "firm support, according to their need." The poet boasts that he has passed beyond his childhood innocence of acting without knowledge of duty, but even he, "no sport of random gust," and "being to himself a guide," has too often acted without full consciousness of reality, having reposed his trust too blindly. Only when he knows the fullness of reality, which is the primary obligation of the ego, can the poet relieve "the weight of chance-desires" and be not only a guide to himself but also a master of his fate. "Duty" is about as impersonal a version of the super-ego as Wordsworth can construct: to that degree it qualifies as a healthy function of mind. He places before his reader a set of paradoxes that make eminently good psychological sense, as in this stanza (removed from the 1815 text):

> Yet not the less would I throughout
> Still act according to the voice
> Of my own wish; and feel past doubt
> That my submissiveness was choice:
> Not seeking in the school of pride
> For 'precepts over dignified,'
> Denial and restraint I prize
> No farther than they breed a second Will more wise.

The "wish" is fulfilled by identification with an ideal of strong authority. Therefore, "submissiveness" is choice, because it is a conscious subordination of instinct to idea: "quietness of thought" controls "chance-desires." This policy or calculated deliberation is itself an ideal. The poet will not be seduced into abandoning his "primal sympathy" while pursuing "the philosophic mind." He prizes denial and restraint only when they "breed a second Will more wise" than one ignorant of Duty. This "second Will" is the organized ego, controlling instincts with their chance-desires, while refusing to be controlled by the super-ego with its "rod / To check the erring." For one so familiar with the complexities of his psyche, Wordsworth could value no other kind of deity than "the light of truth," and to no other kind of deity could he be a satisfied servant. Duty is ego-control projected as an ideal of preeminent social value, because it preserves the delicate balance between "the spirit of self-sacrifice" and "the confidence of reason"—just as the ego itself is a precarious balance between the claims of the id and the commands of the super-ego.

*NAPOLEON* stood as an example of an ego-ideal become tyrant, a constant warning in many of the political sonnets of 1802-1803, included in the grouping he called *Poems Dedicated to National Independence and Liberty.* Four of the first five sonnets in this group were written upon the occasion of Wordsworth's return to Calais in August 1802. They are made from several sets of contrasts, sometimes between England, with its emblematic star of beauty and liberty, and France with its "men of prostrate mind" and "hollow words"; at other times between the France Wordsworth knew in 1791, "when faith was pledged to new-born Liberty," and this present France bent beneath the tyranny of Napoleon when men seem all too prone to slavery. The fourth and fifth sonnets focus upon Napoleon himself, for whom the poet feels an inexplicable grief that such a man should exist to mock "true Sway" and "True Power," but Wordsworth's faith in spiritual power to recover political health is strong even during the trying times of Napoleon's tyranny. In the sonnet "September, 1802. Near Dover," he voices his fear as he stands looking across the Channel toward the coast of France, which seems so near it threatens to overwhelm his consciousness with its threatening menace. Physical power of all kinds, including wind and water (whereby fleets of invasion might one day cross to England), are "in themselves nothing"and might be used by either good or evil. However, Wordsworth holds firmly to his conviction that "by the soul / Only, the Nations shall be great and free."

Wind and water, calm or turbulent, are merely the materials of power—not powers in themselves. Genuine power is power of mind, vigorous and active—not prostrate in slavery. To balance the pernicious effects of Napoleon as an ideal of tyranny, Wordsworth offers tributes to the "great men who have been among us." Most important are those, like Sidney, Marvel, Harrington, and Young Vane, who have "hands that penned / And tongues that uttered wisdom." These are the masters of language, including the poets, and their power is in words well composed—a medium of political, as well as psychological and moral therapy. But the greatest hero of them all was Milton, to whom Wordsworth sends out a call for help in his great sonnet "London 1802." Here is Wordsworth's epitome of the heroic ideal, one who will stand firm with power to aid in the repression of mad chaos, who will not betray with a seduction to tyranny. England itself is vulnerable to the same evils as France, for England has become "a fen / Of stagnant waters" where men have "forfeited their ancient English dower / Of inward happiness."

Wordsworth wants no unseemly reverence paid to power, but he advises a strong respect for what power can accomplish. The "altar, sword, and pen" are emblems of "heroic wealth," all of which were greatly appreciated by Milton and readers of Milton's writings. France seems to have put aside the wealth of altar and pen, at a terrible cost. More importantly, however, both France and England have cut themselves off from the true sources of power, represented in this sonnet by the "fireside, the heroic wealth of hall and bower"—the domestic virtues. "Inward happiness" is a balance, once again, of several competing interests: worship, war, writing, and family affections. Only when these are kept in balance by a strong soul, such as Milton's, can "manners, virtue, freedom, power" again thrive. Like Wordsworth in his "Ode to Duty," Milton was happy because he did lay "the lowliest duties" on his heart.

WORDSWORTH'S "Elegiac Stanzas" are notes toward a better fiction that he can appreciate after looking at his friend's painting of Peele Castle. The poem is an elegy as much for Wordsworth's dead dreams as it is for his dead brother, because the important discovery, or confession, in the poem is Wordsworth's admission that his previous life has been a "Poet's dream," something "that never was, on sea or land," because it existed and still exists only in fantasy. The "Elegiac Stanzas" show Wordsworth's continuing ability to adapt to changing reality, to keep in balance the wishful thinking of the past with a clear perception of the present.

Indeed, "Elegiac Stanzas" is a new exploration for Wordsworth as his great poetry has always been, beginning with "Tintern Abbey," because it makes the present observation an occasion for comparing a present state of mind with previous states, and generating from that comparison a new and more complex consciousness of materials that have previously been unconscious. Since "Elegiac Stanzas" is a response to a painting, it illustrates well the point that art is an excellent medium for sublimating instincts. In this poem Wordsworth describes with loving, gently mocking detail how he might have painted this same picture had he thought to do so when he earlier resided near the scene. In fact, what he is doing is revealing within himself a capacity for doing so *at any time,* because he had no special tendency to "romanticize" nature—he was likely to note the fearful as often as the pleasant qualities in a landscape. But this poem is a confession, nevertheless, that there exists within him an instinct for wishful thinking, for playing with illusions, drawing upon that same light which shed glory all round himself as a child and barely remembered in the "Ode: Intimations of Immortality":

> Ah! then, if mine had been the Painter's hand,
> To express what then I saw; and add the gleam,
> The light that never was, on sea or land,
> The consecration, and the Poet's dream;
>
> I would have planted thee, thou hoary Pile
> Amid a world how different from this!
> Beside a sea that could not cease to smile;
> On tranquil land, beneath a sky of bliss.

When he actually tried to do such things, he wrote poems such as "Descriptive Sketches" or "Home at Grasmere," crippled because the "gleam" was added rather than discovered, or it was isolated for protection from darker visions. Where there was strength in such poetry, it was in the tensions between gleam and shadow, as in the Immortality Ode and here in this poem on Peele Castle.

What he imagines as a possibility for his dreaming vision is, in fact, a confession of his continuing childhood in himself. If he were to yield to his childhood's dream of glory, he would produce illusions, not truth: "Such, in the fond illusion of my heart, / Such Picture would I at that time have made." It would have been a "*fond* illusion" in both senses of the word, desirable and foolish, but only to the mature mind; to a child such a world is the real world, and it is a world which Wordsworth still acknowledges to be a source of strength for healthy minds. This poem is drawing upon that strength even as it shows the limits of its virtue. When the poet says that he has "submitted to a new control," he expresses his continuing desire to construct ego-ideals as compensation for a lost childhood of innocence and unfulfilled wishes.

But when he says that "a power is gone, which nothing can restore," he shakes confidence in his self-consciousness. He leaves an impression that he has surrendered to the control at the expense of the dream, and so has fearfully tipped the balance. In the Immortality Ode he had merely "relinquished one delight" while finding compensation in the "philosophic mind." Here he has lost a "power," which is much more ominous, even if it has resulted in a greater humanization: "A deep distress hath humanised my Soul." On the other hand, his assertion of loss may be another sign of increasing mental health. The "power" that has been lost may be an instinct deliberately sacrificed by an ego that has submitted to a new control: this would be necessary for maintenance not only of a stable mind, but also of vitality in civilization. What has been lost is, in the latter case, a childlike power to delude, to live a life of fantasy, and it has been lost because the ego has chosen to repress it or to use it in new ways. As long as he can say to himself that "the feeling of my loss will ne'er be old," the poet keeps alive the instinct ("feeling") without allowing it uninhibited gratification. His new control is a means to achieve greater social community:

> Farewell, farewell the heart that lives alone,
> Housed in a dream, at distance from the Kind!
> Such happiness, wherever it be known,
> Is to be pitied; for 'tis surely blind.

Blindness again emerges to express Wordsworth's fear or distrust of uninhibited instincts. He well knows that they are blind to all except their own immediate gratification, and that is a power in himself which he has had to struggle to discipline from the beginning of his career in writing. Sacrificing that power is necessary to civilization, although the loss of any gratification is something the mind constantly resists: one does not wish to give up anything that once gave pleasure. Therefore, the ego must turn to another aim, another form, in the new ideal to compensate itself for the pleasure lost. This Wordsworth has done in the image of the Castle. Like the old Leech-gatherer, the star of Milton, the idea of Beauty, or the Happy Warrior, this huge Castle is an ideal of fortitude and control. In itself it has no "feeling," which is good: it cannot therefore be an end in itself for the ego, which might use its "armour" as a defense against instincts of dangerous feeling. However, the ego must not so identify itself with this "unfeeling armour" that it surrenders eros to death.

WHEN finally Napoleon is defeated and the threat of foreign tyranny brought to a happy end, Wordsworth will be able to turn his attention back more forcefully to the needs of his countrymen to behave with the same restraint he describes in Lord Clifford in "Song at the Feast of Brougham Castle." Even during the darkest hours of 1809, when liberty seemed threatened everywhere, Wordsworth counselled restraint although he was often outraged by wars of aggression that forced people everywhere to oppose violence with violence in defense of their homelands. He expresses the desperate plight of the Tyrolese in a sonnet that cries out for those people, "That which we *would* perform in arms—we must!" But even they go forth "a self-devoted crowd, / With weapons grasped in fearless hands" to vindicate mankind. They are themselves the very sacrifices that civilization demands for existence. Should they yield with prostrate minds to usurping tyranny, they would, like children or ego, lose themselves in their parent or super-ego—to commit suicide of imagination.

*Sacrifice* is a key word in Wordsworth's poetry of those dark days. He knows that the price of civilization is high and nearly always worth the expense even of life itself. Sacrifice as a choice of submission to an ideal in the clear light of consciousness is a healthy act of mind. On the other hand, a helpless prostration before power is as pitiable as the helpless blindness of England's poor king, for whom Wordsworth expresses pity in his sonnet "November, 1813." Here is a spectacle that must have been frightening for Wordsworth to consider as a symbol of psychological and political evils in his time: "He sits deprived of sight, / And lamentably wrapped in twofold night." The king's blindness is a sign of political impotence, his madness a sign of psychological chaos. Between these extremes Wordsworth tries to steer a balanced course, opposing the impotence of blind restraint to the chaos of blind instincts.

BLINDNESS may be turned into an "emblem, of the utmost that we know, / Both of ourselves and of the universe," as Wordsworth says of the blind Beggar he once saw in London. However, it need not represent the impotence or the mental chaos that Wordsworth pitied in the old king. It might, indeed, point the way from the outer world of busy sensation into the inner world of mental harmony and spiritual repose. In yet another poem based upon his early experiences in London, the "Power of Music," Wordsworth describes how the music made by a blind fiddler on a London street arrests the frenzied motions of busy Londoners, suspends their thoughts and fills them with a pleasure of self-fulfillment. In this poem the focus is upon the power of art rather than upon the psychology of its creation; this focus is typical of many of Wordsworth's poems of this period. He investigates the qualities of power, whether natural, political, military, or artistic. Just as wind and water "in themselves are nothing" yet contain an awesome "mightiness for evil and for good" ("September 1802. Near Dover"), so may political, military, artistic power be nothing in themselves, yet offer a mightiness for evil and for good.

The power of art is a great good when it provides a release for captive spirits, forced into bondage by the business of a civilization preoccupied with "getting and spending." Wordsworth knows the value of art for satisfying repressed emotions: society requires many sacrifices to maintain its order, but it supplies a base for the arts of civilization which turn those sacrifices into spiritual (i.e., sublimated) achievements. In the midst of all this work, which is necessary, there must still be room for the play of art, as on Oxford Street, London, where the blind man plays while the busy world "roars on like a stream"

> His station there; and he works on the crowd,
> He sways them with harmony merry and loud;
> He fills with his power all their hearts to the brim—
> Was aught ever heard like his fiddle and him?

While the poet seems in the "Power of Music" to tout the

virtues of art at the expense of the world's business, he does not always make it appear so one sided an advantage. There is more balance in a humorous and playful poem dedicated to Charles Lamb, whom Wordsworth later describes as "the frolic and the gentle": *Benjamin The Waggoner* has about it a frolic and gentle quality that is rare in Wordsworth's poetry, but it illustrates an important function of art that he everywhere acknowledges—the temporary release of spirit from necessary bondage. It is a poem in the spirit of Robert Burns' "Tam O'Shanter," narrating the night-time adventures of an inebriated country hero. Unlike Burns' glorious poem, however, Wordsworth's keeps an evenness of attitude between the importance of work to be done and the importance of the play that threatens the success of that work. The hero Benjamin is introduced as a person "of much infirmity" who presently walks secure in his "pride of self-denial," but who will be seduced from his narrow path by the joyful sounds of "a fiddle in its glee." Like the London crowds who are halted from doing the business of Empire, Benjamin the Waggoner is betrayed by his "infirmity" into a lapse that parts him from his team and waggon.

This humorous poem, almost a parody of the subjects which had been more seriously treated by the younger poet in such poems as those dealing with the incidents upon Salisbury Plain, presents a playful mockery of sober hard work at the same time it works hard to demonstrate the evils of playing while working on the job. There is no doubt, nevertheless, that Wordsworth sympathizes with the heroic waggoner, whose virtues are applauded and whose vice is celebrated. Wordsworth analyzes Benjamin's character not only as a burlesque of the tragic hero, but also as the plight of a strong ego always battling to control the adversaries within and without. Benjamin is the ego in command of his animal forces represented by the horses, but he is ever aware of the threatening Master

who, as the Super-Ego, has tied to the wagon a watchdog
of conscience, the "noble Mastiff." When the Ass kicks the
dog, leaving the wound that will break the Master's patience, the episode is celebrated by the poet as an instance
of breeding "better manners." Because the Ass is a sign of
Benjamin's reprobation, an emblem of his having given
way to an instinct, the poet seems to affirm Benjamin's
lapse from duty:

> The Ass, uplifting a hind hoof,
> Saluting the Mastiff on the head;
> And so were better manners bred,
> And all was calmed and quieted.

The most glorious part of *The Waggoner* is the social
happiness of the second canto, where Benjamin and his
newly found friend, the crippled Sailor, cast aside all restraints and join in the revelry of song and dance at the
Cherry Tree Inn. Benjamin hears "a fiddle in its glee" and
recalls that the villagers are celebrating their "Merry-
Night":

> Although before in no dejection,
> At this insidious recollection
> His heart with sudden joy is filled,—
> His ears are by the music thrilled,
> His eyes take pleasure in the road
> Glittering before him bright and broad.

Although the poet-narrator is probably that same "simple
water-drinking Bard" referred to in the first canto, he
joins himself in this festival of unleashed spirits: "What
bustling—jostling—high and low! / A universal overflow!"
Benjamin participates in the "promiscuous rout" of "a fes-
tal company" just as Wordsworth in *The Prelude* says he
did during his first summer vacation, when he passed "the

night in dancing, gaiety and mirth," when spirits "mounted up like joy into the head, / And tingled through the veins." When the Waggoner and the Sailor leave the Inn they are only beginning to enjoy the evening: "No notion have they—not a thought, / That is from joyless regions brought!" The poet joins in to share "their inspiration," to "share their empyreal spirits—yea, / With their enraptured vision, see—O fancy—what a jubilee!" This vision of "shifting pictures—clad in gleams" of "rich change, and multiplied creation!" is the compensation for having broken the bonds of ordinary restraint, just as the poet's own vision of a magnificent morning was a compensation for the young Wordsworth after his night of dancing in 1788.

The difference is, of course, that Benjamin finds his visionary outlet through what Wordsworth in the 1800 Preface condemned as a "gross and violent stimulant" (although it was a metaphor for crude art in the Preface). This is an important difference for Wordsworth, because he believed that the cost of direct expression of instincts was too great for the order of society and the good of civilization. Thus Benjamin's night of revelry may have been a therapeutic expression of his need to gratify pleasure, but it was at the same time a loss to civilization. Gratification of pleasure through art can suffice for most persons; the music of the fiddlers and the story told by the Sailor gratify the small community of listeners' need to play, and to identify with heroic ideals at the same time.

Benjamin knows "a feeling of triumph" only twice in the narrative: once, at the beginning of the story, when he feels "the pride of self-denial," and second, when he "beheld a dancing among the stars" in the third canto, during the night of revelry. His triumph of the first instance is a submission to the ideals of his Master and his Master's world of business, a submission to super-ego; his triumph of the second instance is a submission to demands of instincts which have been long repressed by ideals of his culture. Neither triumph is in itself wholly acceptable, because in either alone is a serious loss of (ego) autonomy. The ultimate price of either kind of triumph is a corruption of civilization, producing a waste of spirit and culture.

The conclusion of *The Waggoner* depicts the poet's dejection as he observes a scene of dismal foreboding. Here the world is "dismal out of doors," where a human caravan "straggles through the wind and rain." In such a world the absence of a strong ego is much to be deplored. This is a muted version of "the world [that] is too much with us," the world where "for everything, we are out of tune." Rather than submit to such a world without emotion, made cold by abstractions of authority, better to be "a Pagan suckled on a creed outworn" and *pretend,* or play, that one is less forlorn. To oppose such a world, in politics or in art, is an heroic endeavor. Wordsworth not only makes his poetry a relief from such dismal scenes, he celebrates the heroes who oppose political tyrannies. In his sonnet to "The King of Sweden," he says that "the voice of song" hails those like this young king who has shown to all a courage to "stand, or fall / If fall they must" with a dignity that earns his heroic ancestors' approval: "the heroes bless him, him their rightful son." It is this kind of courage, to stand or fall with dignity, that Wordsworth examines more closely in *The White Doe of Rylstone,* where the power of art is misapplied and where civilization is threatened by the tyranny of paternal authority.

*RICHARD NORTON, ESQUIRE,* is a figure of unyielding authority, holding to the past without toleration for change and demanding that all his family do likewise. He is a force of political and religious tyranny, once significant for the construction of civilization, but now a threat to the very culture he has helped to build. His Banner is an emblem of that same tyranny, of art abused for arousing direct action rather than for sublimating passions. The

Banner, beautiful and emblematic of filial piety, will nevertheless lead the Nortons to their destruction, vividly represented in the scene of Francis Norton's murder: his "warm life-blood / Had tinged more deeply, as it flowed, / The wounds the broidered Banner showed." It becomes a symbol of religious sublimation; it mixes the sacrifice of God's son with the sacrifice of Norton's son without confirming the value of the sacrifice. As a symbol of political rebellion, the Banner asserts the irony of sons sacrificed to fathers. As Wordsworth said in his 1815 "Supplementary to the Preface," "no poetry has been more subject to distortion, than that species, the argument and scope of which is religious; and no lovers of the art have gone farther astray than the pious and the devout." Norton is one who has taken art astray, because he has tried to use art for religious ends and so he has made demands on it which art cannot sustain.

The White Doe, coming from the wilderness of nature, is offered as an emblem of values which are equally difficult to sustain, because the White Doe is at once a figure of unreflecting nature, a sign of natural grace, and even "a power like human reason." Like the lamb which follows Una in *The Faerie Queene*, the White Doe suggests a kind of religious grace as well, in its companionship with Emily Norton. Wordsworth does not, like Richard Norton, force the symbol as a religious emblem. He does, however, offer it as a force of nature which has subordinated itself to human needs, maintaining for Emily a connection with her past at the same time it provides consolation for her present.

While the active figure of the narrative is Francis Norton, his sister is a disturbing presence, psychologically as mysterious in her own way as the White Doe is in its way. Emily is utterly passive, hardly stirring herself to act even in desperation; she yields to the authority of her brother quite as passively as she had to that of her father. When she is tempted to hope for something that would avert "the coming woe," she immediately represses it, as when she says to the Old Man, while waiting for news of the battle:

"Turn from us all the coming woe:
This would I beg; but on my mind
A passive stillness is enjoined."

She sends the Old Man off to gather news of the family's fortune, and that is the extent of her active intervention in affairs. After the devastation, she endures to sustain an image of something that survives all chances of fate and fortune. She neglects "in imperial state / Those outward images of fate," "carrying inward a serene / And perfect sway." She functions to perform the self-sacrifices necessary for ego to achieve self-mastery. She is also a complement to Francis as the feminine image of the self that makes one's relationship with the father, and she endures as a symbol of the sacrifices necessary for the continuity of civilization. On the other hand Francis Norton is the ego that must make the sacrifices: of his identification with his sister and with his father. Because he cannot successfully sacrifice or repress both identifications, Francis Norton must share the doom of the rest of his family. He is a victim of his own ambivalent attitude toward his father.

This ambivalence is dramatically highlighted by two special episodes of the narrative. First, early in the story Francis attempts to persuade his father from taking up the Banner in defiance of social order. Second, after his father and brothers have been executed, Francis agrees to carry the Banner back to Bolton. In both episodes Francis is a man in a trance. In the first, after he has pleaded unsuccessfully for his father to stay out of battle, Francis felt a visionary dreariness: "in the vacant hall, / He stood silent under the dreary weight,— / A phantasm, in which roof and wall / Shook, tottered, swam before his sight." He stood "leaning on a lance / Which he had grasped unknowingly / Had blindly grasped in that strong trance." Because he wished to join his father at the same time he was divided from him in spirit, the young man's mind is torn from its secure consciousness and thrown into this trance of separation. Because he has seized a lance, he expressed his unconscious desire to participate with his father in the hostilities that follow; however, he might also have seized the lance because of hostility to his father himself. Francis says more than he knows when he tells his sister that "in deep and awful channel runs / This sympathy of Sire and Sons."

In the second episode, after Francis has thrown away the lance with its suggestions of hostility, he joins his captured father and brothers to offer himself in a sacrifice of love (for the second time). His father now accepts his son, but only to ask something he must know is an outrage to Francis. The elder Norton asks his son to regain the Banner and to "bear it to Bolton Priory," where Francis is to "lay it on Saint Mary's shrine." As in the earlier episode, Francis awakens to find himself holding something in his hand, but here the lance has been replaced by the Banner: equally ambiguous and equally troublesome for the son. He has betrayed his faith (or psychologically, his love, for his mother and sister) by submitting to the authority of his father, and he is helplessly condemned to impotence of will. Wordsworth recreates Francis's rationalization for his action as an "unconscious" deed condoned by Providence because "no hindrance" has interfered. When Francis declares that "no choice is left, the deed is mine," there is no doubt that he has resumed command over himself and accepts responsibility for his unconscious as well as for his conscious actions. But "providence" *does* interfere, preventing Francis from fulfilling the mission his father requested.

This providence, however, is another in a sequence of ambiguities, because Francis seems to have invited it as a punishment for his feelings of guilt. His death, made sensational (though symbolic) through its association with the bloody Banner, is the only psychological conclusion possible for Francis Norton. He must be punished on two counts: he betrayed his mother and his sister, and he has thought of betraying his "unconscious" promise to his father. Even though Wordsworth probably would, or could, not have accepted Freud's "castration" theory, he surely has an insight into the fate of Francis Norton that anticipates Freud's speculation that "every punishment is ultimately castration and, as such, a fulfillment of the old passive attitude towards the father. Even Fate is, in the last resort, only a later projection of the father." In the light of his failure to resolve the ambivalences of his relationship with his father and with his faith, Francis Norton shares the "fate" of all sons who do not sufficiently depersonalize the super-ego. This fate is the price of rebellion against authority. It is unavoidable for civilization, as it is unavoidable for Francis Norton.

## CHAPTER EIGHT:

## Bound by Natural Piety

*The Excursion* explores the discontents of civilization. It insists, in the words of Freud, that "there is no golden rule which applies to everyone: every man must find out for himself in what particular fashion he can be saved." The Wanderer enunciates this as a principle of freedom through balance:

> "the innocent Sufferer often sees
> Too clearly; feels too vividly; and longs
> To realize the vision, with intense
> And over-constant yearning,—there—there lies
> The excess, by which the balance is destroyed.

The Solitary's life provides a model for the various ways to strive for happiness. But he has failed to find happiness. The Wanderer recognizes one of the reasons for that failure: "extremes are equally disowned / By reason." The Wanderer's principle of "sound expectations" is based upon a position which reserves the right to choose, to deny the pressures of "over-constant yearning" from out of "the depths / Of natural passions," to resist the "iron bonds / Of military sway." The Wanderer's lesson to relieve the Solitary's despondency sounds in many respects like Freud's education in reality, not the least in its emphasis upon the freedom to exercise "the mind's excursive power."

The Wanderer champions a view of mental health based upon "liberty of mind," anticipating Freud's call for an "education freed from the burden of religious doctrines." The Wanderer exults to see "an intellectual mastery exercised / O'er the blind elements" so that one can hope to "hear the songs / Of humanised society." He strikes a note that harmonizes with Freud's equally strong affirmation "that it is possible for scientific work to gain some knowledge about the reality of the world, by means of which we can increase our power and in accordance with which we can arrange our life." But the Wanderer has at least two problems, or faults, which keep him at some distance from Freud's insights and theories. One is a negative problem, for the Wanderer does not have Freud's understanding of childhood sexuality. His other is one for which he can be more reasonably held responsible: it is one that Wordsworth subjects to some serious and painful criticism in the course of *The Excursion*—this is the more positive fault, or problem, of religion. The Wanderer is a highly religious person, just as the Pastor is, but the Wanderer's religion is not the same as the Pastor's, even though Wordsworth sometimes tends to blur the distinctions between the two.

THE WANDERER attempts to cure the Solitary of his despondency by teaching him, in the words of *The Prelude*, "how the mind of man becomes / A thousand times more beautiful than the earth / On which he dwells." The Wanderer has learned from experience that the beauty and meaning of life derive from the mind's interaction, excursive power, with the sensible world. The Solitary has been too much a victim of the changing time and nature, and so the Solitary must rediscover his essential identification with the unchanging power of the universe, a power that underlies the appearances of mutability—what the Wanderer calls, in his discourse that opens the last book, the "*active* Principle" which, "howe'er removed / From sense and observation, . . . subsists / In all things." The Wanderer says there are three ways to discover, or rediscover, identity with this Principle.

The first is the ancient way of primitive man, the way of superstition but also a way of imagination. The Wanderer tells the Solitary that he should recall how it was possible in the beginning of the creation for mankind to hear "the articulate voice / Of God" borne upon the wind. Even though the Solitary protests against submission to superstition, the Wanderer insists that it would be far better to misconceive a spiritual presence in the passive forms of nature and be filled with joy than to "be joyless as the blind"—which is the consequence of "viewing all objects unremittingly / In disconnection dead and spiritless." Modern man has abused his intellectual power by using it only to reduce the grandeur of nature to the smallest of particles, to break the creation down into a littleness of atoms which merely reflect, in their essential poverty, the dwindled littleness of the probing human spirit. Surely, the Wanderer exclaims, modern man, "for whom our age / Unbaffled powers of vision hath prepared," can obtain from sense and reason more than primitive man did without the aid of science and civilization.

The Wanderer does not seriously maintain that anyone should or could recover the worldview of ancient man. One should not make the attempt because that would merely repeat mistakes already made by the Solitary himself, withdrawing from the benefits of civilization as he did when he sought out "Primeval Nature's child" in the wilds of America; the ideal of primitive joy there disappeared into squalid facts of "superstitious fear, and abject sloth." One *should* not try to abandon one's place in civilization, because one *cannot;* the attempt itself produces disappointment and despondency. Consciousness cannot lose itself to the unconscious powers of instinct and still be conscious. To attempt to regress to the primitive state of mind, as the Solitary did, is to surrender the benefits of civilization in return for the madness of dreams and nightmares.

The civilized person can nevertheless maintain his equanimity in the face of disappointments if he will look forward to the benefits of old age. The Wanderer offers himself as an example to imitate. He is threescore years of age, and he knows of what he speaks. In Book Nine he explains that old age should be thought of as a height attained after laboring to climb the difficult mountain of life. From that height one can look down upon the press of life and feel disencumbered of near obstructions. He suggests loss of interest in the things of this world is an advantage to hope for, since the loss easily converts into a spiritual gain: "fresh power to commune with the invisible world, / And hear the mighty stream of tendency." The mighty stream is a figure for the "active Principle," and the invisible world is a figure for the mind itself. Old Age is not only a liberation from the anchors of sensation; it is also, ominously, a retreat from reality and may be a regression to infantile narcissism.

The Wanderer offers his image of old age as a type of the power which abides in the mind, a power to withdraw from dependence upon a passive world of matter where the only reality is chaos and death. If taken as the Wanderer intends, his example encourages hope for final independence of mind and the courage to face death with integrity of consciousness. However, as the gentle Lady, wife of the Pastor, later whispers to the Poet, one ceases to share the Wanderer's vision the instant the Wanderer ceases to speak. If one reacts to the Wanderer's discourse in the same way as the Lady, then one must share her disappointment and suspect that Wordsworth has portrayed in the Wanderer's optimism an example of a pleasurable illusion which cannot withstand the test of reality.

The Wanderer has a strength of conviction which contains a dangerous weakness at its center. He admits that age forces him to make compromises with nature, gradually surrendering his claims against external reality while he tries to keep all that he has gained from his love for life. He admits in a telling passage of Book Four that he nurses a kind of despondency himself. It is not an arduous task to "relinquish" the happiness and joy which may be had from this world, but, he admits at the same time, it is "the most difficult of tasks to *keep* / Heights which the soul is competent to gain." That the Wanderer knows unhappiness and despondency seems obvious, but it does not come from his failure to keep hold of the forms of matter. His unhappiness, represented by his tendency to "chide the part of me that flags, / Through sinful choice," is that he cannot maintain his separation, or "freedom," from the world. As long as he aspires to that separation he is expressing his need for independence of mind—a healthy ambition of ego. But the Wanderer in fact does not find it easy to "stand in freedom loosened from this world," because if it *is* "the most difficult of tasks to keep" the heights of independence, then it must be the result of a powerful urge to regress, to fall back into an essential dependence upon the world.

He has not finally succeeded in overcoming his instinct to withdraw from reality and seek to recover the pleasure of uninhibited identification with his mother/nature. The Wanderer says that "those fervent raptures are for ever flown," but the speech he delivers at the opening of Book Four, as well as his discourse that opens Book Nine, are both evidence that in fact "those fervent raptures" are *not* flown. Those raptures are experiences of identification with the universe, experiences which Romain Rolland described to Freud as "oceanic" and which Freud speculated to be attempts in the mind to restore the "limitless narcissism" which the infantile ego felt in the womb or at the breast of its mother.

While he does not reduce his hero's yearning to a sexual desire for his mother, Wordsworth does supply some signs that he knows the Wanderer's raptures are fundamentally desires for the same union with nature which the Wanderer remembered from childhood. Desires for reunion, repetitions of childhood's narcissistic egotism, constitute the third way offered by the Wanderer as a means for recovering from despondency. Wordsworth is reexamining the claims of such poems as "Ode: Intimations of Immortality," where mental strength for adults is shown to be a function of the ego's drawing power from its unconscious, childhood strength of intimations from infantile instincts. In *The Excursion,* however, these claims are tested by comparison with other, different claims for ways to freedom and happiness.

The Wanderer asks at the end of the poem why "we revert so fondly to the walks / Of childhood?" he provides his own answer by saying

> "there the Soul discerns
> The dear memorial footsteps unimpaired
> Of her own native vigor."

While the point is close to the one celebrated in the "Ode: Intimations of Immortality," it lacks the courage and the strength of the great Ode, because the Wanderer has fixed his memory, his "intimations," firmly in the very material world which Wordsworth in the Ode accused of imprisoning the child. In fact, the Wanderer seems to be praising those very features of childhood to which Wordsworth denied his special thanks in the Ode: "Delight and liberty, the simple creed / Of childhood, whether busy or at rest, / With new-fledged hope still fluttering in his breast." It was not for these that Wordsworth composed his song of thanks and praise. But the Wanderer does; he goes so far as to base his philosophy of hope upon memories of childhood's feeling of freedom from restraint. In Book Four he raised his song of thanks to the "dread source, / Prime, self-existing cause and end of all" as having wrapped "the cloud / Of infancy around us." The Wanderer prays for this dread source to continue to "endure / For consciousness the motions of thy will," which in infancy was a cloud of simplicity. Whatever else the Intimations Ode has to say, it does not pray for a return to the simple "cloud / Of infancy."

The Wanderer does not always advocate simple regression to childhood states of rapture, much less to the clouds of infancy. Indeed he will have to modify some of his remarks made in Book Eight because of some serious criticism levelled by the Solitary at the Wanderer's simplistic interpretation of civilization. In Book Eight the Wanderer generally deplores the ravages of civilization against nature. He asks "where is now the character of peace, / Sobriety, and order, and chaste love . . . That made the very thought of country-life / A thought of refuge?" His view of the losses to mankind imposed by the advance of industrialization is a view sharply focussed upon a mother at the center of a busy home. While fathers are also mentioned in the same context, the Wanderer abbreviates their role to the province of "domestic bliss." Even more insistently, the Wanderer laments what the State has done to weaken the hold of the mother on her family:

> Economists will tell you that the State
> Thrives by the forfeiture—unfeeling thought,
> And false as monstrous! Can the mother thrive
> By the destruction of her innocent sons
> In whom a premature necessity

> Blocks out the forms of nature, preconsumes
> The reason, famishes the heart, shuts up
> The infant Being in itself, and makes
> Its very spring a season of decay!

A philosophy of nature such as that advocated by the Wanderer is a form of mother-worship and desire for reunion with the mother. The Wanderer will show, however, in Book Nine that he can benefit from the therapy of analysis, his own as well as that provided by the arguments of the Solitary, because in Book Nine the Wanderer attempts to reconcile his affection for nature with his discontents with civilization. Nevertheless, even then he insists that mother nature ("one maternal spirit") binds all together. Civilization, manifesting itself as "country, society, and time itself," is nourished, according to the Wanderer, by the maternal love of nature. Civilization is for the Wanderer not only the force that aims at binding the members of community together, it is also symptomatic of psychic elements which have undergone repression.

*ONE OF THE MOST* outstanding features of the Wanderer's character is that he is stubborn, not to say obsessive, in his religion of "natural piety." This quality of his character can be understood from materials Wordsworth provides through two means: first, from the Poet's narration of the Wanderer's personal history, and second, from the story which the Wanderer tells of Margaret and the Ruined Cottage. Because both of these two means were worked and reworked by Wordsworth from at least as early as 1798, his intentions for explaining the Wanderer's character can be understood best by taking into account the various ways the poet used to tell his character's story. One important feature which appears in all versions and which serves as a common element throughout is the characteristic of *bondage* (or *bonding*): the feelings of the Wanderer are bound to forms of nature, and the Wanderer is bound to the memory of Margaret quite as firmly as Margaret is herself bound to inhabit her deteriorating cottage.

Freud says of the various ways to satisfy the need for happiness (i.e., pleasure), one of the most important is "the way of life which makes love the centre of everything, which looks for all satisfaction in loving and in being loved." The Wanderer's lifetime of restless searching has had its occasions for loving—wives and children. The Wanderer, according to the Poet, "could *afford* to suffer" in sympathy with others because he "had no painful pressure from without." By this the Poet means that the old man had never married nor established a family of his own—"unvexed, unwarped / By partial bondage." Therefore, the Wanderer is a negative illustration of the truth that "we are never so defenceless against suffering as when we love, never so helplessly unhappy as when we have lost our loved object or its love." This vulnerability in a life which makes love the center of everything is what Freud called "the weak side" of the way to happiness.

The Poet believes the Wanderer has never bound himself to any particular human being. The Poet thinks (at the beginning of Book One) the Wanderer has lived with "a just equipoise of love" along a "steady course . . . Unoccupied by sorrow of its own." But the Poet is wrong. There *is* a sorrow in the old pedlar—fixed upon the person of Margaret, the only woman who has bound the Wanderer's imagination in repose. When he tells his tale of Margaret and the ruined cottage, the Wanderer is telling as much about himself as he is about Margaret or about the discontents of civilization (through the image of the ruined cottage). Because Wordsworth knew this about his story, he worked long and hard at uniting the two tales of the Pedlar and Margaret. In some respects, the relationship of these tales to one another is like the relationship Wordsworth intended between *The Prelude* and *The Rec-*

*luse:* an analysis of the mind of the poet as analyst is necessary for establishing the credentials of the poet whose main haunt is the mind of man.

THE WANDERER'S mother had tried to keep him at home, urging him "to teach / A village-school." But the young man was unable to discipline himself to such a task: "wandering thoughts were then / A misery to him." It was a "task he was unable to perform." In MS. E. of *The Pedlar* he is said to have "had small need of books," a trait which Wordsworth retained to describe him even through the last versions of the poem. What reading the Wanderer did was in books that told of martyrs' deaths or in a "straggling volume" of preternatural stories. He peopled his private world with such figures, investing the wild landscape of his homeland with the spectacles of his fancy. Later he was required to study mathematics and geometry, an occupation he pursued because it "deceived / The listless hours, while in the hollow vale, / Hollow and green, he lay on the green turf / In pensive idleness." Even though Wordsworth wished to emphasize in later versions of the narrative that the Wanderer had spent time "in study, and in ardent thought," not even in these later versions does the Wanderer overcome his yearning for "dreams." His real life "was his own, / He made it—for it only lived to him."

He resisted anything that "might tend to wean him" from the nature that "was at his heart." Education might have helped him break away from such intense identifications with nature, but education was a process he either naturalized or resisted: "from his intellect / And from the stillness of abstracted thought / He asked repose." When he was younger, just beginning his education in civilization, he established associations which were never to leave his mind:

> From his sixth year, the Boy of whom I speak,
> In summer, tended cattle on the hills;
> But, through the inclement and the perilous days
> Of long-continuing winter, he repaired,
> Equipped with satchel, to a school, that stood
> Sole building on a mountain's dreary edge,
> Remote from view of city spire, or sound
> Or minster clock!

He went home "all alone" from this bleak and dreary place, "not from terror free," as "the hills grew larger in the darkness." The boy would grow up to have great discontents with civilization.

In earlier versions of the story the explanation of the Wanderer's mental development is more clearly made in terms of his relationships with his parents. The episode of the six-year olds' first schooldays may remind the reader of similar accounts of Wordsworth's own life in his autobiographical poem, particularly in the lines which describe how he took the woodcocks from other people's traps, or, when he borrowed the boat for his evening adventure on the lake and seemed to see a cliff rise up to stride after him, he was troubled for many days afterward by "huge and might Forms" moving slowly through his mind. The Wanderer's childhood experiences of terror are more specifically tied to schooltime associations than are Wordsworth's, but both boys learned by these associations to build up consciences from feelings of guilt and the need to be punished. The growing shadows of the hills that dwarfed the six-year old Wanderer, or the huge and mighty forms that stalked the terrified child Wordsworth—these are psychologically identical with one another, and their relationship to fathers is something the analyst Wordsworth well understood.

The Wanderer's Schoolteacher was also his stepfather:

> From his sixth year the Boy of whom I speak
> In summer tended cattle on the hills
> But in the winter time he duly went
> To his Step-father's School, that stood alone,
> Sole Building on a mountain's dreary edge.

The experiences of this time "lay like substances [on his mind] and almost seem'd / To haunt the bodily sense." In the version of MS P (supplied by DeSelincourt), this information continued to be important to Wordsworth (as late as 1820):

> His Father dwelt; and died in poverty;
> While He, whose lowly fortune I retrace,
> The youngest of three sons, was yet a Babe,
> A little One—unconscious of their loss.
> But ere he had outgrown his infant days
> His widowed Mother, for a second Mate,
> Espoused the Teacher of the Village School;
> Who on her offspring zealously bestowed
> Needful instruction.

When, therefore, the Wanderer's mother urged him later "to teach / A village-school," he found it such a "misery" that "he was unable to perform" the task. The young man could not take the place of his step-father; he could not assume the independent role of a father to carry on the tasks of civilization except in the way of the Pedlar, a way later to be mocked by the Solitary. Wordsworth described in the Intimations Ode how the six-year-old child was subjected to a damaging education under the aegis of his parents: "Fretted by sallies of his mother's kisses, / With light upon him from his father's eyes." Here in *The Excursion*, in versions first written about the same time as the Ode, Wordsworth shows some understanding of what Freud called the Oedipus complex. The Wanderer's great discontents with civilization are, at their foundation, unsatisfied longings for his mother and punishments of guilt from a father whose place he could not take. There is a wonderful complication in the fact that the Wanderer's father was "really" his step-father: Wordsworth's intuition of what Freud called "the family romance."

The Wanderer's unsatisfied longing for his mother explains much about his oceanic feeling of desire for union with nature, and it explains much about his intense feeling for Margaret. He tells the Poet how Margaret's spirit became more obsessed with her wish for her husband's return, driving her more and more into herself and away from her maternal responsibilities (away from reality). The Wanderer's own spirit clings to Margaret as an object of satisfaction; she is an abandoned woman for whose husband he may be a substitute. He loses himself in identifying with her much as he did in his younger raptures of identification with nature. After her death, he is able to maintain his tranquillity because he can replace her as an object of affection with, again, the nature which has filled the void left by the ruin of her cottage:

> "She sleeps in the calm earth, and peace is here.
> I well remember that those very plumes,
> Those weeds, and the high spear-grass on that wall,
> By mist and silent rain-drops silvered o'er,
> As once I passed, into my heart conveyed
> So still an image of tranquillity,
>                    [that] all the grief
> That passing shows of Being leave behind,
> Appeared an idle dream."

The Wanderer consistently turns reality into a dream of wish-fulfillment.

*THE COMPLEMENT* of his yearning for mother nature
is the Wanderer's resistance to the arts of the "paternal
State," his discontents with civilization. In his story of
Margaret he tells how her husband's household affections
not only deteriorated with economic and naturalistic set-
backs, but whose paternal affections actually became sadistic. War and famine wasted the husband's spirit, eventually
drove him to aggression against his own family, and finally
absorbed him completely into the destructive forces of society. Love was put to the service of death in the perversi-
ty of tormenting his wife and children, and then he sacrificed himself totally to the instincts of death and
destruction when he gave up his family to become a soldier. Even this last act was a perversion of love, because he
did it to collect an enlistment reward that he could leave
for Margaret and their children. The story of Margaret's
husband illustrates the truth of Freud's dire conclusion
that "civilized society is perpetually threatened with disintegration," that it is "not easy for men to give up the satisfaction of this inclination to aggression." As long as the
husband remained at home without work, his aggressive
instincts directed his love into sadistic behavior; but when
he became a soldier, he could give full vent to his aggressiveness, even if it meant the sacrifice of his love.

Margaret's husband becomes an agent of the aggression
which Freud identifies as an instinct for death, and so civilization provides an outlet through war for the satisfaction
of that instinct. But aggression turned against the family is
intolerable to civilization. Some way must be found to
control it within the boundaries of civilized society. Freud
suggests that civilization "obtains mastery over the individual's dangerous desire for aggression by weakening and
disarming it and by setting up an agency within him to
watch over it, like a garrison in a conquered city." This requires the individual to renounce his instinct for aggression, driving it back to its source, to the ego itself, where

it creates the conscience, or super-ego, that watches so carefully every desire by the ego to satisfy instincts prohibited by civilization. The Wanderer's hostility to civilization is an expression of his hostility to his step-father; naturally he is much troubled with feelings of guilt as long as he cannot resolve his love for nature with his opposition to civilization. Wordsworth's poem aims for the resolution of this painful conflict in the Wanderer, as it aims also to show how the Solitary's despondency can be corrected with religious faith.

The Wanderer knows that "social industry" can transform some poor hamlet into a huge town, that barren fields can be turned to the production of food for an expanding population. This is a "triumph that proclaims / How much the mild Directress of the plough / Owes to alliance with these new-born arts!" He takes great pride in his nation's commercial and military successes. The bounty and power of nature can be turned, as they often have been, to human advantage, and that is a triumph of mind in which the Wanderer can exult. This kind of feeling is quite different from the religious yearning for a return to mother nature. Indeed, some of the Wanderer's imagery suggests a masculine, aggressive conquest over the more passive, feminine matter of nature.

But the Wanderer knows that the mere conquest of nature cannot produce human happiness. There must be not only beauty, cleanliness, and order, as Freud said, but also a readily available body of ideals—"ideas of possible perfection of individuals, or of people or of the whole humanity." Something like this the Wanderer voices when he says "all true glory rests, / All praise, all safety, and all happiness, / Upon the moral law." When he exclaims that "arts and high inventions" are weak if they are unpropped by virtue, the Wanderer flirts with important psychological truth. He merely flirts, however, because he thinks it has been possible to achieve a culture of "arts and high inventions" without virtue, while, as Freud insisted, culture *is* virtue.

As far as virtue is the exercise of restraint upon instincts of love and death, control over the dark unconscious powers that drive animal being, then "virtue" is the word used to describe the ego's successful renunciation of instinct. To deny immediate satisfaction of instincts, to postpone satisfaction of the pleasure principle, by exercising the reality principle in return for a measure of security and eventual, more largely satisfying pleasure—this is the operation of civilization, which *is* built upon a renunciation of instincts. This then is the price of civilization: renunciation or repression, and deferment of gratification. "The price we pay for our advance in civilization is a loss of happiness through the heightening of the sense of guilt," which may be perceived "as a sort of *malaise,* a dissatisfaction, for which people seek other motivations." The Wanderer is aware of this malaise, this unhappiness that accompanies the progress of civilization, and he is close to the same psychological explanation for it that Freud offered. The Wanderer feels that modern society has produced "most strange issues"; not the least of these is society's self-destructive drive "to produce, with appetite as keen / As that of war, which rests not night or day, / Industrious to destroy." It is easy, then, for the Wanderer to see "the darker side / Of this great change." There is what he calls a "lamentable change" from days of less competitive industry, less aggressive attacks upon nature, so that there seems little to choose from a fate of "pining discontent" or spiritual depression and dejection.

Insofar as the Wanderer believes there is a greater need for moral law and virtue, he believes in the need for more discipline of instincts. He does not understand, to this extent, how much the very accomplishments he praises ("intellectual mastery exercised / O'er the blind elements") depend upon, draw upon instincts for strength—

the instincts and passions are in fact the source of "those gigantic powers" that "have been compelled / To serve the will" of the thinking mind. What finally disturbs the Wanderer most, in Book Eight, is the fact that love and desire must be sacrificed to make civilization possible:

> "Economists will tell you that the State
> Thrives by the forfeiture—unfeeling thought,
> And false as monstrous! Can the mother thrive
> By the destruction of her innocent sons
> In whom a premature necessity
> Blocks out the forms of nature, preconsumes
> The reason, famishes the heart, shuts up
> The infant Being in itself, and makes
> The very spring a season of decay!
> The lot is wretched, the condition sad,
> Whether a pining discontent survive,
> And thirst for change; or habit hath subdued
> The soul deprest, dejected—even to love
> Of her close tasks, and long captivity."

The Wanderer is torn by this scene of conflicts between individual unhappiness and social happiness. He cannot believe that the state thrives upon the unhappiness of its people. He is off on the wrong track when he implies that true social happiness is not possible without a regression to more primitive modes of being. But he is true to his basic character when he suggests that hopes for happiness depend upon the domestic bliss of busy families where children are kept within sight of mothers and fathers. He seems to believe that the virtue he praises was, or still is in some places, active in family life untouched by the demands of larger social units. He would, in other words, limit his definition of civilization to the (nuclear) family.

The Wanderer knows, nevertheless, that there are great benefits for individuals from the accomplishments of his

"inventive Age." He cannot cure the unhappiness of civilization by counselling a retreat from ground already gained
at great cost. When the Solitary challenges his ideal of a
pastoral civilization without discontent, the Wanderer is
speechless of a long time while the Poet describes how they
all retired into the Pastor's lovely parsonage for a respite
from their debates. After the Solitary's rebuttal, this brief
rest in the household of the Pastor is a welcome relief to
the Wanderer. After his rest, the Wanderer breaks silence to
deliver his great speech on the "*active* Principle" of the
universe. The Parson's family, especially his happy boy, has
reanimated the Wanderer's heart from the apparent dejection he felt when the Solitary interrupted his speech on the
unhappiness of civilization. Now the Wanderer can admit
how desperate was the plight even of people living close to
nature. Their basic instincts might have been more readily
satisfied than those of civilized people, but they paid the
heavier price of ignorance. The Wanderer cannot forget

> "The rustic Boy, who walks the fields, untaught;
> The slave of ignorance, and oft of want,
> And miserable hunger."

Without education the mind may not survive the battle
with nature and instinct, or it may become little more
than the tool of society's tyrants:

> "Say, what can follow for a rational soul
> Perverted thus, but weakness in all good,
> And strength in evil? Hence an after-call
> For chastisement, and custody, and bonds,
> And oft-times Death, avenger of the past,
> And the sole guardian in whose hands we dare
> Entrust the future."

He must now admit the need to balance ideals of his

own, ideals which have sometimes conflicted within him, just as he had earlier advised the Solitary to aim for a balanced view of life after so much vacillation between enthusiasm and despair. The Wanderer has not been able to abjure his love of feminine nature, nor has he been able to embrace the advances of masculine culture. But now he has to reconcile the opposing images of children which have emerged from his debate with the Solitary: the happy child of nature, with the miserable and degraded child of rural poverty; the unhappy child of industrialized society, with the bountiful culture produced by that society. The Wanderer in Book Nine proposes a solution to the rift between the individual and civilization, and it is a very interesting solution for him to offer. Since he failed as a school-teacher himself, failed to benefit from formal education, he rebelled against the kind of life represented by intellectual discipline; in doing that he sought refuge from his father (or stepfather) by attempts to return to his mother. His own unhappiness is a product of the tension caused by this unresolved Oedipal project. Now he can see the way to resolve his own problems at the same time he proposes a solution for all society.

To educate the mind is to embrace the authority of the father, to identify with his power to dominate: this is the therapy needed to cure an unhappy civilization. The Wanderer hopes for a future in which the state will teach its children "the rudiments of letters, and inform / The mind with moral and religious truth." He hopes for a time when there will no longer be "a savage horde among the civilized, / A servile band among the lordly free!" The dark discontent bred by ignorance, he hopes, will give way to a beautiful repose when "the whole people should be taught and trained." When that happens, "even the smallest habitable rock, / Beaten by lonely billows, shall hear the songs / Of humanised society; and bloom / With civil arts." These are the mighty issues to be hoped from culture, unexclusively bestowed, preventing any more of the "strange issues" he earlier deplored. Impatient to begin the cure of society, the Wanderer calls upon British law-givers to begin even now this work of urgent need.

# CHAPTER NINE:

## Worlds Not Realised

In the fragment "Beauty and Moonlight: An Ode," the poet is haunted by an image of a girl he loves. While he wanders restlessly beneath the peering eye of the moon, he identifies the moon with his loved one, heightening the eroticism thus:

> might her bosom soft and white
> Heave upon my swimming sight,
> As these two Swans together ride
> Upon the gently swelling tide.

This is a comparison Wordsworth makes in other of his early poems, but in one particularly interesting episode of an early fragment (1791, or 1795-6) he eliminates the swans altogether and brings closer together, more frankly, the associations between moonlight and mother's breasts.

This fragment, Dove Cottage MS. 2, Juvenilia No. XV (b), is one of several related to the Salisbury Plain poems. Wordsworth is experimenting further with explanations for what happens to his character of the Female Vagrant. It is an encounter between the Female Vagrant and another woman (not, as in most versions, between the Female Vagrant and the sailor). Searching for someplace to rest as the evening grows dark, "in the moon's pale light," the Female Vagrant hears a clock toll 2 a.m. just as she notices a wild dwelling. She hears singing come from the house, and she thinks it sounds like "one who sang from very grief of soul." When she knocks she is greeted by "a ragged woman" who tells her she may enter. The sick and hungry woman who lives there then draws a child to her breast:

> Then from a mat of straw a boy she raised
> Who seemed though weak in growth three winters old,
> And with a fruitless look of fondness gazed
> On his pale face; she held him at her breast
> If nourishment thence drawn might lead at length to rest.

The Female Vagrant expostulates that her hostess is too feeble to give the child any nourishment without danger to her own health. But the poor mother, embarrassed that she still tries to nurse a child so old, explains that she must do so because there is no other food than the milk of her own breasts.

Moonlight is a brooding presence of natural light that suggests a power of creativity in the mind. This is a symbolic image of major significance in Wordsworth's poetry. Nature as a mother who nourishes her son (past the age of weaning) under the transforming power of moonlight has obvious connections with scenes of the kind Wordsworth tries to describe in the fragment of verses on the Female Vagrant. Even in the richly complex vision atop Mt. Snowdon, there is an association between the moon and a nursing child: "The perfect image of a mighty Mind, / Of one that feeds upon infinity." In *The Excursion* the Wanderer describes the moon as a symbol of imagination at work: "Within the soul a faculty abides."

This illuminating power within the soul, serving "to exalt / Her native brightness," like the moonlight glowing through a grove a trees, nourishes as it reveals: it is a virtue that "feeds / A calm, a beautiful, a silent fire, / From the encumbrances of mortal life." The Wanderer's symbol has at its center an image of nature as the source of virtue, as the source of an imaginative energy that feeds upon nature's "interpositions and encumbrances."

While moonlight is thus usually connected with maternal security, with nature's nourishment, sunlight is, in a complementary way, usually connected with paternal authority and power. It is often noticed only as it begins to disappear—behind clouds, below the horizon at the end of the day. The setting sun has a very special and personal meaning for Wordsworth, although it may generally be associated with very common notions of death and mortality. In one of his more interesting early attempts at poetry, "The Vale of Esthwaite" (1787), he explores various ways to explain a state of mind which can only be admitted to be "disturbed." Haunted by ghosts, spectres, and demons, the boyish narrator says that he went into the gloomy shades of religious woods at noon. There he heard a "ringing harp" and saw the "druid sons" of Superstition look menacingly at him. He asked in horror, "Why roll on me your glaring eyes? / Why fix on me for sacrifice?" Later he describes an evening of particular sorrow, "when the wintry blast / Through the sharp Hawthorn whistling pass'd": the scene is the one Wordsworth uncovers in Book Eleven of *The Prelude* as a primal scene of guilt for his father's death.

"The Vale of Esthwaite" is another of Wordsworth's early efforts to deal with this scene of inexplicable sorrow and punishment for prohibited desires: "why avails my tear? / To sorrow o'er a Father's bier?" Even now, he says, after the passage of much time, he mourns. But he mourns strangely: "I mourn because I mourned no more," as if he must now suffer for having failed to suffer enough at the time of his father's death. He allows himself to imagine, at sunset, a compensation that "we soon again shall meet"; he hears the whisper of such a promise, "when fades the leaden day / To joy-consuming pain a prey." He imagines that when the time of his own death comes, he will look back to his childhood like the sun itself sinking into darkness, casting its light on the hills whence it arose in the morning. The sentiment of this thought is mixed with his earlier association of his father's death at evening twilight, so that he "becomes" his father in a shared identification with the setting sun. This he needs, even if it mixes guilt with pleasures of happiness, because he has been denied what earlier he wished for—a mother's secure affection:

> For I must never share
> A tender parent's guardian care;
> Sure, from the world's unkind alarm,
> Returning to a mother's arm.

*AFTER THE PICNIC* which concludes *The Excursion* in Book Nine, the Pastor raises a prayer of praise to God, manifested in the beauty of an evening sunset. This prayer is to a God whose "paternal splendours" are accessible only by such degrees and steps as provided by this beautiful sunset, itself a "local transitory type." The prayer is for God the Father to be merciful to His sons. The mercy desired is a "triumph over sin and guilt," so that all "whom Morn awakens, among dews and flowers" will be happy in themselves. The Pastor's own charge is the responsibility of a father to his children. It is on their particular behalf that he lifts an "offering" and presents a "sacrifice": a ritual that repeats the sacrifice made by "Him who bled / Upon the cross." In return the Pastor hopes for a rescue of his children from "all dishonour, cleansed from mortal stain." In fact, the Pastor prays for a speedy end of all time so that "the sting of human nature" will be removed.

This prayer contains most of what Wordsworth considered essential to a Christian faith, not the least of which is the emphasis on the need to make a sacrifice of flesh to spiritual demands. The Wanderer also inclines toward a religion of sacrifice, though he does so with strong reluctance. The Pastor, on the other hand, worships death as a means of deliverance from the "stain" of earthly existence. This stain is specifically known as "guilt," borne by all who are the children of God.

> "Once, while the Name, Jehovah, was a sound
> Within the circuit of this sea-girt isle
> Unheard, the savage nations bowed the head
> To Gods delighting in remorseless deeds;
> Gods which themselves had fashioned, to promote
> Ill purposes, and flatter foul desires.
> Then, in the bosom of yon mountain-cove,
> To those inventions of corrupted man
> Mysterious rites were solemnised; and there—
> Amid impending rocks and gloomy woods—
> Of those terrific Idols some received
> Such dismal service, that the loudest voice
> Of the swoln cataracts (which now are heard
> Soft murmuring) was too weak to overcome,
> Though aided by wild winds, the groans and shrieks
> Of human victims, offered up to appease
> Or to propitiate."

The remarkable thing about this passage is not in its scene of barbarity; it is the scene which has haunted Wordsworth's poetry from his earliest attempt to describe his Salisbury Plain experience. The remarkable quality is, rather, in the juxtaposition Wordsworth makes between the Pastor's attitude of Christian sacrifice and the Pastor's description of pagan sacrifice, uttered in the very act of performing his own religious ritual. The Pastor emphasizes the differences between ancient, hideous rites and modern, "innocent" ones, it is true. But when he refers to "Him who bled / Upon the cross," and when he insists that the children of God are unhappy, stained, guilty, and weary of their earthly lives, the Pastor invites comparison between his religion and the rituals of ancient sacrifice.

The Pastor's wife whispered to the Poet that the old Wanderer's power of rapture ended with the Wanderer's silence, and after the Pastor's ecstatic prayer the Poet describes how the vision of splendor caused by the setting sun dissipates into a gray, faint darkening of the landscape:

> No trace remained
> Of those celestial splendours; grey the vault—
> Pure, cloudless, ether; and the star of eve
> Was wanting; but inferior lights appeared
> Fainting, too faint almost for sight.

The faded sky is an ominous sign of absence. It parallels both the faded vision of the Wanderer and the dying ashes noticed by the Solitary as the group returned from its picnic:

> "The fire, that burned so brightly to our wish,
> Where is it now?—Deserted on the beach—
> Dying, or dead! Nor shall the fanning breeze
> Revive its ashes."

Surrounded by such emblems of impotence, the Pastor's prayer is a strongly ironic conclusion to *The Excursion*.

NOT LONG AFTER he published *The Excursion* Wordsworth composed, in 1817, a poem "Upon an Evening of Extraordinary Splendour and Beauty." Its scene of sunset is a "holy rite" with the power to "sanctify" after a morning of "blissful infancy." Since the glory of infancy, the poet has seen only "gleams," vestiges of feeling that have lingered in his dreams. This present "glimpse of glory" makes him "rejoice in a second birth." He has, for a moment at least, succeeded in achieving the aim of his childhood longing to be his own father.

Sunset is a promise of tranquil and beautiful death, an easy transition from light to darkness. It is also, in the history of the poet's imagination, a reunion of twin glories: the glory of infancy with the gleams of old age. Death is somehow a repetition of birth. The helplessness of those events urges a cry for a father's protection. "The Vale of Esthwaite" was an awkward, almost incoherent, cry for identification with the father whose death deprived the son of security; the Pastor's prayer is an urbane and civilized sublimation of the same cry, projecting as a mythic relationship what originates in the unconscious needs of all; and the poem "Composed Upon an Evening of Extraordinary Splendour and Beauty" is a conscious attempt to recover what has been lost in life's efforts to assert psychological independence. What has been lost, successfully repressed or sublimated, is yearning for the father:

> Dread Power! whom peace and calmness serve
> No less than Nature's threatening voice,
> If aught unworthy be my choice,
> From Thee if I would swerve;
> Oh, let Thy grace remind me of the light
> Full early lost, and fruitlessly deplored;
> Which, at this moment, on my waking sight
> Appears to shine, by miracle restored;
> My soul, though yet confined on earth,
> Rejoices in a second birth!

Wordsworth in 1817 is not intimidated by the darkness. He does not attempt to console himself with a new certainty, not even the kind he found in the conclusion to the "Ode: Intimations of Immortality," when "the Clouds that gather round the setting sun / Do take a sober colouring." However sober, at least there was color to sustain meaning. In 1817 Wordsworth concludes with a much more ambiguous statement: "—'Tis past, the visionary splendour fades; / And night approaches with her shades." Whether this is a courageous defiance of darkness or an infantile submission to threats of terrible punishment, a resignation to reality or a yearning for return to pleasures of the womb, this conclusion indicates that Wordsworth could not fully sanction the attitudes of his Pastor, though he might fully sympathize with the Pastor's desires.

WORDSWORTH'S Pastor thinks there is so much difference between the savage rites of primitive religions and the civilized rituals of his own Christian religion that the paradise once lost to man is almost restored:

> "So wide the difference, a willing mind
> Might almost think, at this affecting hour,
> That paradise, the lost abode of man,
> Was raised again: and to a happy few,
> In its original beauty, here restored."

But that paradise within the "willing mind," even of the Pastor, contains some of the residue that caused Freud to ask whether the dragons of primaeval days are really extinct. Even if the Pastor cannot see these dragons in his paradise, Wordsworth does not shut his eyes to signs of their continuing existence. He knows that in the mind is much to fear:

> Not Chaos, not
> The darkest pit of lowest Erebus,
> Nor aught of blinder vacancy, scooped out
> By help of dreams—can breed such fear and awe
> As fall upon us often when we look
> Into our Minds, into the Mind of Man—

His Pastor may not make the conscious connection between the hideous rites he describes and the Christian Father's sacrifice of his Son, but Wordsworth puts the evidence before his reader by way of the Pastor's own words. While the Pastor does not analyze his own mind for its share of guilt and discontent, he tells many stories which suggest he may understand the connections between religious needs for sacrifice and civilization's insistence upon renouncing instincts of hostility toward fathers. This is the real source of religion, Freud later insisted—*not* the oceanic feeling of identification with mother (nature). In many of the Pastor's stories Wordsworth has put a great weight upon religion as yearning for a father's protection against helplessness.

The Pastor makes a particular point, in one of his stories, to associate the setting sun with his chief character, a pastor himself: "'Him might we liken to the setting sun.'" The active, ardent mind of this priest was tamed of its ambition to serve the great ones of society. He had, like his house, been "trimmed and brightened by the matron's care." His house, once bare, was after several years "screen'd from assault of every bitter blast," and he who had been bright as the sun was hung about with his wife's "soft attendant cloud" to veil his restless energies. The story indicates a sacrifice of instincts for civilization to the constraints of nature; the priest withdrew from the masculine world of aggressive competition into the feminine world of tranquil resignation. The setting sun made mellow by enveloping clouds suggests a character with repressed desires which might better have been satisfied through a more active life. As the Pastor admits, "his harsher passions kept their hold" as he made his adaptation to a new life style. The main reason he kept his passions under control was that his wife restrained him: "'—Those transports . . . his consort would reprove.'"

After the deaths of all in his family, the old priest lived on in a state of divided mind:

> "This Survivor, with his cheerful throng
> Of open projects, and his inward hoard
> Of unsunned griefs, too many and too keen,
> Was overcome by unexpected sleep,
> In one blest moment. Like a shadow thrown
> Softly and lightly from a passing cloud,
> Death fell upon him, while reclined he lay
> For noontide solace on the summer grass,
> The warm lap of his mother earth."

The priest had never truly been separated from his wife any more than he had been away from the warm lap of his mother earth. The shadow of death which passed over his sleeping form is a repetition of the obscuring cloud: wife and mother combine to repress and then destroy the energies of this much diminished man.

The Pastor himself looked to the older priest, whose story he tells, as a father, whom he first saw with childish eyes and who became "the patriarch of the Vale." The old priest's death left a place taken by the Pastor himself, a natural transition made possible by the sacrifice of a father-figure. The religion of the Pastor thrives upon the deaths of fathers, as the religion of the Wanderer thrives upon the triumph of mothers. This story brings the two together in a most convenient way to satisfy both the Pastor and the Wanderer.

*IN BOOK SIX* the Pastor tells a story of a disappointed lover who attempted to sublimate his erotic instinct into a driving curiosity to explore nature. As long as he tried so to master his love, that man suffered symptoms of hysteria: "'A betraying sickliness was seen / To tinge his cheek.'" Although the Pastor assures his listeners that his hero gradually recovered his health with "Nature's care," he paradoxically reports that all the man's efforts to cure himself were "hopeless." And still more strange was the mystery of his death, "hastily smitten by a fever's force." Because he was unsuccessful in his attempt to sublimate his passion, the unhappy lover died—a victim to his own unmastered instincts. His life was, then, a sacrifice to Nature, and so the woman he had loved could rightly consider him "a monument to faithful love / Conquered."

In another story a young man unsuccessfully attempted to break from his parents. The tie with family is, again, very strong, and the result is a split in the youth's personality: "'within his frame / Two several souls alternately had lodged, / Two sets of manners could the Youth put on.'" He tried to act out his aggressiveness as a soldier, "'sworn / Into the lists of giddy enterprise.'" He was a talented, promising man who strangely fell prey to unhappiness. He returned from the wide world to his father's home, where he "'Sought for his weariness a place of rest / Within his Father's gates.'" He returned home "'the ghost of beauty and of health / The wreck of gaiety.'" Three times this happened before he died, never able to achieve permanent independence from his father, to whom he finally yielded his very life as a sacrifice to that strong bondage. The Pastor's final judgment is that this young man was "'content / With neither element of good or ill,'" victimized by his enslavement to infinite contradictions. But the Pastor celebrates what he calls the man's "deliverance" by death, thereby approving the sacrifice of the youth to his paternity. The Pastor considers civilization a lure of evil, drawing life away from families, sons away from fathers; he makes a religion of death itself, as a mechanism of escape from social reality, as that looming shadow of the great Father himself.

Sons may be righteously sacrificed to their fathers, but when fathers yield to unrepressed instincts they might themselves become sacrifices. The pastor tells the story of Alfred Armathwaite as a complement to his tale of unhappy Ellen, since each suffered from pangs of conscience after lapses into passion. Wilfred is the more mysterious because of his having exchanged happy married life for a miserable one of self-torment. He tired of domestic "peace of mind," craving "a substitute in troubled joy." Wilfred made love to a servant girl in an aggressive act of erotic defiance: "against his conscience rose in arms, and, braving / Divine displeasure, broke the marriage vow." The Pastor tells the story as if Wilfred was more intent on rebelling against his conscience than he was of satisfying his lust for the girl. Wordsworth had a difficult time composing the lines which he wanted his Pastor to speak in explaining what motivated Wilfred: he spent much effort (discarding several versions) composing lines for the Pastor to explain what happened to Wilfred Armathwaite after his sexual lapse.

The Pastor wishes to show how divine law works to avenge *any* violation of its taboos. The real source of the Pastor's God is fatherhood, the image of one's self as father, set up within the soul as an authority to punish and restrain. Wilfred attacked this power within himself. In doing so he merely nourished it until he, literally, gave himself over to it in an act of complete sacrifice: "through remorse and grief he died." Even though the Pastor says that he was "pitied among men, absolved by God," the poem says that Wilfred died because "he could not find forgiveness in himself." The textual variants show that Wordsworth wanted to make it clear that Wilfred is "his own world" and that his only god is himself. But the Pastor must translate all this self-torment as a proper religious sacrifice.

The sixth book ends with two stories the Pastor uses to illustrate the ways a father has to compensate for his erotic needs after his wife has died. The first (which ends the final published version of the book) describes how a man apparently succeeds in serving as both father and mother for six daughters. He has all his daughters to himself, virtually acting out a scene from Freud's imagined primal horde. The Pastor admits a strange thing about his own habits when he tells his audience that he sometimes peeps through the windows of this happy patriarch:

> "when the gloom
> Of night is falling round my steps, then most
> This Dwelling charms me; often I stop short,
> (Who could refrain?) and feed by stealth my sight
> With prospect of the company within,
> Laid open through the blazing window."

The Pastor reenacts, as a "peeping-tom" might, the primal scenes of his own mind. What he spied "through the blazing window" was an unhappy man: "Mild Man! he is not gay, but they are gay; / And the whole house seems filled with gaiety."

Wordsworth knows that there is a deep discontent behind the mask of fatherhood. A father may provide authority and security for his children, and he may even enjoy their company of loving respect and dependence. But a father is never so happy as he may seem to be, for he must sacrifice a part of himself to be able to satisfy his role as father. It does not matter what his circumstances, he must make that sacrifice, as all of the Pastor's stories indicate. These have ranged from the example of a lover unable to marry, to a son who cannot escape the authority of his father, to a husband who rebels against his own conscience, to this last story of a father who is not happy when his whole house is "filled with gaiety." Every role demands a sacrifice, and the father can no more be a mother than a mother can be a father. In the rejected conclusion to the sixth book, the Pastor tells a short tale of a father who tried to be a mother to his children and failed, because "'tis not / In course of nature that a Father's wing / Should warm these Little-ones.'" While the Wanderer's religion is based upon his desire to do without fathers, the Pastor's is based upon a desire to do without mothers. In order to reconcile himself to the facts of maternity, the Pastor tells stories which subordinate the value of women to men, and the order of his stories suggests a pattern of increasing independence from women—until finally he must ask the embarrassing question, "can he *feed?*"

In Book Seven the Pastor's masculine and paternal heroes will emerge more clearly as embodiments of civilization. Before he can examine the untramelled social warrior, he has to fill out his picture of the family structure where the father is absent and the mother tries to be both. The story of Ellen, which reminds the Poet of Margaret's travails, is a familiar one that Wordsworth never tired of retelling. It is a necessary link in the pastor's chain of social structures, because Ellen represents the triumphant Mother, the eternal Feminine which persistently clings to and challenges masculine culture. When the mother tries to absorb her son's life into her own, she becomes a perverse monster, such as the woman the Pastor describes prior to telling this one of Ellen.

The prior story is the Pastor's most sophisticated piece of psychoanalysis, possible to him because he can treat his subject as an object; he can see symptoms for what they are—displacements of erotic energy. This mother is fixed in her obsession for her son (the Pastor calls it a "strange thraldom"), but she cannot satisfy her desires for her son without violating terrible taboos ("degenerate" passions). Therefore she becomes obsessively hungry for power and possessions. The Pastor's own defense against such a strong ego is to dwell upon her death as a punishment, not a release (which it has been for his other protagonists). She died unsubmissive to Providence, and so she was seized by a malady that "griped / Her prostrate frame with unrelaxing power, / As the fierce eagle fastens on the lamb." The Pastor's manner of describing this woman's "punishment" reveals his own masculine sexual fantasies of violent sacrifice. On the other hand, he allows Ellen a saintly death for a self-sacrificing life—her reward for proper contrition. When she visited the grave of her infant, she seemed "a rueful Magdalene"; finally, "through the cloud of death, her Spirit passed / Into that pure and unknown world of love / Where injury cannot come."

*BOOK SEVEN* of *The Excursion* contains ideas about the function of poetry, about social progress, and about interpretations of history. As a dramatization of Wordsworth's continuing analysis of social psychology, it is one of the most intriguing sections of the poem. The pastor takes his listeners toward a vision of social commitment which underlies his own drive to identify with the F/ father embodied in Church and State. The book proceeds by setting two kinds of complementary patterns to work: first, the narratives function as pairs, in which characters are made complementary or dialectical; second, they develop a direction of vision from the narrow discontents of individual experience to the broad discontent of civilization at large.

An old woodcutter drives his wagon by and distracts the Pastor from his stories of the dead, to tell one instead of this vigorous old man. It is a story of long-lived and hearty life even into old age, without sign of decay or resignation to mortality. Like the childless couple of an earlier story, this old man seems content and happy—in part because he is a peasant of the lowest class, without the sophistications of learning and ambition. Unlike the pair of handicapped men described in the immediately preceding stories, this man is blessed with all the goods of nature: "with a face / Not worldly-minded, for it bears too much / Of nature's impress,—gaiety and health, / Freedom and hope." The woodcutter is a puzzle to the Pastor, because he refuses to show signs of an "anxious mind." The pastor is amazed that the woodcutter could be a rational creature, capable of foresight, and still not show symptoms of unhappiness.

The content and happiness of the woodcutter are products of the old man's successful life of aggression, enacted without endangering the order and security of civilization. Indeed, the woodcutter's very profession is a service to the development of civilization. He makes his contribution without having to internalize his aggressiveness. On the other hand, the Pastor himself shows some surprisingly aggressive hostility toward the woodcutter:

> "This qualified respect, the old Man's due,
> Is paid without reluctance; but in truth,"
> (Said the good Vicar with a fond half-smile)
> "I feel at times a motion of despite
> Towards one, whose bold contrivances and skill
> As you have seen, bear such conspicuous part
> In works of havoc."

Later, when the Pastor promises that even the old woodcutter will have to die some day, that half-smile has not faded.

He is more comfortable with the truths he can teach through his next two stories of death. In these, one about the death of an infant girl and the other about the sad death of an heroic young man, he finds some comfort after feeling perplexity over the enduring woodcutter. While the death of the infant daughter strengthened the emotional bonds of the family which survived, the death of heroic Oswald did even more: his death strengthened the ties of the community at large. Everyone had looked to Oswald as a glorious leader of the future: "In him the spirit of a hero walked / Our unpretending valley." This young man was intelligent, strong, healthy, and a leader of men. When Napoleon threatened an invasion of England, Oswald was in the vanguard of men prepared to defend their native land. He was prepared to be a sacrifice for his nation, but instead he was the victim of an ignominious accident while washing "the fleeces of his Father's flock." This is not the way a hero is supposed to die. Nevertheless, his comrades paid him "a soldier's honours." The death of a young person brought together in ritual form an entire community, which found new cause for worship—as the Poet understands when he notices the Wanderer react with rapture to the Pastor's tale.

The Solitary, however, reacts differently to this lesson in patriotic sacrifice. The "pining Solitary turned aside." Almost as if he were commenting on the story of Oswald, the Solitary turns to examine the remains of a monumental stone which, the Vicar explains, is all that is left to memorialize the life of a true English soldier. That knight, who lived in the reign of Elizabeth, was a Christian champion who, according to tradition, "came on a war-horse sumptuously attired / And fixed his home in this sequestered vale." Sir Alfred Irthing's life of social contribution, fighting wars for the faith, seems not to have accomplished more for England than did the unfortunate Oswald, who did not live to fight for Church or Nation. This is not reassuring to the Solitary, to whom mutability is nature's bane. Neither is the Solitary reassured by the Wanderer's observation that everything "this world is proud of" fails, "languishes, grows dim, and dies."

By the story of Alfred Irthing the Pastor has shown the social ends to which men devote themselves and the socially acceptable means whereby men may express instincts for aggression. Though "no trace is left / Of the mild-hearted Champion," still "his family name / Is borne by yon clustering cottages." The product of his life's service is a community bound together in part by his name. Even the Wanderer emphasizes the social importance of the old soldier's life, for the knight contributed to "the vast Frame / Of social nature," however mutable it might be. Faintly hoping for "progress in the main," he proposes that all souls are contributions to the organic process of nature, reunions with mother earth. The Pastor, on the other hand holds that individual lives are sacrifices to institutions, to Church and Nation. Sir Alfred Irthing is a consummate example of the ideal social sacrifice. The Pastor emphasizes the images of memorial remains as if they were a sacred altar. From the family of the disappointed clergyman, through the love-inhibited and lonely lives of the blind man and the deaf man, to the socially approved sacrifices of young Oswald and Sir Alfred Irthing, psychic energies have been channeled into socially binding units. The praise contained in the Pastor's prayer at the end of Book Nine is therefore praise for a social progress based upon religious sacrifices.

*THE EXCURSION* is fundamentally an unhappy poem, unhappy for its failure of resolution as a poem as well as a "drama" of psycho-therapy. No one is spiritually content at its conclusion. The Pastor should be the happiest man of the group, given his pleasant status as husband, father, and priest. But even he occasionally feels an underlying malaise of discontent with civilization at the same time he celebrates the accomplishments of a society that has been built of heroic sacrifices. The most evident form of his discontent occurs in his comments on the old woodcutter, where he admits the importance of the work to cut trees for supplying lumber to a thriving society, but the Pastor wants something more. He wants the security and accomplishments of the civilization which is nourished by this destruction, but he also wants those who must destroy to feel some guilt for their aggressiveness. The Pastor wants to see signs of guilt as the price of aggression, for that is "normal," and since the old woodcutter seems careless and guiltless, he is an affront to the Pastor's vision of normality.

Like many of his characters in the stories he tells, the pastor gave up a wider life of social activity in exchange for "the calm delights / Of unambitious piety." He manifests an urge, or drive (common to all) for a portion of security. The instinct of love is paramount in this drive, and it is served by civilization to achieve the great purpose of eros: "to combine single human individuals, and after that families, then races, peoples and nations, into one great unity, the unity of mankind," as Freud put it. Thus does the Pastor praise God as a Father of the family of mankind, and thus does he give thanks to

> "our wise
> Forefathers, who, to guard against the shocks,
> The fluctuation and decay of things,
> Embodied and established these high truths
> In solemn institutions."

The Wanderer's drive expresses itself as an identification with the mother, as a reunion with nature. By contrast, the Pastor's expresses itself as an identification with the father, as a need for protection from helplessness. Death may be more welcome to the Wanderer, therefore, than to the Pastor, although the Pastor does not always admit his fear of death. Insofar as his religion is a protective reaction to his fear of death, his religion is a weakness of his character because it is an "illusion," in the sense that Freud defined it: "As we already know, the terrifying impression of helplessness in childhood aroused the need for protection—for protection through love—which was provided by the father; and the recognition that this helplessness lasts throughout life made it necessary to cling to the existence of a father, but this time a more powerful one." The Pastor feels this helplessness, and he shows it in his frequent use of such words as "snares," "decay," "blind," "irksome world," "desperate," "strange thraldom," "strange mishap," and "his helpless family." This language is drawn from a source pictured as a frightening landscape filled with snares for blind people, a region where children vanish without warning to leave behind helpless old men and desperate mothers.

The metaphors of the Pastor's understanding are drawn from a terrifying symbol of the graveyard as "life" itself. It is a dismal prospect, such as seen on a

> "wild shore strewn
> With wrecks, trod by feet of young and old
> Wandering about in miserable search
> Of friends or kindred, whom the angry seas
> Restores not to their prayer."

Great bodies of water, lakes and oceans, underlie even the land itself, making it a swamp of uncertain security. Therefore, control of water is a metaphor of critical importance to the Pastor. When he praises his forefathers for their great wisdom in the building of solemn institutions, he characterizes those institutions as being like canals built to direct the flow of life's waters. Reasons' control of instincts is manifested socially in the channelling power of institutions such as state and church. But the Pastor always hovers on the edge of what he himself calls "the great abyss," holding onto his Father to keep from falling or being "snatched away."

When he counsels his listeners to aim for the control of "reason, best reason," he renders advice which corresponds with the goals of Freudian therapy. When he warns that "reason, best reason" is "an effort only," a power "never to be won" but always "to be courted," the Pastor is at one with both Wordsworth and Freud. The Pastor knows that mind is the source of what is best in life, but that it is also the source of what is worst:

> "—Look forth, or each man dive into himself;
> What sees he but a creature too perturbed;
> That is transported to excess; . . . .
> Thus darkness and delusion round our path
> Spread, from disease, whose subtle injury lurks
> Within the very faculty of sight."

When he dares to tread into this haunt spread round with darkness and delusion, *he* needs the helping hand of his Father. But not his creator Wordsworth, who must "breathe in worlds / To which the heaven of heavens is a veil." *He* will "pass unalarmed" not only "all terror That ever was put forth in personal form," but even God Himself: "Jehovah—with his thunder." Wordsworth's refusal to fear *his* Father, Jehovah with His thunder, is a mark of his psychological health that he shares with Freud, who used as the epigraph for *The Interpretation of Dreams* this line from the *Aeneid:* "Flectere si nequeo superos, Acheronta movebo."

CHAPTER TEN:

## Thanks to the Human Heart

The Solitary of *The Excursion* is disillusioned and melancholy, but he is not misanthropic; he is a religious sceptic, but he is not uncivilized. He demonstrates the virtue of independent thought—but at the same time he feels the inevitable suffering which must be paid for that virtue. In Book Three he explains that he is no longer "a child of earth," as once he was when he lived "with joy o'er flowing," not thinking of future needs because present happiness lay all about him. He does not yearn for a return to those days when he was surrounded by the cloud of infancy, and so he does not suffer from the Wanderer's regressive impulses. He may not be any longer a child of earth and he may not any longer feel overflowing joy, but he does not wish to substitute pleasure for reality. He asks, mockingly,

> "what good is given to men,
> More solid than the gilded clouds of heaven?
> What joy more lasting than a vernal flower?"

He has put his childhood completely behind him, renouncing pleasure and the infant's cloud of glory, but he speaks "the bitter language of the heart." He is discomposed and vehement, but he is skillful and graceful at the same time. He explains how, soon after the deaths of his wife and children, he ceased to depend upon the world of nature and circumstance for happiness. He looked within his soul in that crisis of confidence, and what he discovered was that pain is a motive for consciousness and for intellectual power:

> "By pain of heart—now checked—and now
>    impelled—
> The intellectual power, through words and things,
> Went sounding on, a dim and perilous way."

The Solitary's life is heroic in this sense, that he has explored regions of mind and heart which most men have been careful to avoid. He is to be compared with Achilles, Aeneas, and Milton's Adam/Satan. He is heroic in the tradition of the moody Achilles who has withdrawn from battle, of the inwardly confused and sad Aeneas who resists his heroic vocation, and of the dispossessed Adam who bears the guilt of all mankind for his loss of paradise. The Solitary is like these heroes especially in his discontent with the sacrifices required by civilization. *The Excursion* focuses upon his life of sacrifice, of retreat from large social commitments, of exile from paradise (infantile and erotic), and therefore *The Excursion* creates a prevailing mood of unhappiness and nagging discontent in connection with this character. However, he is not only unhappy and discontent: he has acquired a compensation of clear vision and mature independence of mind:

> "How languidly I look
> Upon this visible fabric of the world,
> May be divined—perhaps it hath been said:—
> But spare your pity, if there be in me

Aught that deserves respect: for I exist,
Within myself, not comfortless.—The tenour
Which my life holds, he readily may conceive
Whoe'er hath stood to watch a mountain brook."

What appears to the Wanderer as an impious life of broken faith is for the Solitary a life of many separations, of painful liberations from bondage. The Wanderer would typically deplore a loss of dependence upon mother and nature, seeing it as a sin against natural piety, but Wordsworth wants the reader to discover the importance, even the necessity, for making an independent life out of the pains of repeated separations—and so he allows the Solitary to tell his own story in Book Three. The most important differences to note between the Wanderer's preview and the Solitary's autobiography is a difference of emphasis and focus: the Wanderer sees illusions where the Solitary sees reality.

*THE SOLITARY*, in rejecting both the religion of nature and the religion of sacrifice, has exposed himself to the charge of illness. He is ill, as every reader must recognize, but his illness is a necessary consequence of his civilized achievements, the chief of which is his intellectual independence. His life before marriage had been a time of unmitigated happiness and freedom, when he was able "to explore the destiny of human kind" without inner or outer constraints; indeed, he boasts that he was not, like so many other searchers after truth, wedded to a particular point of view or to a particular object of interest: those "who, in this frame of human life, perceive / An object whereunto their souls are tied / In discontented wedlock." It is more than coincidence that he should so describe discontented searchers, for "wedlock" proved to be of dubious value to the Solitary.

His marriage took him from the happy freedom of his

youth into an ecstatic paradise of erotic joy, united as he was with a lovely and wealthy woman. But he has a curious way of narrating the birth of his first child: his "tender Mate became / The thankful captive of maternal bonds." One might skip lightly over this circumlocution of ambivalence, but the sentence should arrest one's attention. To attribute to his wife the character of a captive in bonds is to betray the Solitary's *own* discontent with the situation—he found marriage itself a kind of bondage, but also, more probably, he was keenly disaffected by the child's arrival to remove his wife from his erotic authority. His most important disaffection with maternal bonds is his instinct for realizing that his attachment to his wife was a very special kind of attachment: it was a transformed attachment to his mother, and it is *she* to whom the son is captive for as long as he is married.

As soon as he says that his wife bore a child, the Solitary explains how he went into a fit of depression:

> "those wild paths were left to me alone,
> There could I meditate on follies past;
> And, like a weary voyager escaped
> From risk and hardship, inwardly retrace
> A course of vain delights and thoughtless guilt,
> And self-indulgence—without shame pursued."

Dwelling on his life of vain delights and thoughtless guilt, he was led into an attitude of prayerful gratitude to someone he cannot fully identify for having rescued him from a life of shameless self-indulgence:

> "There, undisturbed, could think of and could thank
> Her whose submissive spirit was to me
> Rule and restraint—my guardian—shall I say
> That earthly Providence, whose guiding love

Within a port of rest had lodged me safe;
Safe from temptation, and from danger far?"

This emphasis upon his safety, his retirement from temptation, is his retrospective understanding of what his marriage was—a regression to the security of his mother. The
reason he cannot name "that earthly Providence" is that
"she" was his wife-as-mother: his wife being "her whose
submissive spirit" made her the Solitary's tender mate, and
his mother being his guardian who had lodged him safe.
Into this paradoxical image of a submissive ruler he mixes
the idea of nature, as earthly Providence.

The Solitary not only is ambivalent about his gratitude
for having been rescued by his mate-mother-providence,
but he is (and was at the time) also ambivalent about his
debt to yet another curious figure:

"Strains followed of acknowledgment addressed
To an Authority enthroned above
The reach of sight; from whom, as from their source,
Proceed all visible ministers of good
That walk the earth—Father of heaven and earth,
Father, and king, and judge, adored and feared!"

Like a child whose anxiety drives it to repress hostility for
its father, in the crisis of the Oedipus project, the Solitary's guilt feelings came upon him at the time of his own
child's birth; they overwhelmed his mind with an image of
his own father as Father, king and judge.

He began to assume "a patrimonial sanctity" as he grew
into the habit of fatherhood, but that habit circumscribed
his identity: he adjusted to a life "bounded to this world."
His port of calm and his subservience to maternal/paternal
modes of providence threatened to abort his psychological
development. That which he most feared, punishment for
his life of "thoughtless guilt," was realized in the deaths of

his wife and children. His fall from domestic felicity was painful, but it was also fortunate, because it rescued his mind from captivity to maternal bondage. Earlier, after the passage on his child's birth, he said that "the mother's kiss / And infant's smile awaited his return"; then, after the deaths of the children, he was "severed" from not only his children but from his wife as well.

The severing, as if by a sword of retribution, occurred *before* his wife's death; she was raised to an "eminence" where she joined, in the Solitary's mind, with the Father who was "enthroned above / The reach of sight." The severing was a ruthless act by the Father, now known by His minion death, to keep the mother to Himself. It is this conception which made the justice of "Heaven's determinations." The mixture of love and fear for both his Father and his wife-as-mother explains why, as his wife slowly died of grief, he describes the dominant emotion as one of shame: whether it is her "pure glory," or her "silent grief," or her "keen heart-anguish" which is "of itself ashamed, / Yet obstinately cherishing itself"—he does not, cannot make clear.

*PUNISHED* by death for having loved too well, the Solitary withdrew into a cave of suicidal gloom, but he was drawn out of that womb of death by a great social illumination. He was awakened from his trauma of separation, reborn to a new life of commitment to social improvement. He says that "Society became my glittering bride," and his erotic instincts were sublimated into activities on behalf of a redeemed civilization:

> "From the depths
> Of natural passion, seemingly escaped,
> My soul diffused herself in wide embrace
> Of institutions."

Death detached him from his interests in family, but it freed him for contributing to the interests of society. He cannot be happy because he has had to sacrifice direct gratification of his instincts, but he can be healthy because he can keep instincts under control.

Civilization, however, with its order and security, replaced the tyranny of the father with a new tyranny of the group. The Solitary exchanged the Father for a "paternal sway" in the illusion of equitable law after the Revolution in France. That "*mild* paternal sway" turned into the "iron bonds / Of military sway," and drove him temporarily away from all European civilization. He tried to escape the second paternal tyrant by running to America. On board the lonely ship, he suffered pangs of conscience in the form of "the Wife and Mother pitifully fixing / Tender reproaches." He found no comfort from the Bible, and he found no more than exacerbation of his discontent when he observed the new American Republic, calling it "a motley spectacle" of "Big passions strutting on a petty stage." Further flight into the American wilderness led him only to savage instincts in creatures "squalid, vengeful, and impure; / Remorseless, and submissive to no law / But superstitious fear, and abject sloth." As if he has plunged into the very darkness of the id itself, the Solitary found in primitive life the very opposite of civilized values. Civilization must, even with all its discontent and unhappiness, be preferred for its order and security. Once free of old illusions, liberated from the authority of external fathers, the Solitary will not make still another mistake of yielding to the remaining illusion of religion.

He vigorously rejects the use of religious rites for sustaining a false hope. Citing the mournful words of Satan when he first saw beautiful Eve, the Solitary declares

> "If to be weak is to be wretched—miserable,
> As the lost Angel by a human voice

> Hath mournfully pronounced, then, in my mind,
> Far better not to move at all than move
> By impulse sent from such illusive power,—
> That finds and cannot fasten down; that grasps
> And is rejoiced, and loses while it grasps;
> That tempts, emboldens—for a time sustains,
> And then betrays; accuses and inflicts
> Remorseless punishment; and so retreads
> The inevitable circle."

The Solitary knows with full consciousness, after a life of self-examined experience, that religious faith is built upon fear of punishment from the Father "enthroned above / The reach of sight." What he does not know with full consciousness (it is a matter of unconscious guilt) is that his fear is a fear of impotence.

The key to understanding this lies in the allusion to Satan in Milton's picture of the evil that winds its way into paradise where it lusts after forbidden fruit. The greatest pain Satan can suffer, according to *Paradise Lost*, is the pain of impotence, first acknowledged in Book I when he told Beelzlebub that "to be weak is miserable." When he looked upon the beauty of Eve, in Book Nine, he felt the utter misery of his impotence:

> the hot Hell that always in him burns,
> Though in mid Heaven, soon ended his delight,
> And tortures him now more, the more he sees
> Of pleasure not for him ordained.

Satan's only pleasure was to destroy:

> "What hither brought us? hate, not love, nor hope
> Of Paradise for Hell, hope here to taste
> Of pleasure, but all pleasure to destroy,

Save what is in destroying; other joy
To me is lost."

Tormented by his desire but unable to act upon it, Satan
was humiliated like any common lover embarrassed by impotence: "'so much hath Hell debased, and pain / Enfeebled me, to what I was in Heaven.'" Like Milton's Satan,
Wordsworth's Solitary has been punished by a Father, but
unlike Satan, the Solitary maintains a courtesy of manners
and self-respect even while refusing to fall once again under the sway of the tyrant Father.

*WHEN* the Wanderer and the Poet arrive in the valley
of the Solitary's residence, they are arrested by sounds of a
funeral which the Wanderer thinks may signal the death of
the Solitary himself. In this gloomy anticipation, the two
visitors suddenly notice the Solitary—very much alive. He
is at first seen as a gentle man dispensing gifts and words
of consolation to a mourning child. The irony of this encounter is elaborated by the lovely episode of the second
book in which the Solitary conducts his guests into his
humble room where he serves them a refreshing meal, tells
them a moving story of the old man whose funeral was
just concluded, and then, "with blithe air of open fellow-
ship, / Brought from the cupboard wine and stouter
cheer." It is, then, the Solitary who creates the substantial
social atmosphere of the poem, who celebrates life with his
affection for both the child and the old man, and who establishes the terms of a social communion through his service as host. It is *he,* more than either the Wanderer or the
Pastor, who is the comforter of *The Excursion.*
The Solitary has sublimated his love into the tenderness
of affection for the child, because he has successfully resisted the overbearing demands of all authority figures. The
sign of this accomplishment lies primarily in his relationship with the man who recently died, but secondarily in

his relationship with the woman who took the old man in as a pensioner (and who seems to be the mother of the child). In abstract terms, the Solitary displays a balanced achievement of the healthy ego, to which the child is related as a symbol of the id and to which the old man is related as a symbol of the super-ego. But, because the Solitary is "normal" in the sense that Freud would recognize, he is nevertheless something of a neurotic for whom unhappiness is a symptom of unresolved guilt, the price he pays for his civilization (of affection, intellect, and manners).

While hosting his visitors, he tells his story of the old man. He explains how he and the housewife's husband found the poor old man huddled beneath tufts of heath plant where he had sought protection from a stormy evening. The old man had sought his refuge in the ruins of a chapel: a symbolic commentary on the Solitary's main theme—the end of illusions, or, as others might think, the decay of religious faith. He describes the scene as a kind of burial: he was "lying three parts buried among tufts," but he was "breathing peaceably, / Snug as a child." The old man became, psychologically, a child in his search for protection. He had sought out protection by "his mother earth," which proved little more useful to him than did the roofless chapel dedicated to his heavenly Father. Later, the Solitary refers to the old man as "that gray-haired Orphan" who was denied parentage not only by heaven and earth, but also by humanity itself. While the Solitary and the child both loved the old man, others who knew him seem merely to have exploited his helplessness—like the housewife, who "knew full well what she possessed! / He was her vassal of all labour." The Solitary is angered as he thinks of the woman's hypocrisy, having offered her house as refuge but turning it into a "kennel." She sends the old man out on a chore the evening he failed to return, and so she seems responsible for his exposure. The old man did not die, however, until three weeks after the event. It was a death strangely delayed.

Something more than physics is needed to explain the reason for the old man's death. He had earlier died unto his manhood, when he became a child again; his physical death is a confirmation of his psychological regression. He death is, on the other hand, also a sign of the Solitary's victory over all authority figures represented by men older than himself. The fact that the Wanderer had misinterpreted the funeral as a rite for the death of the Solitary is a clue to understand the psychological relationship between the Solitary and the old man, because the Solitary *is* the old man in one essential way: the Solitary has buried all authority, repressed the delusions of super-ego, and cast off phantoms of heavenly fathers.

When he directed the sad company to bear away the weakened old man from the ruined chapel, he followed through the heavy mist until, suddenly, he halted to witness an epiphany that, in effect, mocks the sudden illumination Wordsworth celebrated atop Mt. Snowdon at the conclusion of *The Prelude*. The Solitary says that he saw "the appearance of a mighty city—boldly say / A wilderness of building," created by the intermixture of mountains, mist, and light. He calls it "an unimaginable sight!" in a tone of some irony, explaining that it was a mixture of natural forms "confused, commingled, mutually inflamed, Molten together." This also mocks the vision Wordsworth had when he descended from the Simplon Pass to see woods, stationary blasts of water-falls, and unfettered clouds all together as "workings of one mind" and "Characters of the great Apocalypse." The Solitary's view held him captive momentarily, lost in the scene he characterizes as one where each was lost in each, but even so entranced he could see that the scene was an illusion that withdrew him from the real life of the community: "'I have been dead,'" he said, but in saying so he realized that he had forgotten the dead man:

> "But I forget our Charge, as utterly
> I then forgot him:—there I stood and gazed:
> The apparition faded not away,
> And I descended."

What he left behind was an unfaded apparition because, in fact, the illusion of a heavenly city remains with many (other) people as a distraction from the reality of life and the reality of death. When he descended, he left behind such illusions to return to the humble "dwelling-place of Man" which "lay low beneath his feet."

In that valley to which he returned free from illusion, the Solitary discovered the only satisfaction a civilized person can enjoy: clear vision, affection for his fellow man, and sensitivity to beauty. The episode sets up a contrast of special views between his discovery of "a wilderness of building, sinking far / And self-withdrawn into a boundless depth, / Far sinking into splendour—without end," and his song of praise for the loveliness of his valley with its two huge peaks that he calls "those lusty twins" through which the wind blows to make "music of finer tone." While he will not yield to the arguments from design (pursued by the Wanderer at the opening of Book Three), he can celebrate the harmony of beauty that speaks to the human heart.

His words of appreciation for nature's loveliness cause the Poet to compare the Solitary's voice with the nightingale's last note. He is like the nightingale in his plaintive song of loneliness in the darkness, but he is a self-composed man without illusions, civilized though unhappy. He has combined in his character the only possible resolutions of modern man's psychological problems; he has combined the answers which Freud said men look for in their search for happiness: "The man who is predominantly erotic will give first preference to his emotional relationships to other people; the narcissistic man, who inclines to be self-sufficient, will seek his main satisfactions in his internal mental process; the man of action will never give up the external world on which he can try out his strength."

*THE POET COMES* before the reader a man strangely troubled. The "enfeebled Power" to which he refers at the end of the poem is closely related to his own languid condition at the opening. There he is described as weak, not only from physical weariness. When he describes his movement as a "toiling / With languid steps" that are "baffled" by the very earth on which he treads, he is describing what Wordsworth and Freud recognized as symptoms of inhibitions and anxiety. Why the Poet should be so weak is curious—since he will soon be reunited with the loveable old man he has known since his childhood. But that may in fact be his problem: something in him does not want to renew this relationship, and so he is forcing himself to make his way across the bare common under the oppressive heat of the summer sunshine. He explains that he had suddenly come across the Wanderer the day before, when something "hidden" was suddenly revealed, with the result that the Poet was "stricken" into slackening his footsteps—which has remained with him even through the morning of the next day which opens the poem. Not only was the meeting with the Wanderer "unthought-of," it was also undesired in ways not fully recognized by the Poet.

Wordsworth does not provide an analysis of the *causes* for the Poet's symptoms as much as he recreates the *circumstances* which gradually expose those causes and then which gradually will heal the sickness whose symptoms are expressed at the opening of the poem. The Wanderer had established a relationship with the Poet that fulfilled the role of a father to the boy. Wordsworth was uncertain how best to express this relationship, as in his 1804 MS. of *The Pedlar* when his narrator says that it was *he* who took the initiative of love:

> I was a Boy
> When he first notic'd me, and I began
> To love him, and to seek him, and rejoice
> In the plain presence of his dignity.

Later in the same manuscript the Poet-Narrator says "I honor'd him, respected, nay rever'd." This sentiment is softened by the text of the published version, but it surely indicates how clear it was to Wordsworth that the relationship was like that of a father to son. The Poet as son is carrying on the role of his friend as Father-Poet. One of the most important values he associated with the Wanderer was his skill of song, which was to the boy-Poet as "cool refreshing water."

When the Poet finally meets the Wanderer at the ruined cottage, he notices immediately that the Wanderer's hat is "moist with water-drops." Before he can quench his own thirst from the same spring of water, the Poet must make his way through a plot of garden ground run wild, climb a fence, and search through weeds and shrubs for the hidden well. Cooling his temples in the fanning air, slaking his thirst at the hidden well, and listening to the Wanderer's story of Margaret are parallel events for him. Listening to the story, he says that "a heart-felt chillness crept along my veins," so that he had to walk out into the sunshine, where he "stood drinking comfort from the warmer sun, / That had not cheered me long." After the story is concluded, again he is strangely moved:

> From that low bench, rising instinctively
> I turned aside in weakness, nor had power

To thank him for the tale which he had told.
I stood, and leaning o'er the garden wall
Reviewed that Woman's sufferings; and it seemed
To comfort me while with a brother's love
I blessed her in the impotence of grief.

His weakness is a symptom of grief—"the impotence of grief," which strikes near to melancolia.

Although the Poet describes his feeling for the dead Margaret as the love of a brother, he also feels toward her the repressed feelings of a son for a mother. It does not matter whether he feels like brother or son, because the love he feels in response to the story is an inhibited love that finds an outlet in his response to the narrative. The Poet's weakened posture vis-a-vis the Wanderer is the attitude of a son intimidated by the authority of his father, particularly with regard to prohibited objects of erotic desire. This relationship is continued into the next book where the Poet and the Wanderer set off on their journey to visit the Solitary. On the way they encounter a throng of people celebrating May Day, and the Poet wants to join the festivity. He is moved by the sounds of music and the feelings of happiness, but especially he is moved by the sight of the May Pole itself:

                    Like a mast
Of gold, the Maypole shines; as if the rays
Of morning, aided by exhaling dew,
With gladsome influence could re-animate
The faded garlands dangling from its sides.

But the Wanderer will allow no departure from their route. Like a father still, he continues to exercise his authority over the Poet.

When they reach the valley of the Solitary, the Poet responds to the beauty of the region again in terms suggest-

ing that what he needs from nature is erotic satisfaction.
His easy attitude (in a spot "so perfectly secure") is possible because the response is in a sublimated form, approved
by authority of civilization. Even so, as Freud speculated,
beauty seems to derive "from the field of sexual feeling.
The love of beauty seems a perfect example of an impulse
inhibited in its aims." When, therefore, the Poet approaches the house of the Solitary, leaving behind the scenes of
natural beauty in exchange for this symbol of domestic
love, he again undergoes a strange feeling that verges
upon anxiety:

> Homely was the spot;
> And, to my feeling, ere we reached the door,
> Had almost a forbidding nakedness.

He recovers his poise and self-control only when he redi-
rects his attention to the scene of beauty outside the window. Although he will later express his self-satisfaction in
having found happiness in "the blessings of domestic love"
(in Book Five), he certainly has some difficulty in dealing
with this scene at the beginning of the visit to the Solitary's valley. As long as he is in the company of the Wanderer, he continues to be anxious about erotic matters,
however domesticated, until they all relax on the picnic
that ends the poem.

WHILE THE Wanderer overwhelms the Poet with the
eloquence of his powerful stories, "Poured forth with ferv-
our in continuous stream," it is an eloquence received in
ambivalent ways: the Wanderer graces "his doctrine with
authority / Which hostile spirits silently allow." To view
the Wanderer as a man "bound to earth by ties of pity and
love," but "from injurious servitude was free," is to say
something about how the Poet himself feels concerning
his relationship with the Wanderer, whose power depresses

him into weakness at the same time it lifts him into rapture. He can be free from that authority in two ways that are not very satisfactory through most of the poem: first, he can continue to sublimate libidinal instincts through identification with the beauties of the natural landscape, and, second, he can sublimate them through construction of ideals and ideologies that leave him strangely discontent.

To take the second solution first, the Poet's various attempts at sublimation through ideals are among the worst poetry of *The Excursion*. They may be lame attempts at mockery, as in the passage when the Poet imitates the Solitary in criticism of epicurean and stoic philosophies, but even in these the Poet hints that he has sympathy for dreams of ways to "improve the scheme / Of man's existence." Later, he insists that the "dignity of life is not impaired / By aught that innocently satisfies / The humbler cravings of the heart." Love for those who depend upon one is important, but the more important kind of love is that which is cultivated for "others, far beyond this narrow sphere, / Whom, for the very sake of love, he loves." Love "for the very sake of love" is supremely good, and it is something the Poet can easily articulate in the presence of the Wanderer, because this kind of love is so well sublimated (abstracted) that it poses no threat to authority.

Just before they meet with the Pastor, the Poet reads the "admonitory texts" which have been inscribed in the walls of the Church he enters with the Wanderer and the Solitary. He is most interested, it turns out, not in the admonitions but rather in the tales of successful love, as when he reads the story of "a Knight / Tried in the sea-fights of the second Charles." He takes a more than casual interest in this story, as he "gives voice to the silent language." This story allows him to articulate some of his own suppressed feelings—not only of erotic desire but also of hostility to authority.

His responses to beauty in narrative art and in nature are therapies for the Poet's inhibited instincts, whether of eros or death/aggression, and therefore he is saved from some of the pain of his unhappiness. Civilization cannot do without beauty because civilization must convert instincts into the order of society at the same time they are channelled into the controlled reaction of life. If the instincts for love and death are allowed uninhibited expression, individuals would perish in the struggle for domination. The nearest the Poet can come to this kind of experience is to imagine himself as but another of the elements in a scene of stormy nature, seemingly bent upon violent destruction: "what a joy to roam / An equal among mightiest energies," he exclaims. He imagines this feeling of release made conscious:

> "And haply sometimes with articulate voice
> Amid the deafening tumult, scarcely heard
> By him that utters it, exclaim aloud,
> 'Rage on, ye elements! let moon and stars
> Their aspects lend, and mingle in their turn
> With this commotion (ruinous though it be)
> From day to night, from night to day, prolonged!'"

The parenthetical expression, "ruinous though it be," speaks volumes for indicating what the Poet has to suppress. After venting this identification with the power of nature for destruction, he yields his place once again to the authority of the Wanderer, who "takes from the Poet's lips / The strain of transport," leaving him silent once again.

MEETING with the Wanderer was an anxious occasion for the Poet, because it aroused buried feelings of insecurity and hostility toward the man whose place as poet he would himself have to take. Gradually, however, as the company enlarges to include the Solitary and then the Pastor, the Poet is able to assume greater and greater control over his feelings of insecurity, until he is able at the end of the poem to assume an authority of his own even in the presence of the Wanderer.

Wherever he finds himself, whether in the secluded valley of the Solitary or in the church of the Pastor, the Poet exercises a "desexualized energy" of his ego that is gradually gaining in its strength to synthesize. When, at the end of the poem, he revels in the company of the Pastor's wife and children, he shows how strong he has become—able even to apply a technique of spiritual therapy that reunites "antipodes" of the mind, accepting the authority of the father as discipline and duty while he acknowledges the importance of gratifying erotic instincts. In the final scenes he recovers the strength he so strangely had lost at the opening. These final scenes develop as a ritual of initiation or return to paradise. Wordsworth here dramatizes and narrates efficacy of beauty as a therapy of mind. The Poet finds a way to balance all the solutions represented by the Wanderer, Pastor, and Solitary, a way that combines the needs of eros with the need to control. It is a way that utilizes techniques Freud worked out for psycho-therapy many years later.

The main technique of analysis is a controlled method for overcoming resistance, which tries to prevent the emergence of certain feelings. Significantly Freud attributed to Friedrich Schiller authority for explaining that "poetic creation must demand an exactly similar attitude." This attitude Wordsworth recorded as a discovery he made while trying to compose a poem to consecrate his joy at the opening of *The Prelude:*

> For I, me thought, while the sweet breath of Heaven
> Was blowing on my body, felt within
> A corresponding mild creative breeze,

> A vital breeze which travell'd gently on
> O'er things which it had made, and is become
> A tempest, a redundant energy
> Vexing its own creation. 'Tis a power
> That does not come unrecogniz'd.

The power to create *comes* though it "does not come unrecogniz'd," and that is similar to the technique for analysis, when the conscious mind lies on the lookout for unconscious activity. That consciousness alone cannot force experience from the unconscious is a sad truth Wordsworth learned on that auspicious occasion which opens *The Prelude.* When he attempted to excite again his energy of creativity, purely by force of will, "the banded host / Of harmony dispers'd in straggling sounds / And, lastly, utter silence." When he said "'Be it so,'" he more truly exercises the will of which Freud and Schiller speak, because Wordsworth thereby "lets" his "unconscious being" *be.* From that moment his poem could be born, as he yielded his conscious mind to a state of "evenly suspended attention" that noticed everything without interruption of experience.

THE POET JOINS his companions in an ease of mind that encourages even the Solitary to open himself to the flow of experience. While this has been the situation for some time prior to their retirement into the home of the Parson, it is particularly there that the group achieves its ideal condition for openness of mind. They achieve this through "desultory talk" that does not discriminate "trivial themes" from "general argument." This is very important as a technique of psychoanalysis, because the patient must allow "innumerable ideas to come into his consciousness of which he could otherwise never get hold." The conversation proceeded "as accident or fancy led, / Or courtesy prescribed," thereby distributing psychic energy, not allowing it to concentrate for use by the critical faculty. The result is a dropping of resistances and a flowing of consciousness in the forms of unselfconscious speech: "question rose / And answer flowed, and the fetters of reserve / Dropped from every mind" as this "various conversation" went the way of unconscious needs.

This ease of manner and openness of mind allows for the articulation of normally repressed feelings. It is repeated, as a structural parallel to the "various conversation" of the men, by the two young boys who burst onto the scene to interrupt the group. Like the children, the adults have achieved an "animation" of discourse that frees their feelings through "eager discourse." Unlike the boys, however, whose delight is checked by "confusion," the feelings of the men are *allowed* to flow. The comparison of the boys' talk with "a bold brook that splits for better speed" is a part of a larger pattern employed by the Poet to describe the nature and effect of speech that brings spiritual and emotional refreshment the way water does to the hot and thirsty body. Therefore do listeners drink in the words of speakers in the poem.

The ease of conversation which opens up the mind from its customary reserves is achieved after consderable talk which has not been so easy in its debate and rhetorical eloquence. All of the speakers have waxed philosophical at times, interrupted on few occasions by periods of rest and repast, but for the most part the Poet has been more a listener than a speaker. He has practiced the technique of "hovering" or "evenly suspended attention" which Freud recommended for analysts. The Poet has employed a "pensive ear" for taking in innumerable details of sounds, both human and natural. He heard the music of the local Wake in Book Two, the ticking clock in the house of the Solitary, the humming bee and tinkling rill in the valley of the Solitary, and the Solitary's own falling voice as if it were the nightingale's "last note." The Poet has exercised a power of listening without prejudice, rendering himself a receptacle into which words and sounds can pass without interference: he describes how the Wanderer's words "sank into me, the bounteous gift," and then he immediately describes how the sun set in a beauty of "resplendent lights, his rich bequest." The bequest of nature confirms the gift of speech.

Over and over the Poet describes how he hears and sees with an openness of mind that will eventually work to heal his languor and discontent. He is very much aware that his is a journey of "self-examination," quite as much as it is a pleasure excursion—in fact, pleasure is an important part of his therapy. The importance of his experience is summed up in this passage in which he is apparently confirming the scepticism of the Solitary:

> "Earth is sick,
> And heaven is weary, of the hollow words
> Which States and Kingdoms utter when they talk
> Of truth and justice. Turn to private life
> And social neighbourhood; look we to ourselves;
> A light of duty shines on every day
> For all; and yet how few are warmed or cheered!
> How few who mingle with their fellow-man
> And still remain self-governed."

Looking to one's self is a necessary part of the method of achieving "self-government" and responsibility for truth in the substance of words. "Untainted speech," as he later calls it, is a product of a healthy mind and, by extension, of a healthy society.

The image of a healthy society is not to be found in the ruined cottage of Margaret, or in the ruined chapel where the Solitary found the old man; neither is it to be found in the apparition of the "mighty city" which the Solitary saw in the mountains; and certainly it is not to be found in the "crazy huts / And tottering hovels" that the Solitary describes in rebutting the Wanderer's ideals of rustic life. The health of society is, like the health of the individual, a dynamic control over passions and over authority. For the Poet that control is a function of eloquent speech, self-examination, and openness to experience. He finds this at work in the community described at the Parsonage and on the lake where the group has its picnic. The scenes which conclude *The Excursion,* in Books Eight and Nine, are pastoral in setting but social in theme; these scenes are images of social love, natural beauty, and contented consciousness. The parsonage, with its "feminine allurement" joined with its "solemnity," is itself an image of the ideal to which the poem takes its reader; it is a reconstruction of Margaret's ruined cottage into a symbol of spiritual and mental health. The lovely garden surrounding the parsonage is a symbol for the recovered nature that had fallen into ruins of overgrowth and tangled weeds around Margaret's cottage. The wonderful lake where the group has its boating expedition is a refreshing balance to the dry heart and broken well of the first book.

However, the most important images for the Poet in the last scenes are the images of the women, the daughter of the Parson ("a radiant Girl") and the Parson's wife ("the lady of the place"). Surely one reason the party is successful for the Poet is that these women satisfy, as objects of attraction, his own erotic desires (sublimated as affection and controlled as courtesy). The Poet is civilized, no barbarian who gratifies without restraint, and so his relationships with these women are established within the controlled forms of ritual. When he describes them, however, he transcends ritual: the Girl, fresh from the garden, is "light as the silver fawn," and the Lady, attending the household, is "so bright, so fair" that she is "godly" in the eyes of the Poet. The Lady is compared with a "stately ship" made beautiful by experience, and the Girl is compared with water itself, as she serves to satisfy the longing he has had, since the opening of the poem, for emotional refreshment.

# CHAPTER ELEVEN:

## High Instincts

Wordsworth in his 1815 Preface, describing the powers of the soul, says they are "almost divine." This *almost* is a sign that he is uncomfortable with the term *divine*, although he knows that as a term of value it works well to describe the worth of consciousness. As always, he wants to do the work of psychoanalysis, "to make something from the id conscious," as Freud put it, but also "to correct something in the ego." The analyst's work is constantly swinging like a pendulum between a piece of id-analysis and a piece of ego-analysis. Wordsworth could have accepted such a description of soul-analysis, because he knew the pressures of the super-ego, though he would call it by its conscious name of "conscience" or by its unconscious name of "anxiety," "sorrow," or "guilt" and "fear (of death)." He would use various metaphors to describe the super-ego's nature and operation, although the word "stain" is a favorite. Wordsworth is inclined to emphasize its importance as a source of restraint in the maintenance of civilization. He could have agreed with Freud that the principle is one of balance and moderation, because as a force of resistance against primeval instincts, the super-ego ("conscience") is not only desirable but necessary. He realized as Freud did that we owe to the evolution of culture "the best of what we have become, as well as a good part of what we suffer from."

*IN MANY OF HIS POEMS* Wordsworth described the temptation to deny one's feelings of guilt, and he often associated that with society and culture, as in "The Pass of Kirkstone" and "Memory." But wherever the causes of suffering originate, in the individual, in culture, or in nature, they may be removed by the power of the individual's own mind. Wordsworth does not attempt to remedy the social order through legislation or rebellion, nor does he suggest the Christian dispensation of atonement. Guilt and suffering are symptoms of individual psychology, to be dealt with through the power of individual minds. His poetry supplies the stimulus for activating that power, as he explains in the sonnet of dedication for *Memorials of a Tour on the Continent*. Only the reader "can supply / The life, the truth, the beauty," because these poems do not attempt to provide merely "a mirror that gives back the hues / Of living Nature." Instead, they show how "within the mind strong fancies work," as in "The Pass of Kirkstone," where the speaker rejects the temptation to lose himself in mists which "veil the sky, / Mists that distort and magnify," even if they can "subdue" memories of care and guilt.

This poem explores the deluding power of mind when it participates in the temptations of nature to trap and contain, to seduce away from the world of man, with his society, culture, and virtues as well as vices. No one can appreciate civilization, unless one explores the realm represented by the Pass of Kirkstone: "Who comes not hither ne'er shall know / How beautiful the world below." The "pass" is a boundary: between sanity and insanity, between truth and illusion, between the driving instincts of "the insatiate Prodigal" and Druid sacrifices, and the "threatening brow" of duty and conscience. The "pass" is a region of the ego itself, where the terrain is treacherous unless all claims are made conscious (lifting the mist) and kept in balance with one another (the "dread" with the "delight").

There is a danger in the discovery that one's mind exercises a power "almost divine," because like all power, it can be abused and misused, as shown in "The Pass of Kirkstone." When it magnifies and distorts guilt, the mind may lose itself in a frenzy of masochistic torment, punishing itself for old faults of childhood or primitive ages—old faults which must be exposed to the healing power of adult consciousness: thus the mockeries of fancy at work on nature's forms are exorcised by the strong mind of the speaker in "The Pass of Kirkstone," and reality can then be maturely considered. On the other hand, the mind's almost divine power can magnify and distort pleasure as well as pain, as in "Composed Upon an Evening of Extraordinary Splendour and Beauty." Here the scene of a magnificent sunset is striking because it does not quickly disappear. If it had been of short duration, the poet would merely have given it a look of "blank astonishment" and passed on his way. But because it lingered, had a "power to stay," it seemed to insist upon his lingering response. This lingering constitutes the poem itself. The scene arrests time and extends space until the mind is transported.

Not only does the scene suggest "what *can* be," rescuing nature's beauty from the ravages of time, it also restores a feeling of what *was* "in the morn / Of blissful infancy." This is a recovery of childhood's power of autonomous imagination. It also can be a regression to the primitive status of infantile instincts which make themselves known as "dreams" or wishful thinking. As long as the dreamer can awaken from his dream, and as long as the speaker can stand rooted in the solid earth of reality while he wishes for an eternal source of "magnificence," then the mind is secure. One can keep in touch with the rich resources of instinct (represented here by the glory of "blissful infancy" and the "god-like wish" for transcendental magnificence), but one must also keep these resources under restraint, by recalling "Nature's threatening voice." Although the poem ends problematically, warning that "night approaches with her shades," and the beauty of the evening is beginning to fade, the speaker has recovered something in himself that was almost lost to consciousness: "My soul, though yet confined to earth, / Rejoices in a second birth." Like the bird in "To a Skylark," the poet here represents the need to keep in balance "the kindred points of Heaven and Home," aspiring to the limitless as a promise of continuing growth and power, while remaining conscious of the limited as a restraint upon instincts clamoring for immediate gratification.

*Memorials of a Tour on the Continent* express a sentiment Wordsworth often felt on the occasion—that travelling is like life, hoping through change of prospect for "the something more" that always seems just over the horizon and so encourages movement and growth. But travelling on to the new, searching out the potential, requires a price to be paid: leaving behind the familiar, the trusted, and the beloved, as well as the disliked and the undesirable. Wordsworth keeps his imaginative eye on the past with its pleasures of home quite as much as on the future with its promise of escape from pain. This seems an advance from the escapism of poems like "Descriptive Sketches" and even "Home at Grasmere," made possible by the continuing self-analysis of *The Prelude*.

While passing again through the Simplon Pass during his tour of the Continent, he does not repeat the experience of his youth and recorded in *The Prelude*. Instead, in the "Stanzas Composed in the Simplon Pass," he marks his "sadness" as more clearly a "nostalgia," a yearning for home. He is giving something up, willingly this time, in order to reverse the direction of his movement, but he makes this as a conscious decision: "The beauty of Florence, the grandeur of Rome, / Could I leave them unseen, and not yield to regret?" Unlike the sudden seizure of disappointment, lost as in a mist, which he felt when he was young, the poet here is not a victim of his unconscious desires but rather a master of his mind: "if in sadness I turned / From your infantile marvels, the sadness was just." He can turn away "contented," giving up the possible to return to the probable and the certain— represented by "home." Home is not merely a place for Wordsworth, nor is it only a retreat (for, as his many trips to the Continent show, he was never satisfied to remain in retreat). Home is an idea of control, of security that has been achieved through discipline and devotion. Home carries a symbolic force of ego mastering its environment.

WORDSWORTH'S EGO longs for the sublime, to dehumanize scenes of nature, to abstract aesthetic patterns of sound from their natural sources and so, in effect, to purify beauty of its mortal taint. Thus, "At Dover" takes note of a "strange release / From social noise," when the roar of the ocean overpowers "life's common din," to allow one to hear "God's eternal Word, the Voice of Time." The poet realized that his desire for escape from social noise and life's din was a serious symptom of failing imagination and growing social neurosis. He devoted special attention to the importance of "sound" itself. He composed a poem "On the Power of Sound" in 1828, at the conclusion of a period when he began to have doubts about his ability to hear truth as well as to see it through / beneath mutability. If he can trust himself to escape the "tyranny of the eye" by concentrating on the "voices" that issue from out of the "dark abyss" into the "silent light" (described in *Prelude* Fourteen), then he must resolve this crisis of confidence.

"On The Power of Sound" begins with a dark intimidation, that the mind is a frightful mystery. Sound is the key to consciousness, and the ear is a model for the mind. It contains a mysterious interior that belies the simplicity of its exterior form. Wordsworth varies common understanding about "vision" when he describes the ear as an "organ of vision," the thesis of his poem. Consciousness is an inhabitant of this organ, existing as "a glancing mind" whose companion is "a Spirit aerial." The interior of this region is, like a cave, dark and blind. It is an "intricate labyrinth" which challenges thought to enter and find its way. What does enter, what seems to thrive, are "sights," "whispers," "shrieks"—all to enslave the heart or abuse the flesh. However, there also enter the musical tones of "warbled air," "hosannas," and "requiems"—to calm the frenzied spirit and comfort the frightened soul.

The world of space and time is explored as if it were constructed by this organ of vision. The poem itself is a "power of sound," winding its way through the reader's mind, from darkness that opens the poem to great light that concludes it. Through these winding mazes are several themes that work out right relationships of conscience to passion, and art to nature. The single most important principle that defines these relationships is freedom, only to be known as an economy of forces between mind and nature, between individuals and governments, and (within mind itself) between instincts and consciousness. When the relationship is "right," having brought forces into a proper balance so that life can proceed in dignity, the mind has achieved not only its functional freedom but also the pleasure that comes from art. In language harmony as visionary order resides, established there in a consciousness which the poem celebrates as, "A Voice to Light gave Being."

Wordsworth compares the art of sound and language with the power of conscience, which liberates because it corrects and restores passion to a rule of order. Passion and insanity are healed by the power of sound, and civilizations are built on its model of order: "The Gift of king Amphion / That walled a city with its melody." Beyond the social order, in the depths of animal passion represented by "the creatures of the sea," music works to "humanize" them until, like Arion astride the dolphins, man "the Master rides." In the opposite direction, into the silent heavens, sound reaches to participate in the "one pervading spirit / Of tones and numbers" that regulate the order of the universe. Thus does "Deep to Deep" call out for "all worlds, all natures, mood and measure to keep."

WORDSWORTH'S conception of art is becoming increasingly didactic, as it becomes increasingly concerned for the larger welfare of society viewed from a long perspective of cultural history. He is beginning to advocate an art which aims for greater formal control at the expense of spontaneity and passion. He sees the process of artistic achievement in terms identical with the process of civilization. He accepted the loss of spontaneity as a gain for strengthening the ego. As Freud has said, "we owe to that process the best of what we have become, as well as a good part of what we suffer from." The suffering is not ignored by Wordsworth, but his poetry suffers from an increasing celebration of "the best of what we have become."

This can lead to what Freud described as "the ideal condition of things," where the community subordinates its instinctual life to the dictatorship of reason. Wordsworth composes poems which champion an aesthetic function of displacing instinctual aims, as in "The Last Supper, by Leonardo Da Vinci, in the Refectory of the Convent of Maria Della Grazia—Milan," where he is thankful for the moral achievements of the painting, which has begun to deteriorate under the wear of nature and from the tampering of poor artists. In his sonnet "Go back to antique ages," he says the progress of culture is marked by artistic

monuments to instincts which have had to be repressed
and displaced by milder forms of expression. The artifacts
which survive the barbarian past may still serve a moral
and didactic purpose—to teach the civilized present how
tenuous its hold really is on sanity and balance.

One of his most elaborate surveys of this function of art
is "The Pillar of Trajan," in which he takes note of the exemplary features which mark this Roman artifact. It has
stood the test of time and survived all kinds of natural dis-
asters, including "the passions of man's fretful race" which
"have never ceased to eddy round its base." The pillar has
embossed or carved on its sides "historic figures" which
ascend for the spectator who circles the artifact. If one allows one's self to be "charmed' by the scenes, one can
participate in the ascending progress of history represented
by the column. One might identify with the person of
Trajan and "commune with his heart and mind" through
this "classic art." Because art abstracts, it may properly ex-
clude "things that recoil from language," intending instead to represent only the best in human nature as an
ideal for the ego to identify with and use to repress baser
instincts. The "fine illusion" of art can produce "a vision
of the Mind" which helps to resist both instincts and the
tyrannical super-ego. In this poem that generally admires
the achievements of Trajan, Wordsworth points out how
the hero, "thus disciplined," also tried to "enslave whole
nations on their native soil." "The Pillar of Trajan" shows
how "glorious Art" raises a model for psychological identification. However, because it defies "the power of time,"
it also shows its shortcomings when measured against
ideals of progress in civilization: ideals which seem relative
when viewed through a perspective of history as progressive displacement of instinct.

Art, as a tool of that displacement, is assigned the task
of "discovering generalizations, rules and laws which bring
order into chaos," as Freud said. He went on to say as

well, that "in doing this we simplify the world of phenomena; but we cannot avoid falsifying it, especially if we are dealing with processes of development and change." A product of the abstracting imagination (as Wordsworth described it in the 1815 Preface), art must for the sake of its order leave out (repress) the undesirable. Thus "The Pillar of Trajan" is a statement of that process at work, but only as it is seen in the product of the Pillar itself. Being a product of a later stage in the historical process, Wordsworth's *poem* can afford to admit the faults of the hero whose achievements are recorded on the Pillar. The poem marks an advance in the control of mind over its archaic heritage, just as (from this point of view) future generations will be able to claim a similar advance over the inadequacies of art from Wordsworth's time. Still, the poet works very hard to invite critical scrutiny as a part of rational responsibility, whether in aesthetic responses or in political participation. Otherwise, that "sublime consciousness of the soul" for which he aims might never be possible; he may fall far short of realizing the "mighty and almost divine powers" which particularly identify the mind in a state of cultural health.

*IN 1816 WORDSWORTH* composed a series of odes and sonnets which have sometimes embarrassed, even startled, his friendly readers on account of their shrill patriotism and martial spirit. Those poems express his fear of a wholesale rush to a democracy seduced by a "system founded upon abstract rights" and "novel expectations." This kind of behavior must lead to the same tyranny of ideas that brought France to the ruin of Napoleon's reign, and so Wordsworth writes to warn his readers from yielding to a similar temptation. He says, in a note to his "Thanksgiving Ode," that he hopes his poems "will survive to counteract, in unsophisticated minds, the pernicious and degrading tendency of those views and doctrines that lead to the idolatry of power, as power." Power as an end in itself can be seductively attractive. It combines ambition of ego for control, with instincts of id for love/destruction. When the mind identifies with an object of power like Napoleon, it satisfies a need for protection once provided by the father.

Wordsworth's attitude toward God in these poems is a more complicated one, though it is related to his attitude toward Napoleon. God can be invoked to justify use of force to preserve civilization with its "rational liberty," but God can also become merely another name for "Napoleon." To avoid the error of making "liberty synonimous with license," people must defer to an authority of restraint, imposed from without, or accepted from within, as a principle of reality, of "expedience": thus a balance of "conscience regulated by expediency." People must, therefore, to be civilized, submit to the authority of God and law. However, to prevent "aristocratic oppression" and "idolatry of power," they must learn to exhibit "a tenderness of undeceived humanity" alongside "a sternness of enlightened state-policy." People can keep health only by avoiding extremes of aristocratic oppression and flaming democracy. In his note for the "Thanksgiving Ode," Wordsworth hopes his poems will not only counteract a tendency to worship power, he hopes they will clear away the "false splendour" of power used "without reference to a beneficial end." He defends his poems, with their "martial qualities," as means for

> imparting knowledge, civil, moral, and religious, in such measure that the mind, among all classes of the community, may love, admire, and be prepared and accomplished to defend, that country under whose protection its faculties have been unfolded, and its riches acquired.

In 1845 he separated a section of the long "Thanksgiving Ode" to publish as "Ode 1815" ("Imagination—ne'er before content"). This poem has attracted much scorn and caused some perplexity for its original version of lines 106-109, which included the attribution of "Carnage" as the "daughter" of God, who uses "mutual slaughter" among men as a means of "working out a pure intent." This is far removed from the Wordsworth of such poems as "To Toussaint L'Ouverture" or even the "Ode to Duty," with its "stern daughter of the Voice of God." Wordsworth withdrew the objectionable imagery, but he retained the original idea, that God uses "most awful" means to work His "pure intent."

The poem declares that "the God of peace and love" will not "such martial service disapprove," because this is the God of death as well as the God of life: "His drought consumes, his mildew taints with death." Wordsworth does not shrink from the idea of God as Destroyer; indeed, he seems to enjoy this litany of destructiveness as he describes the mysterious and ambiguous nature of his "Tremendous God of battles." He invites pleasure while contemplating God as death in lines which express the guilt of both victors and defeated:

> For Thou art angry with Thine enemies!
>   For these, and mourning for our errors,
>   And sins, that point their terrors,
> We bow our heads before Thee, and we laud
> And magnify Thy name, Almighty God!

Consciousness of one's own sinful nature magnifies the power of God as righteous punishment. Wordsworth unites in a common humanity the victors with the victims of war, because all are equally guilty before God and eternity. He also complicates the ambiguity of the military theme with an ambivalence of attitude toward God the Father, feared and loved, punisher and protector.

The sonnet "Emperors and Kings, how oft have temples rung," warns that too many times have men given thanks to God for the wrong reasons: temples have often rung "with impious thanksgiving," empty trophies of triumphant wrong have hung over ambiguous altars. Triumph, even the victory of Waterloo, is misdirected unless it is for a "Heaven-sanctioned victory," for individual liberty to love, admire, and defend. Emperors and Kings are warned, therefore, that they hold in trust an authority to maintain the virtues of liberty achieved at Waterloo: "from duty fear to swerve!" or be prepared to fall beneath the power "of popular reason," a description of the motive behind military victories which are "heaven-sanctioned." "Popular reason" echoes similar ones in the pamphlet *Two Addresses To the Freeholders of Westmorland* (1818), such as "rational liberty" and "rational acquiescence," or in the note for the "Thanksgiving Ode," with its "rational patriotism."

When he considers the great price paid for civilization, Wordsworth is in awe and is sometimes uncertain that the gain is altogether clear. He praises the English soldiers who gave their lives at Waterloo as "Heroes!—for instant sacrifice prepared," though they, perhaps above all others, had every reason to love life in a free land. But, when "duty bids you bleed in open war," "death, becoming death, is dearer far" than life itself. As long as he believes individual sacrifices are genuine extensions of the principle of cultural sublimation, Wordsworth can accept these deaths of young men as meaningful. However, in a later sonnet, "After Visiting the Field of Waterloo," one of the poems published as *Memorials of a Tour of the Continent,* confronting the scene of the battle itself, he shrinks from his earlier enthusiasm for the "tremendous God of battles." He watches the glory disappear from the field: "A winged Goddess—clothed in vesture wrought / Of rainbow colours . . . She vanished." Then he sees a "prospect blank and cold," feeling "as men *should* feel / With such vast hoards of hidden carnage near, / And horror breathing from the silent ground!" Confronting this reality, or even the remnants of reality, the poet feels a new expediency grow upon him. He has removed from his own satisfied imagination "that false splendour" which loses sight of the ugliness in power unless it can be justified as directed to a beneficial end. This sonnet returns to the truth of death as a frightening loss, meaningless while naked of the glory which the idea of sacrifice confers. And yet the last image of the sonnet conveys a message of meaninglessness for all life, when it is trapped by tyranny or overwhelmed by passion, when it is confronted by deaths imposed rather than deaths that are chosen.

"Feelings of a French Royalist, on the Disinterment of the Remains of the Duke D'Enghien" describes how death uses the punishment of shame as a salutary sting on remorseless hearts. Ironically, "blind worship" of power ("their monstrous Idol") has already made men impotent. This reminder of tyranny's ruthlessness may restore the moral vision people need to recover life. Sacrifices of authority figures in revolutions, as in the execution of the Duke D'Enghien, repeat rituals of father-killing. They in turn lead to a return of the dead (the repressed) to haunt the minds of the guilty (with shame). The sonnet ends with an unusual twist, deploring the present necessity to observe restraints of civilization. As Freud observed, and as Wordsworth well understands, "it is easy for a barbarian to be healthy; for a civilized man the task is hard."

The conclusion of the Ode "Who rises on the banks of the Seine" is a plea for the health that comes from helping the mature ego master old traumas:

> change the creed
> Which hath been held aloft before men's sight
> Since the first framing of societies,

Whether, as bards have told in ancient song,
Built up by soft seducing harmonies;
Or prest together by the appetite,
    And by the power, of wrong.

The poem asks for a new disposition (from the "supreme Disposer") of energies achieved through a new construction ("creed") of the ego's defenses against the instincts of eros and death ("seducing harmonies," "appetite," and "power"). The poet-analyst prescribes a method for strengthening the ego by correcting "inadequate decisions made in early life." In his *Two Addresses To the Freeholders of Westmorland,* he explains in terms of political economics how an incorrect solution to life's traumas works upon unsophisticated peoples in his own time: "The People have ever been the dupes of extremes, VAST GAINS WITH LITTLE PAINS, is a jingle of words that would be an appropriate inscription for the insurrectionary banner of unthinking humanity." The People are a vehicle for unthinking instincts seduced by dreams and wishful thinking into "the iron grasp of military despotism," repeating in social structures the mechanism of psychological neuroses.

Vengeance and retribution are appropriate political responses against tyrants because the expediency of government is one of its main principles of operation, and power applied in terms equal to an opposing power is an expediency necessary to achieve the goal of government: "rational liberty" based upon a salutary equipoise of varying interests. Vengeance and retribution are appropriately psychological responses to fear of conscience, because they weaken the ego's dependence upon the super-ego. Wordsworth's ode exposes the mistake of an incorrect first response to a love object (the tempting beauty in the first stanza), and then hopes to correct that error (which resulted in the sickness of tyranny) by a strengthening of independent will, which turns its death instinct out against the authority of death itself. The poem is a justification of rebellion against tyrants, but it is also an analysis of psychoneuroses which can be cured only by a correctly directed gratification of the death instinct.

*THE MECHANICS* of retribution, as a religious, moral, political, and psychological operation, both intrigue and trouble Wordsworth. "Dion" analyzes political tyranny and the guilty pleasures of punishment. Dion was a benevolent ruler of appreciative people. He had trained himself in the philosophy of Plato, acquiring from that training a "dignity austere" and "self-sufficing solitude." He aspired to share the benefits of his training with others, and so he turned into a philosopher-king. He returned from exile to his native Sicily, where he was welcomed by enthusiastic crowds: "Pure transport undisturbed by doubt or fear / The gazers feel." He is virtually worshipped in "rites divine," and he is called upon "as if a very Deity he were." The paradox, and the pity, of his career is that Dion's desire for the divinity of wisdom and his duty to the ideal path of right intersected with his people's desire for a hero-king: their "breath of popular applause" raised him to the eminence of "divinity."

Dion was a victim of circumstances which compromised his integrity, transformed his pure mind into a guilt-ridden hallucination. But Dion cannot be easily explained. His ambition for power "overleaped the eternal bars" and plunged him into an abyss of political corruption. He suffers from the symptoms of a manic-depressive, described in lines that echo parts of "Resolution and Independence" and the "Ode to Duty":

> For him who to divinity aspired,
> Not on the breath of popular applause,
> But through dependence on the sacred laws
> Framed in the schools where Wisdom dwelt retired,

Intent to trace the ideal path of right

. . . . . . . . . .

And oft his cogitations sink as low
As, through the abysses of a joyless heart,
The heaviest plummet of despair can go—

Dion has loved power too much, and he has murdered to
maintain it. He "hath stained the robes of civil power with
blood, / Unjustly shed, though for the public good." Perhaps he has been an agent of retribution against tyranny,
perhaps he has rescued society from a previous bondage,
but he has violated his own conscience at the same time.
He has, in effect, to make a sacrifice of himself on behalf
of the larger good of society. Dion's death is a release
from the burden of his own guilt as much as it is a release
of society from his own tyranny. Inasmuch as he was a
symptom of society's guilt, his death is a punishment of
that same society. His career justifies the moral that pleasure and peace are possible only to one "whose means are
fair and spotless as his ends," but Wordsworth leaves this
as a problematic conclusion to his poem of sympathy for
Dion.

He was not always sure that peace and pleasure come as
rewards for those whose means are as pure as their ends.
In the "Ode, 1815," he recognized the justice in God's
use of violence to achieve a pure intent; in the "Thanksgiving Ode" he claims that the ghastly sight of "Bleeding
war is one of pure delight," because tyranny has been sub-
dued and "the sway of equity renewed"; and in his *Two
Addresses* he elaborates the politics of "conscience regulated by expediency." He ridicules the policies of Charles
James Fox for having failed to achieve political ends that
were impossible because of "the naked absurdity of the
means." But Wordsworth does not deny the greater importance of ends than means.   Indeed, he later insists that
only ignorance and pride "could prevent us from submit-

ting to a partial evil, for the sake of a general good."

The "Ode on the Morning of the Day Appointed for a General Thanksgiving, January 18, 1816," or "Thanksgiving Ode," is one of Wordsworth's most ambitious single poems of this period. It is a celebration of the victory over Napoleon and a thanksgiving for all the fruits of liberty which were supposed to fall from that victory. It is also an elegant ritual of cultural and psychological analysis, examining the nature of guilt and its reparation in a poetry that sometimes rings with the majesty of the "Immortality Ode." With its vision of Europe caught up in "the fatal web" of Napoleon's tyranny, then rushing to prevent Napoleon's restoration, rising like the ocean itself to be cast "on that offensive soil," like waves upon a thousand shores, and hearing when "the trumpet blew a universal blast," this poem sometimes achieves the splendor and grandeur of Blake's "Europe," with its trumpet blast of revolution and apocalypse. The "Thanksgiving Ode" is a poem for the public and for the private reader, expressing a public and a private belief. The public believes it has progressed in its discovery of God behind the Sun; the private person believes he has progressed in his discovery that God may exist only as the boundary of his own mind. The Ode is a celebration of victory over tyranny, but it says that the source of that tyranny may be in the very minds whence came the strength for overcoming the tyranny. Evil and Good are functions of a constitutional ambivalence in the mind itself.

Proceeding through a logical as well as visual dialectic, the poem asks questions, provides answers, and those in turn are subjected to new questions. The question about the worth of military victory is turned into a question of whether indeed it is a victory after all. The first answer is that there has indeed been a victory, but not by "the vengeful sword"; it was, instead, "by dint of Magnanimity." The military victory at Waterloo is a symbolic projection, a trophy, of an internal spiritual victory and mental equipoise achieved by the victory of Britain. The face, however, which Britain puts on to meet military challenges should not be mistaken for the substance of its spirit. People who wear military masks should not lose themselves in those masks, or they will miss "the sole true glory," a lesson in humility—which only those who explore their own dark depths can know: they must dive "through the abyss of weakness." Wordsworth is proposing not only a Christian therapy of humility. He proposes that the best correction to pride is a reminder that the base upon which that pride is built is a treacherous region of the primitive unconscious.

When people defending civilization lose sight of their true sources of power (in themselves), they will suffer from a "distracted will" and they will achieve a discipline which is merely "passion's dire excess." This is the "fatal" web drawing out, from minds and souls, to cover all Europe. Such discipline can produce little more than "shadows of redress" for the grievances of civilization. But suddenly the poet feels himself falling too deeply into an "abyss of weakness" himself. He banishes the imagery of distress to announce that "the guilt is banished, / And, with the guilt, the shame is fled; / And, with the guilt and shame, the Woe hath vanish'd" with the victory of Waterloo.

After so much violence and after so much noise of battle, even after the loud sounds of celebration, what is most needed as a sign of internal victory is quiet peace of mind. When the boundaries of moderation and balance are broken by noisy passion, then stern conscience raises its voice of warning; the poor ego is torn between the noise of the crowd and the chilly judgments of dictators. When the violence accelerates, as it did in the wars of Napoleon, the last appeal for relief may be death—the ultimate punishment, and the ultimate silence. This is not quite the peace of mind which the poet hopes for. It is a reminder that if quiet is not a function or product of equipoise, it may be a sign of death and disaster.

"Fort Fuentes" suggests a quiet which is a phase in the civilized rhythm of life for individuals and cultures that strive for balance:

> O silence of Nature, how deep is thy sway,
> When the whirlwind of human destruction is spent,
> Our tumults appeased, and our strifes passed
> away!

The fortress fell, "upheav'd by war's sulphurous blast," just like "this sweet-visaged Cherub of Parian stone" which the poet finds at a distance from the fort. The extremes of value in civilization, the fort and the cherub, have both given way to the quiet working of nature. The explosion followed by the collapse, the power by the helplessness, and the music by the silence, are phases in the continuing rhythm of an underlying process.

Therefore, when the noise of shrill opinion or the sounds of martial violence threaten to unleash again the power of uncontrolled passion or the tyranny of harsh repression, the poet counsels a summoning of the mental powers he calls "consciousness" in his sonnet "After Landing—the Valley of Dover, November 1820." Here is a scene empty of "noisy followers of the game / Which faction breeds," a scene of peace and quiet, much like that which overcame Fort Fuentes—except that here it is a quiet of civilized life. Lizards, snakes, birds, and the wild vine climb over the fragmented cherub of Parian stone cast out from Fort Fuentes, to dramatize peaceful repossession by nature over a civilization threatening to destroy itself. But, as an alternative to that kind of peace and quiet, Wordsworth proposes the scene he found after landing in the Valley of Dover, dominated by "majestic herds of cattle, free / To ruminate, couched on the grassy lea," and where the only sound is the mellow horn. This rural stillness generates "consciousnesses" of profound calm, the reward for a society which accepts a government of conscience regulated by expediency.

The conflicts with Napoleon, after the disturbing events of the French Revolution, raised his spirit to a pitch of anxiety for the security of all people and for the beauty of all European civilization. After the successful repression of Napoleon, and the Continent once again safe for travel, Wordsworth could again extend his view to celebrate the loveliness which had been so seriously threatened for much of his lifetime. He was particularly attracted to the beauty of the city of "Brugés." He describes (in two sonnets) the play of evening sunlight reflected through "silent avenues," where people move with a dignity of nun-like grace. There the "Spirit of Antiquity" is enshrined in the architecture and expressed by the very motion of the people, who carry their concerns with a regard for the precious artifacts of the past. The city is, therefore, a symbol of the civilized beauty that can contain not only "the vulgar throng" but also the "grace within the mind," brought together by "social cares from jarring passions freed."

*"TO ENTERPRISE" SEEMS* regressive to eighteenth-century allegorical odes of the kind composed by Collins and the Wartons. It attempts to establish connections between individual endeavor and the progress, or evolution, of civilization, with enterprise the "spirit" which provides continuity. The first two stanzas outline the source of enterprise (in allegorical terms of abstraction) and then trace its operation through the history of man's conquest over nature: from eastern regions of Eurasia where beasts are companions and competitors, through regions where primitive religion draws upon the spirit of enterprise (raising al-

tars for sacrifice), to modern times in western Europe where religion is measured by "severer discipline"—which Wordsworth illustrates with the example of a nun taking her vows. Contemporary religious attitudes owe as much to Enterprise, then, as did ancient ones when "Demigods" trod the earth. Now human endeavor is impelled by a divinity as powerful, but more civilized because more disciplined and more devoted to the improvement of human welfare. Nature is still conquered with as adventurous a spirit as when men competed with the eagle itself, for now men fly among the clouds "with bolder than Icarian flight," dive into the deeps of the silent ocean, and cross the oceans in defiance of wind and contrary waves.

"Enterprise" is very much related to God, Duty, even Imagination. It is a bold Spirit residing "among the starry courts of Jove," a guide to Demi-gods, a divinity impelling young people to lives of self-sacrifice, such as the aspiring Virgin who kneels to receive the hallowed veil. Enterprise is the source of knowledge ("for philosophic Sage"), as well as the source of dreams (for "high-souled Bard"). The source, then, and the peak of progress for enterprise is in the mind itself. It originates in the unconscious aggressiveness of primitive mind, but it fully reveals itself in modern times in the very conscious "world of mind." Therefore, "a single Mind" may be the most important resource for a whole nation, providing "the Patriot's Soul" to inspire others to lives of restraint ("the quickening impulse to control"). Enterprise is the joining of instinct with conscience, controlling impulse in the service of life ("From source still deeper") but for an ego-ideal ("of higher worth"). Not only is Enterprise at work through the history of civilization. It is also at work in each individual person's own lifetime, as ontogeny recapitulates phylogeny. This is what Freud called, with his Lamarckian bias, the "archaic heritage" of each individual from a cultural heritage of acquired traits. Wordsworth distinguishes the enterprise of the young from the enterprise of the old as being a matter of modification for the individual, parallel with the modification that has occurred in the character of culture from primitive to modern times.

Like the culture of which he is a part, Wordsworth as a modern mind and modern poet hopes even in his old age to participate in the show of mental vitality making modern civilization. One definite sign of that continuing spirit of Enterprise would be, not only Hope during a time of political discouragement, but more especially an enduring love, which is "proud to walk the earth" with Enterprise when it is "worthy" of its name. And so he composed many love poems at this time. He set himself a strenuous task of translating a great poem of love, *The Aeneid,* which elaborates many of the themes most interesting to Wordsworth in his maturity. These themes are, of course, love and war, but also the right relationship of piety to politics, and the evolution of civilization out of ancient contexts of violence toward an ideal of disciplined peace. Wordsworth said he would translate no more than the first four books. He completed three, and a few lines from Books Four and Eight. His concentration on the first three books indicates his current preoccupation with such matters as the artist's responsibility during war, the relationship of aggression and conscience, and the psychological sources of religious values.

Aeneas's words of encouragement and "patience" to his crew during the storm at sea which opens the poem articulate words and feelings which Wordsworth as mature artist speaks to his troubled times. The private uncertainty which underlies Aeneas's public posture as leader and hero equally well describes the private conditions of Wordsworth's public voice, of any modern poet's voice, when that poet is so forcefully aware of the uncertain foundations for social order in conditions of fear and aimless violence. Neptune calming troubled waters, Aeneas repressing his own pains to counsel endurance with patience—these are actions appropriate to responsible leaders during public crises, and they are exemplary for artists during war or political upheavals. In his pamphlet *To the Freeholders of Westmorland* (roughly contemporaneous with his translation of *The Aeneid*), Wordsworth echoes Neptune and Aeneas:

> our forfathers were tried, as we have been tried— and their virtue did not sink under the duties which the decrees of Providence imposed upon it. They triumphed, though less signally than we have done;—following their example, let us now cultivate fortitude, encourage hope and chearful industry; and give way to enterprise.  So with prosperity return.

Aeneas must learn to submit to the authority of Providence, through love of his father (hence, his renowned "piety"), before he will be spiritually prepared to carry forward the aims of history. So must all persons do the same, in the increasingly conservative view of Wordsworth—who goes on in his pamphlet to warn that "the lessons of History must be studied;—they teach us, that, under every form of civil policy, war will contrive to lift up its head, and most pertinaciously in those States where the People have most sway." This warning is a result of his increasing regard for the precious and precarious achievements of civilization. He entreats "that the discontented would exercise their understandings, rather than consult their passions," lest they be hurried into a false "tranquillity under the iron grasp of military despotism." Thus *The Aeneid* provides, for Wordsworth at this time, a study of the right and wrong ways to recover civilization after great social and personal chaos. The scene of Aeneas carrying his father and leading his son out of burning Troy is a special occasion, or image, for Wordsworth's translation. He had been deprived of the opportunity to carry "the freight" of his father's "old age" upon bent shoulders. He had to settle for carrying, in his piety, the burden of art and culture through a deteriorating political and spiritual scene of Europe. His translations from *The Aeneid* emphasize an achievement of piety through renunciation of instincts, of love and death. Love is a snare of the death instinct itself unless the mind can rise to heroic heights of repression—with the assistance of divine authority.

# CHAPTER TWELVE:

## More Habitual Sway

*The Aeneid* is a great poem of great loves. But, because it shows how dangerous lust can be when eros is joined with death, its greatness does not follow from a celebration of erotic love. Instead it is a poem of love as *piety,* identification with the father whose blessing is a source of discipline. Love-contained, then, is the norm for erotic behavior in *The Aeneid,* and so it is in Wordsworth's love poetry in this later period: a love poetry that easily could give way to devotional poetry ("piety") of a religious kind. "Laodamia," one of the best poems he composed during this time, is a love poem qualified by religious sentiments. However, by choosing a subject from classical materials, Wordsworth is able to keep the religious tone in balance with the erotic theme.

"Laodamia," owing much to Book VI of *The Aeneid,* is in a manner Wordsworth's translation of Virgil's subject from that Book. Aeneas tries to embrace his dead father's phantom, as Laodamia does her husband, but of course neither is gratified in desire. The difference is that Aeneas is able to accept his father's counsel of self-restraint and thus goes forward to fulfill his heroic mission, while Laodamia is unable to accept the teaching of Protesilaus, who tells her "to control / Rebellious passion." Because her "fervent love" moved the gods to answer her prayers (inspired by "fruitless hope"), Laodamia has her love intensified by the appearance of her husband's ghost. She even asks for a "nuptial kiss," which causes the heavens to darken and her spouse's lips to turn "a Stygian hue."

When the time allotted for the visit of Protesilaus expires, so does Laodamia expire. He leaves in dignified silence, and she perishes in despair. The "just gods" are rigid in their demands, like an unrelenting conscience or super-ego; Laodamia is chaotic in her desires, like an undiscriminating id. The standard of ego-control is Protesilaus, obedient to the ideals of heaven and still hopeful of reunion with his beloved Laodamia. It is Protesilaus who learns to sacrifice immediate desire for the sake of order and security, giving himself to fulfill the designs of providence (like Aeneas). If Laodamia represents the failure of mind to comply with the demands of reality, driven to her destruction because she cannot measure up to the high demands for self-denial, she illustrates the tragedy of civilizations which ask too much of people. On the other hand, "the just Gods whom no weak pity moved" represent impossible demands for the surrender of all passion to sublimated order.

*WORDSWORTH COMPOSED* several love poems to his wife and sister at this time, stressing once their united identity (in the poems "to Lycoris" in 1817) and another time (in 1824) his indebtedness for renewals of emotional strength. The "Ode to Lycoris, May, 1817," is a summons for lovers to enjoy springtime pleasures even though they are in the autumn of their lives. Like the call by Protesilaus to Laodamia, the poet here tells Lycoris that "life requires an *art* / To which our souls must bend; / A skill— to balance and supply." Therefore, it is even more important that they indulge the pleasures of springtime as they decline in years, else they will overset the balance to which they should devote themselves: "blossoms and the budding spray / Should inspire us in our own decay." There is no submission here to the power of age and time, both strong weapons of the super-ego. Love, paradoxically, supplies the poet with the continuity he needs for identity, feeling as he does that he is "a bard of ebbing time, / And nurtured in a fickle clime."

His short, exquisite love lyrics of 1824 are simple expressions of appreciation for the saving love of his wife. She is his contact with earthly reality, with the common things which make for substance in life and which guarantee a continuity of identity. He declares that he is devoted to her, in part, because she is not perfect: "Let other bards of angels sing," because he loves truth and reality, not bodiless abstractions. Wordsworth's love poems are not witty metaphysical conceits, nor are they courtly Petrarchan hyperboles; because he refuses to exaggerate the importance of eros (as Laodamia does), he makes himself vulnerable to charges of being trite and mundane in his love poems. He tells his wife,

> Heed not tho' none should call thee fair;
>> So, Mary, let it be
> If nought in loveliness compare
>> With what thou are to me.

This lyric compares favorably with his earlier poem to Mary, "She was a Phantom of delight," in which the lover gradually cleared his vision to see truth and beauty identical in common life. There was still in that poem, however, a tendency to exaggeration, as in the idea of "a perfect Woman," a tendency overcome in this later poem, where the poet says that "true beauty" is a product of a mystery tied to love, "whose veil is unremoved."

*"THE THREE COTTAGE GIRLS" DESCRIBES* three girls who have not yet fallen prey to "Love's uneasy sovereignty." This is a playful poem, but it concludes on a serious note that suggests how eager the poet is to keep in touch with the freshness and vigor of youth, to stimulate erotic desire. By taking all three into his imaginative vision, bestowing upon their figures "the gift of immortality," he has created an erotic triptych of evolving types of love: from the Italian girl's self-sacrifice through religious sublimations, to the Highland girl's undetermined potential for continuing self-expression. Love is a demanding sovereign, whether His realm be the Church, the family/ nation, or nature's self.

"The Triad" presents the poet as Prospero who summons maidens to dance across the lawn as prospective wives for a young man standing beside him. He says he will not, as did poet-magicians of old, try to trick the groom with Naiads, Dryads, or Sea-Nymphs. Instead, he will present "mere mortals." But they fail to appear when he commands them to begin their dance. Frustrated, he admits, "I sing in vain." Hyperboles have failed. It is time for simple truths:

> But why solicit more than sight could bear,
> By casting on a moment all we dare!
> Invoke we those bright Beings one by one;
> And what was boldly promised, truly shall be done.

This, it turns out, is the "spell" that works—a submission to reality and truth.

"The Triad" scorns to make use of classical tricks of personification, but it is anxious to cast a spell of enchantment over the scene of presentation. When it concludes, the Poet says "The Charm is over." Ominously, "the mute Phantoms are gone, / Nor will return," as if these were mere fictions, illusions of love. Teasingly, he pauses a moment, and then says to the "favoured Youth" in search of a wife, "droop not": these phantoms were an "apparition" that "obeyed a summons covetous of truth."

Love is liable to the charge that it can delude and confuse. Wordsworth sometimes fears that "charm" may end before the end of life. His career has been in many ways a struggle to retain the charm of natural truth, to reunite mind and nature in a spousal verse of intellectual consummations with natural instincts. To say, then, that the charm is over may be more intimidating than it is a promise of deliverance from illusion. When he tries to write poetry without benefit of "charm," to describe or narrate naked truths, then he is likely to produce in art what he advocates in ethics—a moderation that at its worst may be only banal, at its best merely efficient. His love stories of *The Russian Fugitive* and "The Egyptian Maid" are liable to these faults, although they are interesting experiments in erotic adventures.

The child of *The Russian Fugitive* flees the false protection of the social order, appeals to a mythic order implied by the idea of "foster" parents, and returns to the protection of the order of marriage—nature and society united. When that union is threatened, as in *The Russian Fugitive,* or actually broken as in "The Egyptian Maid," all charm ceases. Or, rather, charm is abused, because "charm" is really a mode of power, and power may be imposed, suffered, or mutually engaged. In *The Russian Fugitive* charm is broken because it is suffered. In "The Egyptian Maid" it is broken because it is imposed—by Merlin, envious that something so beautiful as the "bright ship" could have been built without his approval or assistance. Echoing Shakespeare's Prospero again, Wordsworth describes how Merlin uses, abuses, his magical power to cause a storm to destroy the ship of "The Water Lily" and drown the Egyptian maid. When Galahad, the favored knight, extends his hand at the end of the tale to resurrect the girl, Wordsworth describes the scene using imagery long a favorite erotic symbol for him: Swans (of Venus, identified in the "Ode to Lycoris"), here compared with serpents,

> He touched with hesitating hand—
> And lo! those Birds, far-famed through Love's dominions,
> The Swans, in triumph clap their wings;
> And their necks play, involved in rings,
> Like sinless snakes in Eden's happy land;—
> "Mine is she," cried the Knight; —again they clapped
>   their pinions.

Death yields its sovereignty to Eros, and civilization survives through the union of this couple, Christian and Pagan, nature and soul, in the ritual of renewal, holy matrimony.

The charm of marriage, as ritual or as metaphor, is the power that renews and restores, in poetry and in life. This is an issue in the companion poems, "The Wishing-Gate" and "The Wishing-Gate Destroyed," which elaborate the function of a highly symbolic gate as a therapeutic device for anxiety-ridden people. The wishing-gate is art as sublimation of natural instincts. It leads into the natural, and it allows for the indulgence of wishful thinking. For many people, who know of no other resource for relieving anxieties (of love), this gate has served a useful psychological function: to make reality more bearable with constructions of fantasy. However, the second poem insists that the best therapy is reality, that which remains behind when "the charm is fled" at the destruction of the gate. The poet is torn between deploring the loss of the charm rendered by this symbol of ancient superstition, and the triumph of reality over fantasy which the destruction represents/ produces. He must, as a champion of "truth and love," finally submit to the virtue of a life lived without the "props" of wishful thinking. Even though mankind should acknowledge its debt to the artifacts of superstition, it should move on in its civilized maturity to an art of "truth informing mind and heart."

So that the truth of mind not overcome completely the truth of heart, Wordsworth insists in such poems as "Ode, Composed on May Morning" that mankind continue to observe the living symbols of nature—which can never be outdated. Fearful that civilization might press too urgently the need to outgrow wishful thinking, with its charm, he reminds readers that the May-day rituals *will* continue even if people *will* try to ignore them. Better to join with "all Nature which welcomes May whose sway / Tempers the year's extremes" and to enjoy "the balance of delight." Love and the heart must not be forgotten in the effort to break free of superstition, because after all, superstitions were functional activities of love and heart. To keep the balance of mental health, the poet requires a mature regard for the facts, though not at the expense of the heart, where those facts are humanized by the affects of eros and death.

*THE CHARM* that Wordsworth has most difficulty overcoming is, as every reader of his poetry knows, the power of nature to bind his affections. His poetry has thrived upon his vital relationship with the objective world of reality. As long as there was a living interchange between the human and the natural, the mental and the material, he was satisfied and his poetry was vigorous. However, if the interchange broke down, as when the mind becomes subject to the tyranny of the eye in its passive dependence upon external scenes, or when the external scene disappears into a mist of subjectivity, as in the disappointment of the Simplon Pass, the interchange begins to fail, and so does the vitality that depends on the balance of tension. In his later poetry, Wordsworth tends to concentrate more often on the human side of this interchange emphasizing the attributes of mind and heart; he tends to be preoccupied with human relationships of love and war in society, or in history and tradition as recorded by the cultural artifacts of architecture, painting, and poetry.

Transition between stances of observation are noticeable in that later poetry in which nature is ostensibly the main subject, but turns out to be a convenience for imagination—as if nature were (merely) a great storehouse of metaphors, supplying bridges between ideas and affects of mind. Wordsworth, like his Wanderer, keeps returning to great Mother Nature for nourishment, but rarely does he yield to the temptation which seduces the Wanderer, to worship her. Neither does he, like Coleridge (or Blake or Keats), turn against nature as a "witch." The great marriage he once celebrated between mind and nature has not broken down, but it has lost much of its original vitality. It has become a comfortable domestic arrangement, convenient for maintaining creature comforts for the man of culture.

One of the dominant metaphors he draws from nature is imagery of autumn, classically and conventionally appropriate for expressions of declining age. While the metaphors of this imagery encourage the poet to adopt terms of mellowness and ripeness as norms for qualities of life, they also serve as continuing reminders that death is not far away. In the poem "Departing summer hath assumed" the main imagery dominating the first half is *fading, fainting, failing,* and *fever.* This motif develops a theme of decay and disintegration to a climax where the poet refuses to despair. He contrasts the fading decay of old age with springtime "ecstasies, / And passions' feverish dreams." Of special interest psychologically, he implies an identification of "dreams" in youth with the fears of old age—both are fantasies of mind conditioned by environment and internal "economics."

"Departing summer hath assumed" announces that the

poet can "temperately rejoice" despite the narrowing of life. It asserts that the range of possibilities for "undiscordant themes" remains wide, and that freedom to choose from among them remains as strong as ever. In fact, the poet's freedom may be greater now than it had been, because he has under his conscious control more of the energies that had earlier been bound to unconscious anxieties. Unless self-control is an illusion (and even if it is, it is still a conscious "ideal"), he may exercise his powers of writing to contain any subject he chooses. Yet, what he chooses does not always strike one as the most interesting or the most rewarding (this has always been a problem with Wordsworth's poetry, as several critics from Jeffrey on have complained). Even in his later years Wordsworth considers the real challenge to be in one's ability to raise mind above the universal banalities of existence, to confer some dignity of meaning upon those banalities, and thereby to affirm the essential worth of human experience. To throw one's self as a writer into any extremity of being (of feeling, or of thinking), is to risk loss of individual autonomy, the source of dignity and meaning.

The sonnet "Not Love, not War, nor the tumultuous swell" boasts a poetry devoted to celebration of the common—not the bizarre or extravagant. While there is little to admire in the sonnet's advocacy of the quiet life of "meek aspirations," there is interest in the focus on the river as an image to resolve the poem's theme. The slow movement of the river is a virtue for its effect of producing clarity, a quality Wordsworth associates with consciousness and truth: both of which might be lost in the raging floods of a swiftly moving river. The river is a source of life and beauty, it is a metaphor of the mind, and it is the basis for an analogy between natural process and human life, as in *The River Duddon Sonnets,* where Wordsworth engages in one of his favorite poetic forms as subject of nostalgic interes . He traces through thirty-four sonnets the course of the Duddon from its source in the mountains to its disappearance into the ocean. He describes this course as if he were strolling along its banks, commenting on the associations of various locations with persons and events from history, but mainly reviewing the stages of human growth and development as if in the form of this river's course.

From the very first sonnet of morning light and clear air in mountain heights, there is a faint consciousness of something rejected/denied, in darkness and sleep left to those who "toil from dream to dream." Life is in the light of the mountains only because there is a mature adult who is able to travel back to sources and examine primeval beginnings: this the adult is able to do *because* maturity *is* a light of consciousness. This adult consciousness rejects the dreams of those who toil in sleep rather than awake to the freedom of depth, or "height," analysis. This search into one's infant past produces a new control, the key concept for the sonnet sequence. A person's life might then, like the poems themselves and the river they describe, flow with the same slow, easy clarity of the crystal river in the sonnet "Not Love, not War, or the tumultuous swell."

What the mature consciousness can discover is that its own clarity arose out of darkness and perhaps out of destruction; its clarity is a consequence of its control. The "child of the clouds" might have been "remote from every taint / Of sordid industry" at its origin, but "Desolation is its Patron-saint." The birthplace of the river is surrounded by signs of this desolation, a "ruthless Power" which is as evident as the brilliant moss, "instinct with freshness rare." Both the ruthless power of Desolation and the rare freshness come from the same foster-mother Earth. With the positive freshness is born the negative desolation, combining from the beginning the dual instincts of love and death. The ambivalence of these dual instincts is what underlies the main image of the fourth sonnet, where the "cradled Nursling" "appears a glistening snake." When it runs into a playground where "ruddy children" sport under the careless eyes of their mother, the poem makes a subtle but strong connection between sex and death.

The sequence winds toward its conclusion following the river in its descent into the sea, coming to a halt near a graveyard in Sonnet Thirty-One, beneath the towers of a provincial church. The "Conclusion," in Sonnet Thirty-Three, looks out over the bay into which the river empties, hoping for the same peace and calm of transition from life into death as the river Duddon exhibits when it falls into the sea. This analogy of sea and death, although a common enough figure, carries a conviction that whatever death may be, it is a natural function and it is a release/fulfillment of the course of life itself. Wordsworth's way of accepting the inevitability of death, in these sonnets, is not to interpret it as a just punishment for guilty thoughts and deeds, but rather as a quiet consummation of life's (psychic) energies. It achieves its ultimate climax of release from containment/tension, and, triumphantly, this release is at the same time an enlargement of identity, a new freedom acquired through a new identification with power greater than one's self. It is as though Wordsworth, through this analogy of the river seeking "that receptacle vast" with life driving into death, has found a mechanism for identifying himself with his father, the end as well as the beginning.

*ANXIETIES OF LOVE* are among the afflictions of life for which many persons resort to poetry, looking for some consolation, as Wordsworth explains in the "Essay, Supplementary to the Preface" (1815). To turn to poetry for this purpose, he suggests, is to ask from it what only religion can finally provide. As well as a consolation for affliction, poetry as religion may also provide for "a protection against the pressure of trivial employments." He suggests, by his parallel construction, a parallel of meaning between "consolation for the afflictions of life" and "protection against the pressure of trivial employments," so that poetry as religion could in fact be a mode of fantasy for escape from reality. It could, then, be a defense against the afflictions, or pressures, of conscience, the super-ego bent upon punishing the ego for guilty desires and failures in life. It is quite likely, as Wordsworth also says, that most readers of poetry for religious needs are persons "in middle and declining age," when they have begun to be preoccupied with death, but also when they have begun to question themselves about what exactly they have accomplished with their lives.

He warns "we shall find that no poetry has been more subject to distortion, than that species, the argument and scope of which is religious; and no lovers of the art have gone farther astray than the pious and the devout." He aims to "send the soul into herself, to be admonished of her weakness, or to be made conscious of her power." Poetry which remains true to reality and religion can achieve effects of comfort and defense, but not at the cost of truth. If poetry keeps together, as "the commerce between Man and his Maker," the experience of "elevation" and the "pressure of the trivial," the urge toward the "infinitude" with the anchor of the finite, the sublimations with the "substitutions," and the ideals with the "sensuous incarnation," then it can be poetry and religion at the same time. The end result will be "sublimated humanity." The goal of poetry is to bring together the present (ego) with the past (id and super-ego) in a mode of power to deal with the future.

His tour of the Continent in 1820 led Wordsworth into many situations of confrontation with religious beauty which threatened to compromise his convictions about truth and reality, but he usually overcame his English and provincial Protestantism to recognize a value and virtue in

Roman Catholic beauty. He was uncomfortable with a religion that made so much of the soul's relationship with its Holy Mother, that seemed to encourage a form of infantile regression. He was also uncomfortable with a religion so ready to defer to papal authority, that seemed to encourage a kind of infantile dependence upon paternal protection. Wordsworth's Protestant heritage, although it was modified as Anglo-Catholicism is modified Protestantism, was mixed with his personal history of early orphanage, to produce more than usual conscious ambivalences toward religious authorities. He avoids expressing his personal feelings of commitment to religious figures, especially in his poetry. It is rare to find there any evidence of an emotional tie to God, unless it is awe or fear, or even to Jesus, who is less a person than an idea for Wordsworth. It is more likely that the mother of Jesus will evoke an emotional response from Wordsworth, but when that happens he is quick to qualify his feelings with very conscious defensive reactions.

The most neutral of religious figures are Angels, symbols of the connections he insists upon between heaven and earth. Angels are agents of "the commerce between man and his Maker." They help to satisfy religious need without sacrificing truths of natural reality. The sonnet "In the Cathedral at Cologne" invokes the aid of angels "to complete / This Temple," an idea inspired by a beautiful but uncompleted design. The power to bring ideas and ideals into material shape is the power of "angels." If the poem, like the cathedral, is a gift to the father as well as to the Father, this poem constitutes a crisis for the self that fears its "aspiring heat / Hath failed." The product aimed for is a sublimation of desire, an artifact of culture. The Angels are agents of consciousness converting energy into matter according to the form of an idea: "Angels governed by a plan / Thus far pursued (how gloriously!) by Man." But the artifact is incomplete: as long as it is pursued with an eye to the approval of God the Father it may never be completed. Wordsworth's point is gained by his assertion that "aspiring heat / Hath failed," referring to the deferential attitude of the men who had been "studious that *He* might not disdain the seat / Who dwells in heaven!" This studious respect has been intimidating and incapacitating for the makers of the art.

The poet himself is not undergoing a crisis of confidence of powers. He is pointing to the unsatisfactory qualities that obtain when artists try to shape their art with a conscious aim of pleasing authorities, including even God the Father. Angels might be summoned, therefore, to break the barrier of conscious and conscientious regard for authority, or they might be summoned to convert through their ambiguous natures the "aspiring heat" into the "vast design." They could do this because of their dual natures and dual functions: they are bisexual, and they inhabit the conscious as well as the unconscious realms of being. In the little poem on a "Scene on the Lake of Brientz," Wordsworth says that only two things are known about angels, "that they sing and that they love." They are nicely convenient, therefore, for representing powers of sublimating humanity, freely converting love into art and art into love. Watching the "harvest Damsels" as they "float / Homeward in their rugged Boat," Wordsworth imagines them as the very Angels who "harvest" song out of love.

To humanize the natural and to sublimate the human compete for priority in Wordsworth's art. The poem "Processions, Suggested on a Sabbath Morning in the Vale of Chamouny" sketches various ways of reconciliation that lie behind the scene Wordsworth witnesses during his tour of the Alps in 1820. He is very interested in the developing history of rituals and ceremonials, from primeval times (such as he images for the Druids) to the most recent High Church masses of Roman Catholicism. He casts an artist's eye on the beauty and the order of these ceremonials, which typify the need to civilize. But he also looks at them with his modern bias of naturalistic psychology. To look at them in this way is to see that ceremonials may become not only habits, but also systems of ignorance and symptoms of spiritual sickness (neurotic defenses of compulsive behavior). The "solemnities / That moved in long array" through the history of mankind have been defenses against divine wrath, releases of pent-up emotions, and constructions of hopes or wishful thinking.

He witnessed a Roman Catholic ceremonial in The Vale of Chamouny, where the "white-robed Shapes" of the Catholic Votaries seemed to merge with the white streams of "glacier Pillars" in "solemn guise / For the same service, by mysterious ties." The slow motion of the human stream seemed the same as the even slower motion of the natural stream, as natural as wearing a human face. Wordsworth says that he can still see that scene "in the vivid freshness of a dream," a dream that haunts him. He is unable to rid himself of its power, although he ambitiously celebrates it at the same time. He concludes the poem with this warning:

> Trembling, I look upon the secret springs
> Of that licentious craving in the mind
> To act the God among external things,
> To bind, on apt suggestions, or unbind;
> And marvel not that antique Faith inclined
> To crowd the world with metamorphosis,
> Vouchsafed in pity or in wrath assigned;
> Such insolent temptations wouldst thou miss,
> Avoid these sights; nor brood o'er Fable's dark abyss!

His poem is itself a ritual, a solemn ceremonial of art. He issues his trembling warning because he knows the power of seduction by such religious forms. The artist intensifies ordinary human desire "to act the God among external things."

Now his understanding is modified to call this a "licentious craving," to devour all nature, all reality, by absorbing it into the self. This is a symptom of mania, of a sickness that can be explained as either infantile ("antique Faith") in its unrestrained demand for satisfaction, or infantile in its fearful projection of guilt ("Vouchsafed in pity or in wrath assigned"). The reader is well advised, then, not to let his vision be usurped by religious ritual or to retire from reality to "brood o'er Fable's dark abyss" in an impotent imitation of God at the beginning of the Creation. The "Essay, Supplementary to the Preface" (1815) proposes that poetry should make the soul "conscious of her power," though not at the expense of her sanity. Poetry has to balance the goals of strengthening ego, restraining id, and restricting super-ego ("to be admonished of her weakness"). Religious poetry should not encourage superstition. It should, instead, make the mind "passionate for the instruction of reason."

WORDSWORTH ADMIRED his native England as the refuge of liberty—political, religious, and intellectual. The rest of Europe had been for so many years of his life a continent darkened by political tyranny, religious superstition, and widespread physical violence. He celebrates England as a bastion of real freedom. He composed a tribute to England's history of evolution from a darkness of ignorance and superstition to present intellectual enlightenment in the *Ecclesiastical Sonnets* (published in 1822 as *Ecclesiastical Sketches*). In this sequence he shows his bias for a dematerialized conception of God: idol worship can bind imagination and enslave intellect. Too abstract a notion of God, however, might atrophy the driving passions, which could be even more threatening to imagination. The rise of tyranny is a consequence of the failure by ego or government to maintain firm control over unruly instincts.

Therefore, the first step toward freedom, intellectual or political, is to establish and maintain discipline. Wordsworth considered the progress of the mind to have made a great leap forward when Christianity was first established in England. Then, when the rise of papal power darkened the spirit and intellect of Christian Europe, there was a set-back of grave proportions. The achievements of Protestantism as a triumph over the materialistic religion of the popes are worth celebrating, because those are primarily intellectual achievements—restorations of what Freud called "the high level in things of the mind."

The *Ecclesiastical Sonnets* begin in a hesitating manner. They reach for conjectures in the intellectual darkness that covers the primeval past of British religious history, when Druids practiced their baleful rites on "this savage Island." The poet looks for clues to explain what motivated the religions of primeval people. This proves to be a darkness of the unconscious as much as the darkness of historical ignorance. Sonnet V, "Uncertainty," alludes to Wordsworth's Salisbury Plain crossing in his youth to make an analogy with crossing into unknown regions of the historical past:

> Darkness surrounds us; seeking, we are lost
> On Snowdon's wilds, amid Brigantian coves
> Or where the solitary shepherd roves
> Along the plain of Sarum, by the ghost
> Of Time and shadows of Tradition crost.

The lonely explorer of darkness is a self-image which fits Wordsworth's conception of his own task as artist (projected in the more famous description of Newton in *The Prelude,* "Voyaging through strange seas of Thought, alone," or drawing more deeply upon his childhood fears of exploring dark and lonesome moors). The *Ecclesiastical Sonnets,* however, suppress the personal note most of the time, though they occasionally hint that he is exploring personal origins as he explores racial and national origins. He suggests a collective unconscious, as he does a collective consciousness, when he uses metaphors of dreaming to explain some of the more irrational or morally ambivalent episodes in British religious history. Religious history under the reign of the popes is a dream of power unleashed. Most of Part II is a nightmare of history from which Britons struggle to awaken, and the rest of the sequence is a history of full waking consciousness working hard to keep dreams under control. At the beginning of the third part, the poet needs visitations of hope to keep his "midnight dream" from turning into a nightmare of renewed cultural chaos.

The last sonnet of the sequence returns to use the image of a stream to observe that its "living Waters, less and less by guilt / Stained and polluted, brighten as they roll." This symbolic image concludes an important theme of the sequence: the spiritual process of moral purification, the psychological process of controlling guilt, and the historical process of sublimating instincts into art and ideas. This theme is developed through imagery as well as through narrative, and its main image is this one of polluted or stained water—which begins in utter darkness and only gradually, slowly and erratically, flows out into light and cleanliness. This history of guilt that originates in ancient darkness is an important ingredient of that "primal truth" Wordsworth searches for early in the poem.

Guilt is a feeling of punishment for having done something wrong, or for having wished to do something wrong. The guilt suffered through religious history is particularly the punishment of children for having disobeyed and rebelled against their parents. Wordsworth uses family relationships as a source of metaphors to describe the cyclical development of religious history in Britain. From the beginnings, sons have rebelled against fathers to establish independence; even though rebellion is painful and debts of guilt are incurred, that rebellion is necessary for spiritual health and for the progress of civilization. Tribes and nations are like children and parents, as the Druids are to the Romans, the Britons to the Saxons, and the Protestants to the Roman Catholics. Each "family" of history has its internal quarrels, tensions, and dissensions, until the family breaks up to extend itself in new directions with a new consciousness born of that painful break. In his progressive view of ecclesiastical history, however, Wordsworth believes that the gains from all the pain have produced, in England at least, a lasting treasure of mental riches. These are the ideals of equity, freedom, and security, and they are expressed in the religious sublimations of Anglican church ritual.

Equity as an achievement of individual mental health is the basis of a community's political and religious health. It is an "economic" idea, in Freud's way of using the term, because it represents a balance of power between forces within the mind as well as between persons within the community. This economy changes with changes in circumstances: the balance is always precarious. The drama that interests Wordsworth in the ecclesiastical history of his culture is a drama that comes from this balancing of mental forces, sometimes tipping toward the extreme of unconscious passions, at other times tipping toward the extreme of super-conscious idealistic tyranny. However, it always restores itself to the balance of a nation governed by toleration and charity, but vigorous in its application of the laws of self-defense. Because cultural growth is analogous to individual growth from childhood dependence upon authority, individuals and groups must pass through the dangerous strait of passion *versus* tyranny. To make the break into independence, passion must be drawn upon for the power of separation, and ideals of autonomy (modelled upon the father) must be projected as goals of achievement. Wordsworth's ecclesiastical history is fraught with the dangers of such alliances: it is a family romance turning into a national history.

A pope convened the Council of Clermont and ordered all Christendom to recover the Holy City from the infidels. Catholic England suffered some of its darkest days while under an interdict by a pope during the era of the Crusades. It was a time when papal tyranny showed its destructive and punishing side without mercy, causing "cheerful morn / To grow sad as night," when death was wedded to love (imagined as weddings in graveyards). Emperors were forced to stoop before popes in acts of "outraged Nature," and the "world is in the Pope's hand" to be wielded as if it were "stuff / For occupation of a magic wand." Although the children of the Church were denied opportunities to grow into independent adulthood of mind and spirit by the tyranny of the popes, that was a phase of ecclesiastical history which also would have to break up those dark days of papal tyranny.

One pernicious result of papal tyranny was the spread of superstition, and one very serious consequence of superstition was the enforced doctrine of Transubstantiation. The true God is "the Invisible," not to be held in bondage to the sense of man through nature. The authority figures in this cycle of Church history are the Protestant rebels against the Catholic father. Those were "youthful heroes" temporarily diverted from criticisms of the pope and the Church in England, where in the fifteenth century the Yorks and the Lancasters fought until "temporal power" was weakened further in favor of "spiritual truth," which proceeded "from infancy to lusty youth." This "lusty youth" will grow to full manhood in the persons of such martyrs as Latimer, Ridley, and Cranmer, but that will require the violence of Queen Mary's revival of popery to make the occasion for ritual sacrifices to purge England of ancient guilt.

Meanwhile Roman Catholicism in England was deteriorating into a routine of hypocritical sensuality (in its extreme form)—a natural consequence of submission to papal tyranny. When Henry VIII dissolved the monasteries, therefore, the English Church began the necessary purgation, though it was painful for many well-meaning persons. Among those forced to depart the realm were the Saints (as "the old idolatry"), about which Wordsworth expressed ambivalent feelings—since those figures (such as St. George) were useful symbols of emotional values that needed expression. Even more ambivalent is his lament for the destruction of the Holy Mother, the image of purity and "mother's love," mixing "celestial with terrene." But her Image too fell to earth, as it had to in the continuing process of breaking with parents.

*IT WAS POSSIBLE* Queen Elizabeth could have taken the place of the Holy Mother, but she never combined "mother's love with maiden purity," as did the "idea" of the "Woman! above all women glorified." Instead, Elizabeth had to follow after the unfortunate reign of her sister Mary, who tried to pull England back into the papal fold and thereby ended the ideal of the Holy Mother whose name she shared. Elizabeth represented an error of movement away from the sensuality of the mother, toward the cold abstractness of the virgin. When she ordered the execution of Mary, Queen of Scots, Elizabeth took on a guilt of such blackness that her reputation was forever stained. Women in the history of religious development and civilization are in Wordsworth's interpretation quite as subject to guilty feelings of ambivalence as they are in Freud's theories of the infant's Oedipus complex. The "Idol" of the Virgin Mother cannot survive the test of reality or the necessity for growing up.

In Part II of the *Ecclesiastical Sonnets* Wordsworth, by interjecting a personal note, suggests a resolution of the conflict between ideals of the mother. He encounters "the figure of a lovely Maid" whose presence convinces him that she was "no Spirit," that "she was one I loved exceedingly." While he gazed at her, he fell into a reverie in which the maiden "melted into air." The sonnet ends with a dissolution of vision. The poet's love is responsible for the visionary quality, but his love cannot sustain the elevated mode of his perception. The lovely Maid may have been Wordsworth's daughter Dora (as he identified her to Isabella Fenwick), but in the poem itself she is without a personal identification. The second sonnet, "Patriotic Sympathies," offers an interpretation of the vision's meaning, for "that Vision spake / Fear to his Soul," raising in him a strange "sadness which might seem / Wholly dissevered from our present theme." The sadness is a warning that however "lovely" is the Church, as this lovely Maid, it is subject to dissolution as an ideal. If the visionary maiden is an embodiment of religious spirit (though "no Spirit"), of the Church itself, then she is intimately connected with the welfare of the nation as well. The second sonnet makes this connection by saying that his "beloved Country" also visits his sleep of midnight dreaming. These poetic maneuvers echo Dante's tropes of Beatrice as Wordsworth deconstructs and reconstructs the analogy of citizen to Country, soul to Church, and son to mother through visionary experiences of "filial love."

Wordsworth's filial love for his country as if it were his mother is complicated in this sequence of visions by his earlier reveries of love for the "lovely Maid," especially if that lovely maid was a (his) daughter. If he made the identifications more explicit, he would be saying that a daughter is an embodiment of the mother. But he is unable to unite the divided images of womanhood, after all. The lovely Maid is kept separate from the beloved Country, just as the Virgin Mary was separated from, first, Queen Mary, and then from Queen Elizabeth. The best is to maintain the visionary quality of the Maid as an ideal (with no personal identification), known in the heart as emotional affect of love, intellectualized as a "dissolution" of "corporeal presence." As an ideal of chastity (in the widest sense), the Maid inspires regard for the ideal of Country as the Mother whose chastity is always in danger, like that of the "image" of the Virgin Mother in Sonnet II-25, falling into the dust of guilt and shame—as the nation is made to do during the reign of Charles the Second.

The poet's need to recover images of motherhood from the dissolution of dreams, from the destruction of material Images, continues through the last section of the *Ecclesiastical Sonnets* until he describes the sublimating powers of Anglican religious rituals. In the sonnet describing a child's first catechism (III-22), he interjects one of his rare personal notes into the poem, more rare because it alludes to his long-dead mother:

> From Little down to Least, in due degree,
> Around the Pastor, each in new-wrought vest,
> Each with a vernal posy at his breast,
> We stood, a trembling, earnest Company!
> With low soft murmur, like a distant bee,
> Some spake, by thought-perplexing fears betrayed;
> And some a bold unerring answer made:
> How fluttered then thy anxious heart for me,
> Beloved Mother! Thou whose happy hand
> Had bound the flowers I wore, with faithful tie:
> Sweet flowers! at whose inaudible command
> Her countenance, phantom-like, doth reappear:
> O lost too early for the frequent tear,
> And ill requited by this heartfelt sigh!

The memorial to his mother functions, in the context of remembered catechising, as a sublimation of his love for his mother into the forms of religious rituals of instruction. His Mother has "become" his Church and his Country, "in truth a second Mother," as he describes the "Sponsors" for baptism. Church and Country are the same in ideal, as Daughter can be Mother to the man whose love has been properly sublimated.

After the successful reformation of the English Catholic Church and the rebellion against papal tyranny, there arose another kind of paternal tyrant, a pale imitation of the pope in the persons of the Stuart Kings. As would be fitting to the conclusion of a religious cycle, the second Stuart King was executed, "sacrificed," to purge the subjects of their submission to his tyranny. As "children" those subjects are visited with a return of guilt and punishment in the form of the Puritans, with their irrational insistence upon severity of conscience. Wordsworth's praise for the Latitudinarians (III-4) is praise for the norm of a balance between extremes, a norm of ego control over passion and conscience, in that "sole temple of the inward mind" where "rich words" articulate "thought's defence." The arrival of William the Third heralds the restoration not only of legitimate Protestant monarchy but also, more importantly, the restoration of mental and spiritual health for the nation: William is "the Hero who comes to liberate, not defy," driving out "the vacillating Bondman of the Pope" (James II).

When Sacheverel became a celebrated cause of Church politics, he was a renewal of the always present danger that the precarious balance would be tipped again. Wordsworth is very sensitive to the insidious ways language can be abused to drive the group mind into defensive reactions. Referring to the irrational usages of the terms "High and Low" as wings of the Established Church, he concludes his sonnet on Sacheverel with this note of caution:

*HIGH AND LOW,*
Watchwords of Party, on all tongues are rife;
As if a Church, though sprung from heaven, must owe
To opposites and fierce extremes her life,—
Not to the golden mean, and quiet flow
Of truths that soften hatred, temper strife.

The religious treasure of the English Church is measured by its moderation of such extremes. What is essential to the identity of the Church is identical with that is essential to the identity of the Nation and, in Church and Nation, to the identities of each individual: religious piety, natural piety, and political moderation are identified by a common denominator of ego-control ("expedience governed by conscience").

The result of practices employing the sublimating rituals of English Christianity is a civilization which faces the truth of its inherent anxieties, admits the truth of its growth out of ambivalence and darkness, and maintains the truth of a mixed nature in man and world. The virtue of such a civilization is the habit of mind which can entertain conflicting claims in climates of toleration. Therefore England, as the mother of such a civilization, welcomes all nature's children to her bosom, including even the "Emigrant French Clergy" of Sonnet III-36, who fled the tyranny of England's traditional adversary nation and adversary Church. Wordsworth boasts that English civilization offers a consummation of the essential meaning in Christian Catholicism, exemplified by this sanctuary for the French Clergy: "Creed and test / Vanish before the unreserved embrace / Of catholic humanity." This "catholic humanity" can become "sublimated humanity" through achievement of Charity, the goal of English ecclesiastical history: "Thus all things lead to Charity," which is defined, in "Congratuation," as an achievement of the State, "balancing herself between / License and slavish order, daring to be free." Wordsworth's special task as poet is to produce an equally "daring art" of individual freedom that respects the value of filial duty: he fulfills his task by continuing to be an analyst of the mind and soul of the nation—proper subjects for one who has already made himself the subject of a daring poetic psychoanalysis.

# CHAPTER THIRTEEN:

## A Sober Coloring

Wordsworth's poetry of the period between 1828 and 1847 reflects the occasional strife of public and private experience, but it always searches for balance and often it shows ways for the reader to achieve or maintain that same balance which the poet found for himself. This balance is a matter of adaptation and integrity in social, psychological, and religious subjects of concern. Poems with social concerns range from the public events of the nation to the private relationships of the poet with friends and family; these included such matters as political reform in 1832 and 1834, the building of railways through the Lake Country, the deaths of Charles Lamb and S.T. Coleridge, and the departure of Walter Scott from Scotland to Italy. Poems with psychological concerns range from reevaluations of nature, to urgent redefinitions of art. Poems with religious concerns, fewer than one might expect, avoid argumentation but insist upon moderation while entertaining possibilities for spiritual transcendence.

The most interesting creative labor of this time is Wordsworth's reworking of his *Prelude* manuscript, especially during the years between 1828 and 1839. This reworking of materials, which were themselves often records of having reworked earlier materials, has excited the endless curiosity of critics and scholars at the same time it has created an enormously complicated task of bibliographical and textual clarification. Wordsworth's continuing labor at the composition of the poem on the growth of his mind is a process of self-therapy maintained in the healthy interests of ego-control. By this continuing reworking, he is continuing his self-analysis, lifting old repressions, bringing into control of consciousness old fantasies, and rejecting or repressing old fears which may have lifted themselves in disguises of symptoms that were not recognized for what they really were at the time the poet first constructed his self-analysis. This continuing self-analysis serves to release intellectual and imaginative vigor from bondages to earlier (sometimes infantile) instincts, restoring the ego to autonomy of control over the passions of both id and super-ego.

His continuing self-analysis is an answer to Freud's question whether there is "such a thing as a natural end to an analysis?" In that Wordsworth's record of his past, embodied in manuscripts written many years earlier, is a "construction" of his mind, his poem *is* himself as a patient *to* himself as analyst. Since, as Freud maintained, "the work of analysis aims at inducing the patient to give up the repressions (using the word in the widest sense) belonging to his early development and to replace them by reactions of a sort that would correspond to a psychically mature condition," Wordsworth's later analysis of his earlier constructions aims for a therapy of mind as well as a revision of text and modification of style.

The reader, with resistances, identifies with the poet as analyst with *his* resistances, trying to lift repressions which are held onto by a mind and a text which does not want to give up what it has adjusted to accept as organic parts of itself. The text is itself a form of resistance, embodying a construction of the mind which has taken on an independent existence from its creator the analyst. Because even that piece of now-independent self is a *symptom* isolated for examination, it is itself the very resistance of the analyst's own ego. The poet's revision of his revisions of his life's constructions is a process of continuing self-therapy: lifting repressed fantasies, releasing misused and abused energies, and redirecting instincts toward culturally approved objects of satisfaction.

*WORDSWORTH HAD,* as a younger man, been sympathetic with the positions of Charles James Fox; as an older man, he corrected that attitude, separated his feelings of approval from Fox and focused them instead upon Edmund Burke, an ego-ideal to which his conscious mind has fixed its energies with determination. When younger, Wordsworth might have been prepared to identify with Fox, sympathizing with the younger man's hope to replace the older one, to exercise his own "power of words." Now that he is older, Wordsworth has not only found outlets for his power of words, he has become all that Burke had come to mean to him. What had been a part of himself, expressed in the fragment of identity added to MS A of *The Prelude* sometime after 1819, has become an important image of his mature integrity in the revision added for the 1850 text. What he most identifies with in the image of Burke is the mature person ("old, but vigorous in age") beleaguered by foes of order and liberty—beleaguered, but not without power to stand true. Burke has become, more clearly to the analyst-poet of 1828-1832 reexamining himself as he was decades earlier, the super-ego of the poet: "he forewarns, denounces, launches forth," and his main adversary is the unruly crowd of instincts clamboring to escape ("explode") from their "cave" of the id. By this revision, therefore, Wordsworth strengthens what had been primarily a symptom, a mechanism of defense by his ego, drawing upon passion to elevate an ideal of order for the self and for the state.

The importance of this elevation is emphasized in a passage added to Book Ten, removing the line, "with desires heroic and firm sense," and substituting his more reflective/reflecting statement, "Nor did the inexperience of my youth / Preclude conviction." The later statement corrects the enthusiasm of the earlier, younger one. Wordsworth wants to retain the substance of the remark, that someone of strong mind and integrity was needed to inspire the masses to move with conviction in right directions, but he wants also to mitigate the younger tendency to hero-worship. This is important for the older Wordsworth, because he wishes to exalt an ideal of authority which awakens an heroic instinct in all people, but he does not wish to celebrate tyrants.

His trust in an abiding instinct of discipline, expressed in lines 179 through 190, added to the 1850 text, is a trust acquired in maturity. The "sovereign voice" of line 183 is not, however, a tyrant of the soul drawing exclusively upon the instinct of death, as might the super-ego (or Napoleon). The poet's trust is in a balanced mind, unwavering between authority of ideals and temptations of passions. His trust is in the ego, self integrated as judge and arbiter:

> A sovereign voice subsists within the soul,
> Arbiter undisturbed of right and wrong,
> Of life and death, in majesty severe
> Enjoining, as may best promote the aims
> Of truth and justice, either sacrifice,
> From whatsoever region of our cares
> Or our infirm affections Nature pleads,
> Earnest and blind, against the stern decree.

The complex syntax of this clause produces an effect of suspended judgment, and it expresses the poet's *present* release of energy (in thought) which had earlier been bound to a more narrow image—of repressed fear and uncertainty (more conscious when composed for the 1805-6 version than when first experienced, but now in this revision even more conscious, though more complex).

Wordsworth's need to revise is expressed as a need to complicate. The revisions of lines 369-381 in Book Ten of the 1805-6 text show that this need to complicate is actually a concession to reality—not a repression disguised as sophistication. In his 1805-6 description of the nightmares he suffered while in Paris after the September massacres, he says parenthetically, "I speak bare truth." The poet had perhaps spoken "truth" when he spoke "bare truth" for the earlier version, but the *bareness* seems to the older poet to have been, in effect, a repression of painful associations; truth, then, was *not* fully told when it was told as "bare truth." Thus the older poet elaborates the experience, and in so doing he is analyzing (putting a construction on) materials which were themselves at one time an analysis (a construction) of meaning from a dream. Wordsworth provides particulars which seem to him now to have been repressed in the earlier version: the "ghastly visions" had shown him, he now explains,

> innocent victims sinking under fear,
> And momentary hope, and worn-out prayer,
> Each in his separate cell, or penned in crowds
> For sacrifice, and struggling with fond mirth
> In levity in dungeons, where the dust
> Was laid with tears. Then suddenly the scene
> Changed, and the unbroken dream entangled me.

That the dream had been a defense of some kind was clear to the poet as analyst, because in his dream he broke into "long orations," striving "to plead / Before unjust tribunals," which he described even as a wish for his own death. But surely it was a wish for punishment of someone, possibly his father, in himself.

As a present symptom, this elaboration of the dream (now seen as having been an entanglement and frustration) suggests that one of Wordsworth's motives for writing is "to plead / before unjust tribunals." Certainly it is a motive that, if paraphrased somewhat, can explain much of his interest in politics and government, as well as reveal his unconscious defenses against the guilt he harbors toward his father and mother: making poetry would in itself be a defense mechanism, with pleasures of punishment for guilt. These details say what the older Wordsworth *values* in the fear he remembers to have had—they may say, furthermore, what he presently fears from threats of social upheaval. What is most clear-minded about his revision, however, is Wordsworth's more courageous description of the location, and cause, for the dream of death and terror from tyranny.

In the 1805-6 version, he concludes the passage by confessing that what frightened him most was his realization that this scene "of treachery and desertion" occurred "in the place / The holiest that I knew of, my own soul." In the 1850 version he more specifically identifies the source as a "death-like" sense, and he naturalizes his soul as "the last place of refuge"—a flight into himself, away from responsibility, with a frightening attraction to death itself. The older poet is more conscious of the attraction, and he is more "truthful" about the meaning of the experience (a point open to dispute to the biographical critic as well as to the psychoanalytical critic, since Wordsworth's guilt may be consciously connected with his "desertion" of Annette).

The material of Book Ten, covering the period of his residence in France, draws toward a crisis of will and identity for the young man—as he felt it in 1792. When the older Wordsworth came to describe it for his first version of his mind's development, he explained that he was "sick" and "yielded up moral questions in despair." But he did not (could not) focus on the despair itself, on the sickness as he knew it was, as more than metaphor. Wordsworth shifts from his acknowledgment of sickness and despair with little pause, to describe how he sought to deal with his problem:

> I lost
> A feeling of conviction, and, in fine,
> Sick, wearied out with contrarieties,
> Yielded up moral questions in despair,
> And for my future studies, as the sole
> Employment of the enquiring faculty,
> Turn'd towards mathematics, and their clear
> And solid evidence—            (1805-6)

This was in itself symptomatic behavior, avoiding what he wished to admit. He sought to simplify what had been complex, to substitute clarity and solidity for confusion and uncertainty. What he had tried to do was not only to deny the humanness of his experience, but to avoid discipline and reprimand. He had lost the power to regulate his conscience and his passion. "Regulate" is what he says in 1805-6 Coleridge helped him to do: as if Coleridge had become the father-analyst correcting the errant child-patient.

The poet of 1805-6 knew clearly what he had done in 1792, turning for external regulation when he could not find it, or yield to it, in himself, and avoiding problems by displacing energies of attention onto other objects. He knew that Coleridge had helped him to recover his balance, as a regulating influence; he also knew that his sister, "the beloved Woman," helped him to recover—she spoke to him "in a voice / Of sudden admonition." Together, the "precious Friend" (Coleridge) and the "beloved Woman" (Dorothy) repeated psychotherapeutic functions of the poet's lost parents.

When Wordsworth came to revise this same passage, he interrupted the transition between "despair" and avoidance behavior, to elaborate and "confess" what had been the nature of his sickness—which he more readily named a "disease." The very complexity which he had attempted to simplify by displacement and avoidance was avoided again by the older poet as he described it in the 1805-6 *Prelude;* the resistance continued even into the composition at that earlier date. But now, more than two decades after the first analysis and construction, the poet fights his resistance more consciously. He details the features of his disease and he recognizes that it was a crisis:

> This was the crisis of that strong disease,
> This the soul's last and lowest ebb; I drooped,
> Deeming our blessed reason of least use
> Where wanted most.                    (1850)

Although it is possible that the older poet is still dealing with an old repression by pretending that it occurred only in his past, by turning it back onto the past with its fictional self, the fact remains that Wordsworth is able very late in his life to reexamine his avoidances with courage. He goes on for another twelve lines to describe what had characterized his disease of despair. In this new description he draws to a focus upon elements of "obligation," and "law" set against "passion" and "folly." He explains that he was afraid of becoming a "dupe of folly, or the slave of crime." A law-breaker despite his best efforts: this is the way he saw himself, or rather, the way he now believes he had fancied himself to have been.

He needed to prosecute himself, but he did not have the strength to submit to prosecution. He punished himself anyway: "depressed, bewildered" are the words he uses to describe symptoms of unconscious guilt. His "real" crime, as the older Wordsworth can now understand it, was to lose faith in himself, in his capacity to live up to the ideal of the man he thought himself capable of becoming (the father in himself). Certainly his turn to the study of mathematics was an acceptable way of rebellion— acceptable to his super-ego, which could not have allowed him to punish himself in a frenzy of sexual license (suggested by his denial that he lived among "scoffers, seeking light and gay revenge, from indiscriminate laughter") or in a lethargy of "utter waste" and "sloth." By turning to mathematics, the young man had turned to "*pains*-taking thought," to "work" for an agent, or agency, of his mind, "enthroned" high above "the disturbances" of life. He withdrew into himself, into a "high" notion of himself— into his super-ego, an agent of mind which allows "no admission" from the unruly mob of instincts clamoring below and outside.

Finally, the mature Wordsworth can name not only the beloved Woman as his beloved Sister, he can also identify the Friend as someone more than a person nearby: the Friend was "the bounteous Giver of all good" (not otherwise named in the later text). This "Giver" was the source, so the older Wordsworth says, of his salvation in 1792, for this Giver gave him his sister. Although Coleridge was earlier credited with having helped to save Wordsworth, he is now removed. Out of the deeps of his mind, the older poet has lifted up a repressed psychic fact for present recognition: behind the image of Coleridge was this "bounteous Giver of all Good," who may be God, but, since He particularly gave Wordsworth the "gift" of Dorothy, He must also be the father as well as the Father.

*DURING HIS* last years, Wordsworth writes often of an old theme—freedom: a liberty from external restraints, and now a "contentment" as well. In the only speech he is known to have delivered (subsequently printed in a local newspaper), he addressed his neighbors on the occasion of laying a foundation stone for a new school. It was appropriate that in his only public speech he should have talked about education, the advantage of culture achieving real freedom of mind. This freedom is an exercise of spirit that he calls "contentment," which "is better than riches," because it is essential to real happiness and "moral dignity." Contentment is the feeling of self-fulfillment, having survived "various trials" and having performed "diverse duties" laid upon one by time and place. To achieve this feeling, one must recognize the truth "that *most* men must end their temporal course pretty much as they began it." However much might remain to be done to improve the social and economic welfare, there is an even more important improvement for which education must aim. Wordsworth's speech is a definition of this special aim for contentment.

"Education, according to the derivation of the word," he explains, "comprehends all those processes and influences, come from whence they may, that conduce to the best development of the bodily powers, and of the moral, intellectual, and spiritual faculties which the position of the individual admits of." Education is a matter of individual self-fulfillment, and so it is "an education not for time but for eternity." Only those who set their sights on the limited improvement of material and social conditions will be content with an education "for time." They will in the end be truly discontented unless they also adjust that kind of education (a mere arrangement of things) to one which balances inner needs with outer realities, inner resources with outer demands. An education which balances all dimensions of the human, including "bodily powers," "moral, intellectual and spiritual faculties," is an education which aims for real freedom for the individual— experienced as "contentment."

Social adjustment is possible only if one has an awareness of inner connectedness with others. That may be possible only for those whose family life is secure. Wordsworth's speech insists that parents are as responsible for true education as public school teachers. The quiet example of parents, taking "care over their *own* conduct," makes formal education into a humanizing process that concludes in contentment. Parents' "own well-regulated behaviour" provides "the silent operation of example" for the formation of their children's mental and spiritual habits; therefore, "parents become infinitely the most important tutors of their children, without appearing, or positively meaning to be so." Parents are, he says, the source of conscience for their children: they add the dimension of moral faculties to an otherwise narrow conception of mental structure and operation. He emphasizes, with the conviction of a psycho-analyst, that parents are tutors even without "positively meaning to be so." The child's relationships with parents determine the nature of super-ego.

The right relationship between parents themselves is crucial, then, for their healthy relationships with children. Some of Wordsworth's late poems focus on this right relationship between husband and wife, father and mother. Here also the word *contentment* proves a useful term of description and evaluation. "The Armenian Lady's Love" describes how a man who has lost his freedom in a foreign land is able to recover that freedom only as a renewal of his marriage. The first half of this poem works out various obstacles of self-doubt that have prevented the protagonists' flight into freedom. Once they have accepted the boundaries of their separate definitions, they set out to discover a true state of fulfillment. The Christian knight will be reunited with his wife, and the Armenian lady will be united with them together. She had looked to him as a possible lover, and he had seen her as a father's daughter. When they reach his home in Christendom, she accepts her role as a "handmaiden" to his desires, but in fact she seems to have become his "daughter"—the only role he could accept would be "father" since he has been a party to her rebellion against her real father. Their contentment and emotional freedom are functions of their balanced acceptance of parental and filial roles. Wordsworth, however, describes the Armenian lady as "a sister, loved" by the knight and his wife. Then he closes the poem with an ambiguous image of the trio in their tomb together, where their effigies are sculptured thus:

> Mute memento of that union
> In a Saxon church survives,
> Where a cross-legged Knight lies sculptured
> As between two wedded Wives—

Whether as daughter-substitute, sister, or second "wife," the Armenian princess has been a redeemer (for herself and) for the Christian knight. She has been his spiritual wife, helping him to remain constant in his affliction, and so she made possible his reunion in contentment and freedom.

Achievement of identity through union of husband and wife, overcoming divisions of time and space, is possible only as long as the noble instincts are allowed expression. In the sonnet that begins, "Why are thou silent!" Wordsworth addresses his wife with an expostulation that absence should not produce a "treacherous air" that withers the plant of their love. Then he changes his metaphor to say that if his beloved does not affirm the life of their love through words that break silence and treachery of distance, his heart will be empty as a bird's nest in winter. More chilling is his fear that silence will fall on his heart, as snow drops to fill an empty nest. Lovers are related as birds to their soft and warm nests, and words renew feelings with a force equal to that of united bodies. The cold emptiness of snow in abandoned nests is a frightening im-

age of separation and desertion. Another sonnet composed
eight years later gives thanks to a Thrush for snapping the
chains which have bound the poet to his fireside (in
"Hark! 'tis the thrush, undaunted, undeprest"). The bird
awakens the poet from his domestic lethargy, and excites
his imagination with a song of "love and nest." The poet
declares that he will join the bird to sing

> So loud, so clear, my Partner through life's day,
> Mute in her nest love-chosen, if not love-built
> Like thine, shall gladden, as in seasons past,
> Thrilled by loose snatches of the social Lay.

*His* words, then, are finally necessary to renew the life of
their partnership in love.

Love between husband and wife is liberating as well as
fulfilling. Fronting the inevitability of death, as the Thrush
fronts the darkening skylight and its roaring wind, the
poet grounds his security in identity shared with his wife.
His poetry is a song for their marriage, but it is also a
song for society ("the social Lay"). If he can keep his love
"awake," gladden his wife, with his art, then he will also
serve the integrity of his nation and human society. Both
of these sonnets convert warmth of lovers' affection into
the ties of society. They also make clear the danger of
loneliness, isolation and separation when words fail. Settled marriages, established relationships of long duration,
or any human arrangements may be useful to maintain
identities, but they are not self-renewing, and they do not
insure security without vigilance. Even the healthiest of relationships can develop internal conflicts, fall into emotional paralysis, or destroy the spirit, if they are not carefully attended.

*IF ONE IS CONTENT* with life because one has settled
accounts with reality and because one has achieved a bal-

ance among psychic powers, then one may look upon the world with some of the ease that Wordsworth feels in a late poem such as "Rural Illusions." In this he admits that nature, even as "Maternal Flora," is deceptive. She allows one to mistake leaves for birds (a "transient deception"), and she permits blossoms which have "dropped from twigs" to be taken for the "live growths" of "tiny flowers." Nature may be beguiling, but she is amusing; on the other hand, "the World's illusive shows" leave "the undeceived" with feelings of melancholy. There is a playfulness in nature's "transient feignings with plain truth" that appeals to the poet, whereas the shows of the "World" strike him as signs of emptiness and aimlessness. By contrasting these two shows of illusion, Wordsworth points up the continuing base of "plain truth" that underlies the processes of nature and the contrasting emptiness of changes in worldliness. At the same time, he reveals some anxiety about the deceptive and illusory character of "plain truth" and natural process. His easy acceptance has a twist at the end, when he concludes that Nature's feignings are pleasing most, and most often, to "those fond Idlers . . . Whom oftenest she beguiles."

The security of relationships with mother nature is a type for, a product of, having had a secure relationship with one's mother. A child's earliest object of love is its mother, with whom it first identifies and depends upon. When Wordsworth writes a poem on the birth of his grandchild (born to his son John), beginning, "Like a shipwreck'd Sailor tost," he makes it a poem of tribute to the baby's mother, to all mothers. It is dominated by images of struggle, labor, helplessness, and "storms of life." A mother's labor in delivery is a danger from which both she and the child are happy to have escaped. Wordsworth sees in their mutual struggle for life a prefiguration of the problems which all must face together. Birth is a trauma which must be accepted as a first test, a training for later

survival. It is a disaster if there is no succeeding comfort
and care by the mother. The power of "labouring Nature"
must be balanced by the power of the "gentle virgin
heart," in a paradox of great importance for healthy psychological development, since the mother is always the
child's first lover.

This poem makes an even more startling connection between mother and baby, when it sees in the calm of "this
*one* release" (the feeling of having escaped dangers of
childbirth) a prefiguration for the final release of death.
To make this connection for the *mother* is no great feat of
special insight, but to leap forward in making the connection for the infant *is*, especially when that connection is
between the child's peaceful rest upon its mothers' breast
and its last though "holier rest." Depending upon the
nursing mother for comfort after painful trial of birth, the
baby is

> In all trials sure to find
> Comfort for a faithful mind;
> Kindlier issues, holier rest,
> Than even now await her prest,
> Conscious Nursling, to thy breast!

To perceive in the nursing infant evidence of the final release, or at least evidence that a mother's protection is a
preparation for accepting the final rest, is an insight not
simply the result of an old man's constant thoughts of
death. Nor is it simply the metaphysical conceit that finds
in sexual experience a pun on death. For Wordsworth, the
point is psychological and it is profound: to know that the
mother teaches contentment even unto death quite as
much as that the "child is father of the man."

The poet's own contentment is disturbed, however, in
one of the most intimate poems he ever composed, the
"Lines Suggested by a Portrait from the Pencil of F.

Stone." Here he invites his reader to join him as he looks at the portrait of a lovely young woman. He points to the painting,

> Look at her, who'er
> Thou be that, kindling with a poet's soul,
> Hast loved the painter's true Promethean craft
> Intensely—from Imagination take
> The treasure,—what mine eyes behold see thou,
> Even though the Atlantic ocean roll between.

Then he begins a word description of the painting, but he is not content merely to put into words what is contained by the line and paint of the portrait.

Beguiled now by art rather than by nature (as in "Rural Illusions"), he is drawn more deeply into himself as he is fixed by the painting. The mystery of the painting's attraction is felt as a kind of hypnotic bondage, wherein he gazes and notices how "stillness charms the air." He invites the reader to participate in a view of the portrait as a deepening meditation on the power of art to lift its audience from common cares. This power is "soul-bewitching," not the least because it teases the observer into unanswerable questions: "make me / Thy confidant!" he exclaims, wanting to know whence the girl of the painting has "derived the air / Of calm abstraction?" He sees her on the point of becoming a woman, on the boundary between her childhood and womanhood. Shortly he will drive to the heart of this girl's mystery, because, when he fixes his attention on the blue flower she holds, he says (with certainty more than speculation) that it is a special flower, it was "her Mother's favourite." Images of femininity and sexual awakening (the crescent moon, the gates of womanhood, unpierced hearts, and now the blue flower) have brought the poet's attention to the heart of the matter: the girl's identification with her mother, now dead. The girl loves the flower for her "departed Mother's sake." This association makes the painting special:

> Words have something told
> More than pencil can, and verily
> More than is needed, but the precious Art
> Forgives their interference.

He is moved by the power of the painting to associate love with death, a girl on the verge of womanhood with her dead mother, and now the timeless with the temporal. He concludes by returning to the intimacy with which he began:

> And I, grown old, but in a happier land,
> Domestic Portrait! have to verse consigned
> In thy calm presence those heart-moving words:
> Words that can soothe, more than they agitate.

Grown old, Wordsworth still hearkens back to the heart-breaking loss of a mother in the dawn of life. As an artist himself, he perceives the force of the painting in terms of its details of representation, but that force is emotional rather than formal. The permanence of the girl's portrait is a memorial of her love for her mother, and so the dead mother lives on in the "living" portrait of her daughter. Wordsworth here may pay tribute to his own mother as an inspiration of his own art, and this time he does not mean mother nature (in fact, the portrait has drawn the poet's attention away from "that fair scene / In Nature's prodigality displayed / Before my window").

When separation is forced by the death of a parent, art and analysis can provide a controlled withdrawal of emotional investment to prevent mental illness. The girl of the portrait is made into a woman by her abilities to adjust to her mother's death, which she has done by way of symbolic substitutes—and which the poet himself has done by the symbol of his poem that records the insight. When, however, the parent survives the death of a child, and there is no other help for the mourning process, the result can be madness—such as that which Wordsworth describes in his short, three-sonnet sequence of "The Widow on Windermere Side." He might very well have felt the poignancy of this story because of its reminders of his sister's mental deterioration, but he does not make that a special point of the poem. Instead, he concentrates on the failure of a mother (who is also a widow) to keep her mental balance after the loss of all her children: "one by one, the hand of death assailed / Her children from her inmost heart bewept."

He thus returns to an old motif of his poetry, from the gipsy of "Descriptive Sketches," and Martha of "The Thorn," to Margaret of "The Ruined Cottage." What is peculiar to this poem of old age, however, is that the despairing mother makes her grief into a religious delusion. The sonnets are an analysis of connections between individual sickness and religious consolations. Furthermore, they are an analysis of the regressive character of such consolations—perhaps sexual in origin. The poet does not condemn the mother for her failure to keep control of her instincts, because he recognizes her need for something to take the place of great loss. However, he does not in any way offer this experience as anything else than a symptom of madness: "Since reason failed want is her threatened doom, / Yet frequent transports mitigate the gloom." She has transformed her son into Jesus, "her descending Son." She has become the Holy Mother, substituting the world of her wishful fantasies for the world of empty realities.

Whatever else Wordsworth may mean by imagination, he does not mean the fantasies and delusions of the mad, who are pitifully quite as "dead" as those who have no imagination at all. Children grow into adults by virtue of their imagination, a synthesizing power of ego-control able to survive separations of many kinds. They can do this because they have power-giving images of comforting parents. But parents cannot survive separations from children by identifications with those children: they will regress to childlike states of mind themselves. Nor may parents, like this poor mad mother, deny the fact of separation without risk to their abilities to deal with reality: this mother has escaped the reality of death by becoming the divine Mother who sees in nature signs of her eternal Son.

When Wordsworth tried to describe how he felt when his parents died, he had used scenes and objects from natural landscapes. He was nearly paralysed from any kind of statement when his brother John died, and again when his small children died some years later. Finally, when Dora died, he lapsed into silence as a poet forever. Art was no substitute for his personal losses, although he knew that art as analysis could strengthen egos to survive most of life's traumas. Perhaps art, employing the materials of fantasy and wishful thinking, was too close to religious delusions of the kind into which the mad mother fell. Even though, as he says in the "Essay, Supplementary to the Preface," "poetry is most just to its own divine origin when it administers the comforts and breathes the spirit of religion," Wordsworth was uneasy with the notion that poetry can do the work of religion.

He was concerned that readers who look for religious consolation in poetry are likely to be those for whom the range of "passions is contracted accordingly; and their sympathies become so exclusive, that many species of high excellence wholly escape, or but languidly excite, their notice." He does not write poetry to provide religious consolation, partly because that kind of poetry is too narrow, but mainly because that kind of poetry tends to take the mind away from realities of life, and weaken ego controls.

He warns that "no poetry has been more subject to distortion, than that species, the argument and scope of which is religious." Poetry deals with "sensuous incarnation," with finite things; religion pulls the mind away from the finite toward the infinite and indefinite. He resists the pressure to become religious and indefinite, as something tending toward the madness of this poor deluded mother. Poetry should, as he says in the 1815 Essay, be "passionate for the instruction of reason," not "detached from the treasures of time."

*IN TWO VERY DIFFERENT* kinds of poems, one "Written After the Death of Charles Lamb" and the other on the occasion of Walter Scott's departure from Scotland to Naples, "Yarrow Revisited," Wordsworth analyzes the importance of friendship for its protection against loss and loneliness. These are poems of anxiety, but it is an anxiety analyzed and controlled. This is true even for the strange and often clumsy poem on the death of Charles Lamb: clumsy because Wordsworth had to rewrite his "Epitaph" as an elegiac memorial, and strange because the poem has to struggle against obvious resistances disguised as hints of mystery. The clumsiness and the strangeness appeared in the first version, printed as "Epitaph," composed of the first thirty-eight lines of the completed poem. It is a tribute to the affection and genius of Lamb, whose name is naturally enough an invitation to pun on Christian innocence. Wordsworth not only has to work around Lamb's often expressed distaste for rural life (a "lamb" should know better), but he has also to modify the notion of "innocence." Lamb's was a name

> Wherever Christian altars have been raised,
> Hallowed to meekness and to innocence;
> And if in him meekness at times gave way,
> Provoked out of herself by troubles strange,

> Many and strange, that hung about his life;
> Still, at the centre of his being, lodged
> A soul by resignation sanctified.

He repeats the point that Lamb was provoked out of his meekness by "troubles strange, / Many and strange." Then he retreats from a plain exposition of what he means. Instead, he represses in Lamb what he cannot further explain in the poem.

Later, after completing the "Epitaph," Wordsworth is restless with his earlier account of Lamb's life. He is uneasy with himself because he has not been forthright: it was an "imperfect record" whose "aim is missed," because "much that truth most urgently required / Had from a faltering pen been asked in vain." He has suppressed truth in trying to explain what was special about Lamb: he had tried to play the role of censor in guarding the reputation of his friend. He admits that his motives had been guarded as well, having written "with an earnest wish, / Though but a doubting hope." To get at the truth he must dig at the "one root" which held Charles Lamb together with his sister Mary. The subject is sacred and taboo:

> And taking up a voice shall speak (tho' still
> Awed by the theme's peculiar sanctity
> Which words less free presumed not even to touch),

a "theme" which is, surprisingly, "fraternal love."

Surely it is not in itself of a *peculiar* sanctity, and certainly Wordsworth has never before had to be so careful about his thoughts on brotherly love. There were times, particularly in the "spots of time" passages in *The Prelude*, when he did use "words less free" as he approached "to touch" upon tabooed subjects, but there is no hint to this point in the poem that anything like incestuous desire or patricidal thoughts were the frightening things for Lamb that they were for the child Wordsworth. Still, however, the poet does not drive home to his subject. He circles as he moves in slowly to seize his point. He celebrates sexual love in marriage. He uses conventional imagery of vines clinging to trees to express the symbiotic relationship of wife and husband, "enriching and adorning"—imagery which will be picked up later to elaborate a different kind of point about Charles and Mary Lamb ("a double tree / With two collateral stems sprung from one root"), but it is *sexual* imagery in either case, *ex*pressed in marriage and *re*pressed in the love that binds brother and sister.

His own discretion will not allow Wordsworth to say more exactly what he is analyzing here, the "one root" that ties together sister and brother. But what he refers to as the sickness, illustrated by a child around its mother's neck, is the child's love-hate relationship with its parents, a sickness well demonstrated by the problems of Mary Lamb. The Lambs represent fears and anxieties which Wordsworth has the courage to confront in his own self-analysis and which he wants to heal by this poem's analysis of the truth. The love of Charles and Mary Lamb for one another is tragic only because they had to live out in reality the fantasy of children, a desire to kill the parents. They also had to live out in reality the complementary fantasy of incestuous desire for parents. Wordsworth suggests in his poem of "truth" that Mary *became* her mother to her brother, who must have been in her childish and psychotic view a substitute ("recompense") for her father (whom she also tried to kill).

It is a sordid tale which Wordsworth does not want to elaborate, but if he is to say something truthful about Charles Lamb, he must approach the horror of Lamb's life as well as the sweet gentleness of it. The civilized culture of both Mary and Charles Lamb may stand as a paradox only to those who cannot appreciate the psychological facts of sublimation and repression, as well as the compensation. Their quiet lives, purchased at great expense of horrors repressed, were pursued in "dual loneliness" because they were two lonely persons living together. They therefore exemplify the radical loneliness of life in the midst of social amenities. Wordsworth prefers, however, to emphasize their achievements of discipline in the face of horror, their struggles to be civilized when so much mad fury had erupted to threaten that civilization. Mary Lamb exemplifies the terror of the child taking possession of the adult, but her charm and achievements in culture were testaments as well that civilization is a necessary acquisition for a mind to become healthy.

Civilization, however, is not so much an acquisition as an achievement. Friendship is a sign of progress toward civilization because it is a sublimation of instincts which would otherwise be exhausted upon objects of primary desire or destruction. The friendship between Charles Lamb and his sister was not fully "civilized" because it could not be completely sublimated. However disciplined their affection for one another, they could not deny the identity of their shared fantasy, of their single derivation. Wordsworth senses the awkwardness of that strange and troubling relationship even as he analyzes it for its truth. He counsels the therapy of deep analysis ("the remembrance of foregone distress") to defend against "the worse fear of future ill," but this is no easy task and it is no certain relief from the pains of separation. On the occasion of his own separation from his friend Walter Scott, in the autumn of 1831, he had also counselled a return of the self into its past as the best way to gather strength for confronting reality. His poem "Yarrow Revisited" sounds like the earlier Wordsworth who could draw strength from revisiting scenes of earlier experience, because here he makes a memorial from a memory of happy hours and thereby stands strong against the pain of having to bid his friend farewell—

perhaps never to see him again.

Wordsworth encourages his friend to look forward to the place of his destination, Italy, with all its classical beauties. Scott should look forward by looking back; the place in his future is the past of classical beauty. Therefore, Wordsworth suggests a way of triumph for the flagging spirit, when "classic Fancy" may be linked with "native Fancy" to "preserve thy heart from sinking." "Mighty Nature's self" has no human meaning without the help of "the poetic voice." What continues, then, is not so important as what is adjusted to changing needs. Nature is always the same and nature is always disappointing. Wordsworth says he has known this since he first looked upon Yarrow. His integrity, now as then, depends upon his unwillingness to surrender his dreams, his capacity to link past ("classic Fancy") with the past ("native Fancy"). To fit the individual experience into the larger scheme, or pattern, of the racial past of European civilization is to find the strength of mind that is necessary to endure shocks of separation from nature and from time itself. What is past is the dependence of the mind upon nature's accidents, of the child upon the parent. Wordsworth has been on this "border" several times in the progress of his life; in fact, "now" is always a border, though not so much between the past and the future as between different *kinds* of past.

Contentment in the face of constant change and dislocation is possible for one who has learned how to reconcile or blend those two kinds of past, represented by classic fancy and native fancy. Thoughts once centered in nature must be freed from their bondage to the illusion of permanence, a symptom of mental fixation to any kind of perception, whether infantile or animal. The changing lights of perception, represented in the last stanza of this poem as "dream-light," "common sunshine," and "memory's shadowy moonshine," are types of perception which must be made subordinate to the mind always conscious of its acts of perception. Poetry is the product of that action, a training "for hope and calm enjoyment," because it is the "voice / That hourly speaks within us" to link the individual with society, with tradition and civilization. The importance of this link (only possible through conscious processes such as art performs) is a value which Wordsworth explained in 1844 when he fought against efforts to bring railroads into the Lake Country: "features of nature cannot, in their finer relations to the human mind, be comprehended, or even very imperfectly conceived, without processes of culture or opportunities of observation in some degree habitual."

Trying to force nature upon people as an object of beauty is "treating them like children." The main point is not that nature has to be preserved, but that human integrity must be respected: the "true dignity of the species" lies "in a just proportion between actions governed by a man's own inclinations and those of other men." "Personal independence" is the goal of art and culture, as it is the goal of psychoanalysis. It can be achieved only through a conscious balance of ever changing claims against the individual. Nature constantly threatens to spread its shadows over "our inward prospect," but it cannot completely annihilate the mind in its depths (in "the soul's deep valley"). "Independence" is a term of painful relativity, a term of boundaries—between nature ("reality"), between persons, between forces within the mind itself. It is a term for the transformation of things into values, of past into present, and instincts into art.

# CHAPTER FOURTEEN:

## Father of the Man

What is conservative about Wordsworth's last poems is their contentment with an alliance that changes the present into the past. In one of his last compositions, Freud described the super-ego in these terms:

> Thus the super-ego takes up a kind of intermediate position between the id and the external world; it unites in itself the influences of the present and the past. In the establishment of the super-ego we have before us, as it were, an example of the way in which the present is changed into the past.

Submission to the authority of the super-ego is a way of maintaining control over the passage of time, which will register itself as continuous change and as a continuous threat to integrity of self and society. The present may become the past in the helpless way of natural disintegration, or it may do so in the way of tradition, i.e., adding to the building of something: self, art, history as knowledge, or government as a pattern/mechanism of defense and survival. There is no future except as a projection of wishes or fears, and there are no fears more threatening to identity than fears of separation and alienation. To be thrown for-

ward into a future that has no connection with the past is
to be orphaned by history and rejected by culture.

Wordsworth's last poems are defenses against such dis-
connections. They draw upon ideas of authority and order
to maintain a continuity of identity. They may seem to
convert all time into past-time, but they do so in order to
prevent the ego from losing itself in an ever-present
"now," with disorienting loss of directions. To be only in
the present, only in relationship with the external world, is
to be lost as a child cast out into the wilderness. On the
other hand, to be only in the past of one's self is to be in
a prison of ignorance, victimized by the very drives which
require direction: this is the *organic* past, the realm of the
id.

The past which comes into being through establishment
of the super-ego is "more than anything the *cultural*
past." It is a repetition of the parents' experience of time;
it is always being re-experienced as an after-experience.
The ego knows its experience as "an after-experience;" the
super-ego is by its very nature only the after-experience itself. To yield completely to the authority of the super-ego
would be to lose consciousness of the self as an individual
with personal history and with a sense of the present. The
super-ego is infinitely regressive, eternally echoing one parent in devouring relationship after another.

*CONTENTMENT* is the ego turning time-present into
time-past, converting external reality into individual past
through cultural past. Wordsworth's late poems aim for
this contentment of ego, as in "Yarrow Revisited," which
links a present (ominous) reality of individual experiences
with cultural experiences of what it calls "classic Fancy."
The main problem in this poem was to find a way to compensate for an inadequacy of nature to heal human
wounds, and also for the inadequacy of individual memories to lift the mind to discover new grounds of comfort.

The resolution is found in an idea of the past as expressed by poetry itself. Poetry is the voice of the past, of all human experience as shaped and reshaped in continued and repeated after-experience.

Poetry is the ego in its strength, in its health of balance and harmony, and poetry is always in the present because it unites the two kinds of past, the individual and the cultural. No other art is as therapeutic as the art of language, because no other art is made out of consciousness itself. Poetry is the best hope for humankind to realize its potential for being: this is a sufficient cause for its continuity. When, therefore, Wordsworth writes of discipline and obedience in such poems as "Humanity," he is writing about the importance of learning to draw strength from the past to serve the present, just as a child does when it identifies with a parent in the process of building up the super-ego.

The poet is Jacob in "Humanity," presenting a dream of power to ascend and descend without loss of self-control. If all could share in this dream, presumably through this poem itself, then all might through their participation make "the great Vision." It counsels individuals to submit, to close their restless eyes, to relax, to sink, and to find release from pains of resistance and suffering in an unfeeling world. There would be no need to resist and suffer the unnecessary (and unnatural) gains of political and economic oppression if *all* persons, *including* authorities in positions of responsibility, would "bow down before the naked sense / Of the great Vision." Men of power do not "live at ease with self-restraint" and they pass on their disease to those whose lives they repress. Wordsworth does not counsel submission to political authority as an expediency for survival. Indeed he admonishes those very authorities for their failure of discipline, failure of vision.

Leaders who serve merely the present and enforce their authority upon those who depend upon them for leadership are themselves burdens. They are a weight to be borne by people of conscience, like the artists; they are little more than cogs in the machine of nature which they exploit as an ever-present "now." Leaders without a vision of the cultural past, without a blending of high and low, merely urge "on the vast machine / Of sleepless Labour, 'mid whose dizzy wheels / The Power least prized is that which thinks and feels." Wordsworth's poem is an indictment of those captains of industry who have bound themselves to the eternal present in their exploitation of nature, including exploitation of human beings as "property" to be manipulated for immediate gratifications. These are the forces which have made the pleasure principle "an Idol, falsely called 'the Wealth / Of Nations.'" Reality has become little more than "sleepless Labour" and "dizzy wheels." "Power" has *become* what it wants—mere immediate gratification.

Wordsworth calls for a sense of responsibility shared by all. This can be acquired by submission to the discipline of art, which draws from sacred springs of the past a human power that reflects "the poetry of things," restoring "things" to their proper identities. This means primarily restoration of people from the category of things (merely sleepless labor and property), to their individual integrity. Poetry can put the smallest as well as the largest item of experience into the rightness of affection. It illustrates the truth in danger of being forgotten by people on the boundary of an age about to be cut adrift from its cultural heritage: everything that exists, from the lowest to the highest, *is* only because "Infinite Power" makes it so. A respect for the power in "the lowliest flower" is as much a respect for "infinite Power" as might be the respect due the "righteous Gods" themselves. The discipline Wordsworth advocates in his art is the discipline to submit the enormity of one's desires and fears to the lowliest of another's being.

"Submissive will" is a phrase of discipline in one of his

most vigorous poems of his late years, "The Warning."
The vigor is a mark of the poem's aggressive tone, in a
Jeremiad that even Wordsworth believed to be unusually
strong. In his 1835 *Postscript* he explains that this poem
was written because "the Author could not help writing
it." It was published because the "time is surely not passed
away when such a warning could be of least service to any
portion of his Countrymen." He explains that "recent
events have intimately touched his affections, and thrown
him back upon sensations akin to those he was troubled
with in an early period of his life." Until recently, after the
"deliverance" from Buonaparte's tyranny, "the course of
public events was of a less exciting, & therefore of a less
poetic character," by which he means that events until recently have not been "so discordant in their elements."
But in the opening years of the fourth decade public affairs raise the threat of old chaos, and the poet is thrown
back to the discordant times of his youth. He feels a return of repressed fears, rising to meet the public events
that summon those fears. Drawing upon his personal experience of witnessing the breakup of Europe, Wordsworth
warns people of these later times not to repeat the errors
of the past.

"The Warning" itself is a curious mixture of paternal
tenderness toward a sleeping infant and paternal wrath
against the mob, addressed as if the mob were a horde of
disobedient sons. The image used to teach the poet's lesson suggests that "civic strife" can be prevented or controlled only if citizens will learn "the beauty of omniscient
care," represented by "the sleeping pair" of mother and
infant—the image which opens and closes the poem. Citizens of the state are children to their father in this poem,
just as they are described in the 1835 *Postscript,* where
Wordsworth stresses the responsibility of the state to its
citizens (to make the main point that the poor must be
cared for when they cannot find gainful employment):

"may we not still contend for the duty of a christian government standing *in loco parentis* towards all its subjects?"
He argues that people are attached by strong ties to their
country, which they think of "as an indulgent parent, to
whose arms, even they who have been imprudent and un-
deserving may, like the prodigal son, betake themselves,
without fear of being rejected." "The Warning" is addressed to citizens, whereas the *Postscript* is addressed to
administrators of government, and so the emphasis shifts
from responsibilities of the state to responsibilities of citizens, but in both the relationship is filial and paternal.
"Individual dignity" is the value to be cherished by all in
the maintenance of government.

"The Warning" sounds cranky at times, breaking
through a surface of contentment which marks most of
Wordsworth's later poetry. It draws, however, upon controlled fears, converting ambivalent feelings toward parents
into a virtue of political force. The poem is moralistic in
tone and tends to be didactic in its genre of the prophetic
Jeremiad, but it is Wordsworthian because it is compas-
sionate and domestic in focus. It is realistic in its insistence
that public events cannot be separated from private experience; it implies a social psychology that depends upon
family relationships for form and dynamics. A major principle in the poem is the principle of security, the sense of
safety that every individual ego strives for, though not at
the cost of withdrawal; otherwise, one might think that
private experience *could* be kept separate from public
events. There is a terrain of mutual responsibility, a nexus
of interconnections which extend from the self to the family, from the family to the state, and from the state to history and God. All are necessary for the maintenance of
whatever fragile order can be preserved against crushing
tyrannies of uncontrolled passions and narrow-minded ideologies.

Because he insists upon the value of order as fundamental to the hope for liberty, Wordsworth titles his sonnets (most of) which were written on the occasion of the Reform Bill of 1832 *Sonnets Dedicated to Liberty and Order.* While he may sympathize with those who fret beneath unjust administration of laws and who suffer because of unequal distribution of goods, he is wary of the consequences for those same people who might be misled by visionary hopes and illusory dreams. He has always been able to sympathize with the urge to transcendental vision, but he has also usually been suspicious of that urge as a denial of reality and human content. Those who suffer from political tyranny or economic poverty may not expect to leap instantly from their sufferings into a large contentment, if they attempt to reach their goal by means of rebellion against the very order which protects them from chaos. Order may be expanded and extended throughout nature or mind, but it may not be violated without risk to sanity and life itself. Like children who may chafe that they may not gratify their instincts immediately and without deference to the authority of their parents, citizens of a state, regardless of their social or economic status, may be discontent when they are not allowed means for uninhibited satisfaction of wants and needs. Also like children, citizens must respect the authority of the reality principle as a force with the power to destroy. It is also a force with the power to satisfy, if it is dealt with as a complicated balance of multiple claims (which makes it mysterious and awesome). This reality is, at its nuclear centre of human experience, the authority of parents, and it has its cultural equivalent in the nation (or the state) as mother and in history (or time) as father.

Growth and maturation is possible only within the confines of order, a balance between pleasure and reality, instincts and conscience, passions and repentance. Since each generation must be trained to take the place of its predecessors, each generation is doomed to experience much discontent, because each must submit to the authority of prior power in order merely to survive. This requires an internalizing of anger and envy, which may be transformed into principles of self-discipline at the same time they are painful and necessary. Thus Wordsworth says every generation is "locked in our world's embrace through weal and woe," caught up in the love-hate processes of life itself:

> As leaves are to the tree whereon they grow
> And wither, every human generation
> Is to the Being of a might nation,
> Locked in our world's embrace through weal and woe;
> Thought that should teach the zealot to forego
> Rash schemes, to abjure all selfish agitation,
> And seek through noiseless pains and moderation
> The unblemished good they only can bestow.

Noisy pain is understandable in infants and children, but adults should symbolize their maturity of self-discipline through a silent suffering. Noisy outcries will invite noisy reactions, maybe even punishments, that produce "social havoc."

One must live in this life according to the rule of this life. This is acceptance of the reality principle. Discussing issues of reform in the Church, he insists in his 1835 *Postscript* that "our sphere of duty is upon earth," where ministers of the Gospel themselves "should be versed in the knowledge of existing facts, and be accustomed to a wide range of social experience." As children of the earth and heirs of time, all persons must understand "the relations of impure and conflicting things to each other," putting off the hopes of apocalypse as pointing only "to the purity and peace of a future world." The *Sonnets Dedicated to Liberty and Order* appeal for all to put understanding before dreaming, to put the past before the future, and to secure order as the necessary condition for liberty. Respecting the authority of history and nature, all may realize the same truth together and "feel for all, as brother Men!" All must internalize their aggressiveness toward their father(s) and accept their identities as the result of a shared subordination to parental authority:

> Let thy scope
> Be one fixed mind for all; thy rights approve
> To thy own conscience gradually renewed;
> Learn to make Time the father of wise Hope;
> Then trust thy cause to the arm of Fortitude,
> The light of Knowledge, and the warmth of Love.

As a fraternity that respects the authority of the father, they may exercise their rights as heirs to that authority, and they may discover genuine liberty "through impartial law" and "self-sacrifice."

*THE FIRST OF THE Sonnets Dedicated to Liberty and Order* concludes with a note of admonishment to those who would fly like Icarus "on presumptuous wing." When he criticizes those who cry that "'Knowledge will save me from the threatened woe,'" Wordsworth sounds less Romantic than Classical, less confident than resigned, less content than anxious. But his point is better taken as a challenge to find in mere humanity sufficient cause for meaning. Mere humanity is trivial only to those whose definitions have become so inflated that they have lost all shape, or have been so reduced to some fixed, mathematical scale that they have disappeared into the industrialized landscape of machines and things. He was fearful that the minds of his readers might take on the shapelessness of abstractions (as in political slogans hearkening back to the "rights of man") or that they might be locked into the quantified machinery of utilitarians. The kind of knowledge he criticizes is that which, as he says in some epi-

grammatic verses not published until 1885 ("To The Utilitarians"), makes "Fact" into "imagination's Lord." He
bemoans anyone's thinking that such subservience to facts
could be, paradoxically, redemptive: "Not *thus*," he exclaims, "can Knowledge elevate / Our Nature from her
fallen state."

The "economic rage" of the Utilitarians is one of the
spectres threatening to disturb his repose and contentment. It is a serious threat because it not only promises
more than it can deliver, it also invites one to believe that
health and happiness are products of environmental controls more than individual responsibility for control of individual consciousness. Many events in Wordsworth's late
years combine to challenge his peace of mind. These include the deaths of friends and relatives, troubling doubts
that his sons will be independent and happy, the failure of
Dorothy's mental powers, and his own occasional ill
health. These personal causes for unhappiness were private
intensifications of the public cultural issues repeatedly addressed in his writing. Therefore his poems of these late
years are outcries by the man protesting against the indignities of old age, at the same time they are affirmations of
a strength of mind that will not yield to those indignities.

Wordsworth composed several poems of what could be
called "reorganization." He reviews his relationship with
nature and with his art, emphasizing in each instance a
restless, impatient concern with mutability and change. He
shifts his focus from the energies of motion and activity in
nature, from the processes of participation in art, to the
"mute repose" in nature and to the moral piety of art. He
combines his observations of nature with his review of his
art: these together are expressions of self-examination—
made newly objective and given new form. This occurs in
"Gold and Silver Fishes in a Vase," an otherwise minor
piece of writing. It shows the dangers his imagination
courts in its increasing tendency to subordinate itself to

the ends of conscience, the "sovereign voice" of his super-ego.

Wordsworth can, however, still create feelings of playful activity, spontaneous vitality in such poems as "This Lawn, a carpet all alive," with its dance of shadows across the landscape, its stir of breeze and tide, and its medley of boreal lights. Still, these scenes are merely "emblems" of "strenuous idleness," an oxymoron more apt to describe a mind imprisoned by its own futile strivings to escape repressive authority than it is to describe the processes of nature—"Worldliness revelling in the fields." Each of the first two stanzas supplies images for scenes of diminishing activity: the first ends with the word "idleness," and the second opens with a refrain of "Less . . . less." To condemn this as only so much "eager strife" and "ceaseless play," mere shadows that draw attention from "the genuine life" which "grows / Unheeded" in the grass beneath—this is to turn from life to death, with its "mute repose," however much the poet thinks the undramatic grass provides a better index to genuine life. The directions of the poem are downwards, from more to less, from the dynamic to the static. Like the "gold and silver fishes in a vase," the silent grass is fixed in expression and secures its meaning ("repose") at great cost—muteness (surely ominous for a poet).

Sometimes when he wants to celebrate the *changes* of nature rather than the permanence, or the signs of its repose, Wordsworth will turn them into defenses against pain rather than celebrations of joy or pleasure. In the little poem he calls "Thoughts on the Seasons," he describes springtime, not as the coming of new life but rather as the "escape" from pain, "from every hurtful blast." Even though he hastens to describe May as sprightly and the loveliest of the springtime months, he emphasizes her status as the "last" and he sees her as his own "promise of escape." This is disappointing, but it is Wordsworth's way of forcing to his uses the fears of separations. His sense of debt makes its way through to a conscious statement even here, where the earth seems to repay the labors of man with a harvest of gold in the autumn season. The voice of authority that Wordsworth has so often before exploited for beautiful purposes here threatens to make his art into propaganda of religious fantasies.

Knowing its dangers, he makes a little drama of the tendency to write such poetry in "The Primrose of the Rock," which may be taken as a turning point for his style of old age. Here he reviews his experience of many years before, when he saw a primrose tuft hugging onto the sides of a high, though precariously perched, rock. When he first saw it, he moralized it as "a lasting link in Nature's chain," describing how the flowers live by "faith" in their stems, their roots, the rock itself, and the earth beneath the rock. He even celebrated the constancy of the earth in its god-given spherical track. But now he offers an apology for having been so exuberant in his mechanical analysis of natural piety. His enthusiasm he explains as the product of environment ("But air breathed soft that day"), and his song was softly breathed. An "after-lay" he proceeds to deliver in four more stanzas,, to balance the first four of the earlier song, but this "after-lay" is even more didactic and moralistic than the first. These last four stanzas are defenses against "tremblings that reprove / Our vernal tendencies to hope." He reproves himself for his earlier song of interpretation, because it had pretended to find solace in the naturalistic cycle of life as represented by the interdependent parts of the primrose, the rock, the earth, and the springtime rebirths of old fibers. Now, he insists, there can be no help from nature when one is confronted by wan disease, sorrow bent over hopeless dust, and withered age. Instead, imagination must translate itself into a new myth, which ironically the poet describes as "eternal summer." This is one of Wordsworth's most blatant poems of transcendence, proposing a "faith that elevates" and "makes each soul a separate heaven."

By making his errors of interpretation themselves the subject of his poem, Wordsworth objectifies for analysis what constitutes in other poems a symptom of resistance. The source of the resistance is the super-ego, or when it is conscious, the conscience, which makes the poet feel guilty for having made so much of importance from this relationships with nature—a guilt which he can overcome only if he can make it conscious, as he does in this poem. His has been a guilt of misinterpretation as well as of obligation, heavy burdens to bear when he attempts to exercise his being in a free and balanced manner. "The Primrose of the Rock" marks another boundary in his lengthening career. It contains elements of the younger Wordsworth, indebted to his mother Nature, clinging to her like the "living rock" celebrated in the poem; it also points to what the older Wordsworth could have become even more than he did, submitting to the restricting authority of God the Father, who "upholds them all." But what is healthy about the poem, and what rescues the speaker from an imbalance of either extreme, is the middle stanza: it holds to a center of consciousness as the source of control. As an extreme of interpretation by the reader, the poem enacts the mind itself, identifying with the primrose and the rock as sources of natural instinct, then transcending those instincts in an abstracting process of sublimating passions under the aegis of a harsh super-ego: he "turned the thistles of a curse / To types beneficent." But at the center is the ego, looking back in order to correct fantasies and making projections in order to satisfy conscience.

The healthy mind must serve several masters, sometimes seeming to be led by what it is charged to lead itself. Wordsworth tries, as ego, to adjust to a changing world of reality, both within and without. He must catch himself occasionally, or he will yield too readily to the harsh task-master his conscience would make of him, and so he devises poetic strategies for keeping that from happening. It is no surprise that he should have to battle against sternness as the strongest element of his mind, for that seems always to have been the inclination of his character (as he admitted in his lyric "To a Butterfly," in 1802, beginning "Stay near me"). This aggressive streak, which he recognizes as an identification with his father (even as a defense against his father), sometimes makes itself known as a violation, or a threat of violation, against nature. If, then, he can put this before himself as a subject of his poems, inviting readers to see it with him, he thereby makes it conscious and subject to control. From his earliest poetry to his last, Wordsworth strives to outwit his super-ego and the death it constantly threatens.

In one of the oddest poems of his late career, however, he pays tribute to a power within the mind which not only moves independently of the will but sometimes seems to control both will and consciousness. The poem is "Presentiments." It acknowledges the presence of an "Instinct" which he once might have called "Imagination." When he says that it was the cause for mysterious tears and sighs he experienced "in early days," Wordsworth refers to experiences he had identified as signals of imagination at work even when he knew it not. To say that such tears and sighs "seemed fatherless," then, not only ties "presentiments" with "imagination" (which also seemed fatherless to him when he named it is *Prelude* VI), but it also continues his tendency to link his imaginative powers with his orphanage. This he had done, more remotely and more powerfully, in the "Ode: Intimations of Immortality," when he used the metaphors of stepmothers and lost homes; here in his old age he turns the thought in a new direction, or perhaps he merely recognizes more clearly what he had suspected as the source for his power of making—the need to compensate for losses, to build substitutions, to punish himself and others for those losses. "Presentiments" are heaven-born in the psychological sense that they derive from a prior state of being, from as far back as infancy itself, and they "shun the touch / Of vulgar sense" because they are manifestations of that same instinct which he had earlier described as "obstinate questionings / Of sense and outward things" in the Intimations Ode: they are elements of narcissistic libido, drawing the self back into itself. Experienced in old age, they are in the control of conscience or super-ego: "the bosom-weight, your stubborn gift, / That no philosophy can lift, / Shall vanish, if ye please, / Like morning mist."

The main functions of presentiments are admonitory, judgmental, and sometimes even punitive. They "teach us to beware," and to "foretaste the springs / Of bitter contraries"; they reprove, and they are a test. They operate in children and in the childhood of culture ("the cradled Child" and "the naked Indian of the wild"). They move through whole nations, as when "an exulting Nation's hope" grows too large for reality, it is "startled and made wise" by bitter contraries. All of these functions have been served by Wordsworth through his poetry, and to the extent that he has been moved by emotion, imagination, or instinct, he has been moved by these "presentiments." To serve this force within himself is, he now believes, his main duty as a poet. Being able to obey his heart, he is being faithful to his identity as he has been able to know it from childhood. But now, paradoxically he *chooses* to obey what once he might have resisted and nevertheless might have been forced to serve against his will. Here he may consciously serve an unconscious power, which he can know only as well as he can make himself a voice for "the moral Muse." The truth which his moral muse can lay bare is this paradox of the mind, which Wordsworth has always known in his greatest poetry, that consciousness owes its being to forces of unconscious origin; these forces may be "higher, sometimes humbler, guides" to the ego, but they are *instincts* nevertheless, and they are ever present even "when lights of reason fail." Better, then, to know they will exist than to deny them as fictions of illusions. Otherwise, they will create unbearable anxieties and terrors for punishments, which are "unwelcome insights" to be sure, but truth nevertheless. Like the father who has been lost, presentiments are voices of authority which can protect or punish the needful ego.

Wordsworth is as sensitive to reader response as he has ever been in his career. He now writes more poems about the rhetorical and moral functions of poetry, and this makes him sound more tendentious and deliberative than his readers may like. (It causes him sometimes to become the kind of poet that Keats disparages, one who "bullies" the reader "into a certain Philosophy" and if it fails, "seems to put its hand in its breeches pocket.") This would surely dismay Wordsworth, for he wishes more than anything to secure his readers' confidence in his effort to "touch them through the Poet's pen" (as he puts it in some verses of 1841, "Though Pulpits and the Desk May Fail"). He certainly does not want to separate his readers from himself, as he says can be done with a single word— such as the one he once saw engraved upon "A Gravestone Upon the Floor in the Cloisters of Worcester Cathedral." That word, *misserimus,* was but a "solitary word," but is did "separate / From all, and cast a cloud around the fate" of its author. As much as he was interested in tombstone poetry, he did not want his own to be merely a monument to his separate identity. Such a poem would have interested Wordsworth if for no other reason than that he was intrigued with the connections between art and death, but it was a particularly keen concern of his late years that his poetry live and be therapeutic.

In "The Gleaner," which invites comparison with the

earlier "Solitary Reaper," he concentrates on a single detail of the picture he describes (changing the mode of imaginative response form the early poem's sound to this later poem's sight). He now represents the lure of the scene (itself contained by art) as a beguiling "whisper" that invites the "captive mind" of the audience to lose itself in "sweet illusion." Most of the poem is a lingering over this seductive power of art to transport the spectator into an idle search for "long-lost bowers." But, in the turn on the main point of the poem, one particular detail halts the regressive movement of the idling imagination, because the damsel in the picture is moving through corn, not flowers. The picture is no invitation to dally amidst loveliness: rather, it is a call to "Life's daily tasks," and its whisper turns into an "utterance" that the poet interprets as "the prayer / That asks for daily bread." The last stanza is, therefore, another instance of Wordsworth's tendency to throw up defenses in his art, and this particular defense is typical of his later concerns: to emphasize the utility of art, even though he has held onto some of his aesthetic integrity by devoting most of the poem to a loving contemplation of the picture's beauty.

To approach his reader with a palpable moral is perhaps his tendency, the tendency of an ego driven by conscience, but Wordsworth does not take easily to this mode of expression. He protests in another poem that "more ambitious Poets" may try "to take the heart / By storm," but he "would rather win its way / With gentle violence." This statement is interesting for its further discrimination: "more ambitious Poets" try to take the *heart,* but Wordsworth shifts, or enlarges, that term to describe his own goal, as he tries to win his way into "*minds.*" He needs the violence to overcome some kinds of resistances, but he needs the gentleness to secure trust. At least, as an artist of mental experience, he recognizes ambivalence as a characteristic of mind, and he recognizes that reading may itself be a mechanism of resistance.

To overcome that resistance, or maybe even to try to outwit reader distrust, he deliberately disarms himself occasionally to confront the reader nakedly. In a slight poem, "Valedictory Sonnet," which was intended to close out the volume of sonnets published in 1838, he plays with figurative language in a most cavalier way, comparing himself with a gardener who uses his tools (of art) to train "simple Nature" in the "flowers" of his poems. Then, he confesses his trickery: "but metaphor dismissed, and thanks apart, / Reader, farewell!" He throws up his disguises and invites trust in simplicity (echoing, perhaps, Sidney and other sonneteers), after having practiced some innocent deceptions. Wordsworth has always, however, been disarmingly simple, seeming to throw off metaphors even when he is using them, just as he uses unconscious resources to strengthen conscious controls. What is slightly alarming about a statement like this one, however, is that he seems so sensitive to the reader's distrust that he is willing to pretend to pretend. His own defensiveness is threatening to make him dishonest, which would doom him and his integrity as an artist.

*WHEN HE CALLS,* in "A Morning Exercise," upon the lark to "mount / To the last point of vision, and beyond," Wordsworth temporarily yields to a religious urge to transcend the troubles of flesh. Until his poem restores some balance in a halt of that flight which threatens to imitate "the wandering bird of paradise," he seems lost in the pleasures of his vision, a contemplated flight from mortality. Something in him wants to cease, to pause from what he calls "the struggle against Time" in "Elegiac Musings," a tribute to his friend Sir George Beaumont. The thought of death here raises the poet's feelings "and still we struggle." His mind is torn between an injunction to give in to death and its other instinct to build. For the artist, the two instincts may be resolved in the statement of the art itself, which, as an "emblem of our mortal doom," is a sublimation of both eros and destruction. The poem is an unburdening of grief; it is also a defense against the threat of death. It is, despite its tone of calm commemoration, a structure of defense; it protests against the silence and nothingness of his friend's disappearance. It is also a reconstruction of identity because it is a compromise with the expressed desire by Beaumont that there be no eulogy for him. Therefore, Wordsworth defends his words as expressions of loss, not praises for the lost one. But he also praises in the end when he says that Beaumont's virtues will be judged by God alone—in that mode of his now achieved "exalted nature." The poet's contemplation of "exalted nature" raises his feelings from "struggle" to "genuine" relief in a new identity as the Judge Himself. The poet reaches for a level of vision required for the large perspective which he attributes to the dead man, or to God Himself. At least, with the authority of a survivor, he challenges the dead man to deny the propriety of this tribute.

This authoritative and victorious tone marks several of Wordsworth's late works. It is a tone appropriate to the sovereign voice he has assumed in his identification with his father. It is a voice of judgment, but it is also a voice of appeal and sometimes of compassion. It may strike one as sometimes harsh and grating, sometimes condescending, and sometimes simply pompous. Its strength is in its self-assurance and self-command, tempered by an awareness of the struggle necessary to achieve and maintain itself, in such poems as the "Musing Near Aquapendente," "The Cuckoo at Laverna," and the *Sonnets Upon the Punishment of Death*. These poems speak with a voice of authority, but they also contain defenses against fear of death and loneliness, against loss of power and dissolution of identity. When this posture of old age overreaches itself, asserts itself in defiance of passion and threats of death, the voice of the poet cracks under the strain of its own discipline, in such poems as "Devotional Incitements" and "Upon Seeing a Coloured Drawing of the Bird of Paradise in an Album."

The last stanza of "Devotional Incitements" begins with this exclamation that

> the sanctities combined
> By art to unsensualise the mind
> Decay and languish; or, as creeds
> And humours change, are spurned like weeds.

That art should "unsensualise the mind" is a strange function to hope for from a poet who had insisted that poetry is "incapable to sustain her existence without sensuous incarnation." But if art will not or cannot unsensualise the mind because it refuses combination with the "solemn rites and awful forms" of religious sanctities, then perhaps "Kind Nature" will do the work of art. This paradoxical doctrine, characteristic of many of Wordsworth's poem throughout his career, is finally the main lesson of this truncated poem: that the imagery of nature, appealing to the senses, will conduct the mind from its bondage of flesh into a freedom of intellect. To the extent that nature triumphs, art must fail—and that is bad news for the poet. The artful shaping of his materials proves to be a resistance for his instincts, driving him to an identification with the dissolving, disintegrating processes of nature as they are "wafted in mute harmonies" to the skies. Art is the main defense against submission to "the eternal Will," the "divine monition that Nature yields."

"Upon Seeing a Coloured Drawing of the Bird of Paradise in an Album" is an admonition to the artist who presumed to try to represent the bird of paradise in a fixed attitude of repose. The opening lines reprimand anyone who might be rash enough to try such a thing as to say that buoyancy is the same as "fixed repose." While there is an element of tension here, elaborating the ironies of such arrogance, what is missing is the poet's tactful sense of self-criticism. Indeed, Wordsworth could be analyzing his own recent tendencies to "circumscribe this Shape in fixed repose," since he has written much poetry of a kind similar in function to the drawing which is criticized here. When he goes on to say what should be done in drawing a bird of paradise, he is in fact trying to do the thing himself; he only manages to moralize the picture as a search for God. He turns nature's creature into a "Bird of God" and advises that human happiness depends upon achieving an aim like that of this bird: "In never-wearied search of Paradise."

To join the speaker to "uphold our Spirits urged to kindred flight" would be to turn away from the flight of the morning lark, to turn from balance to a kind of fanatic "perpetual flight" (as in "A Morning Exercise"). The conclusion of "The Bird of Paradise" sounds like the conclusion to *The Prelude,* with its summons to celebrate the mind of man as "a thousand times more beautiful than the earth / On which he dwells." The later poem, however, focuses on the morally ugly, not the aesthetically beautiful: "Above the world that deems itself most wise / When most enslaved by gross realities!" Freedom here is not in an independent ego, balancing demands with a balanced consciousness; rather, freedom here is once again a flight, as in the earliest poems, though a flight that now knows its destination is god the Father. Life seems to be a learning how to "conform to the eternal Will" ("Devotional Incitements"), by learning to fly "on wings that fear no glance of God's pure sight" ("Bird of Paradise").

*"MUSINGS NEAR AQUAPENDENTE" MAY NOT BE* the "pearl" Wordsworth hoped it would be, "Fit to be

placed in that pure diadem" which "Wisdom wears." It is
nevertheless a fine poem. It is strong for the vigor of its
descriptions, and it is strong for the vitality of its
thoughts. It is a strong poem in a collection of strong
poems, the *Memorials of a Tour in Italy.* The "Musings"
were composed in 1841 to commemorate experiences of
1837; it is a poem of almost four hundred lines, blank
verse which invites comparison with the undisputedly great
"Tintern Abbey." Indeed, this late poem is a challenge by
the older Wordsworth to himself as a young poet in a
landscape of time much larger and much richer than he
knew it in 1798. Wordsworth concludes his musings on a
Miltonic note of multiple significance. He offers his art as
a balm for "vexed and disordered" times, modestly realizing that it may influence only "a scattered few." Its primary accomplishment, however, is to fortify the mind of
the speaker himself. At the end of his musings, he commits himself to a new life and a new hope: "Let us now /
Rise, and to-morrow greet magnificent Rome." All of the
preceding poem has been a preparation for completing the
journey to Rome, and that in turn is a trope for describing
the spiritual, intellectual life of the speaker.

Wordsworth reaches a summit of understanding and appreciation that not even ancient masters knew; he looks
back with ease because he stands on the height of a time
that is marked by acute self-consciousness. This boast of
the modern is also a threat to the mind, which needs always to remember that there is "no faculty within us
which the Soul / Can spare." The last sections of the
poem are bent upon restoring a model of harmony for
minds which presume too much wisdom because they are
heirs to many generations of knowledge. Wordsworth's
survey of Roman antiquities, through landscape and art, is
a recall of the past as a correction of modern emphases on
the present. History and Poetry may unite Reason with
Imagination to preserve lasting virtue in "bold fictions,"

but they are separately weak powers of creativity; they may be united by "high aims," which draw together powers of individual minds and cultural institutions through the operations of the past on the present. In a startling reversal of some of his earlier poems which call upon readers to rise, to mount toward goals beyond the ordinary human horizon, this poem calls for a descent, as it presumes to correct Christianity itself;

> And not disdaining
> Union with those primeval energies
> To virtue consecrate, stoop ye from your height
> Christian Traditions! at my Spirit's call
> Descend.

To reunite with depth, the past with the present, the instincts with the ideals, classical paganism with Christian idealism, even death with life—this is the task necessary for revitalizing jaded spirits of the old who surrender too often and too easily. It is also the task necessary for preventing modern culture from becoming a mockery of the healthy mind. Wordsworth accuses his time of being "a chilled age, most pitably shut out / From that which *is* and actuates, by forms, / Abstractions, and by lifeless fact to fact." It is not himself alone endangered by the narrowing frailties of old age—it is all who have the mixed blessing of living in the modern period of human history. Moderns make the mistake of believing themselves to be young and unique, when in fact they are the products of old age, drooping "as if bent on perishing."

Not only the secular life of modern culture is liable to the discomforts of a chilled age. In another of the poems from the *Memorials of a Tour in Italy,* "The Cuckoo at Laverna," Wordsworth focuses upon the chilly abstractness of the religious life. Indeed religious life was convicted of a death-like frigidity in the "Musings," but in that poem the point is subordinated to the major concern of consciousness and vision. In "The Cuckoo at Laverna," the speaker is surprised by joy, to borrow Wordsworth's own words from an earlier poem. He hears the cry of the Cuckoo, and he halts to strain in listening. It is a rare treat, not to have been expected so far from home. But of the sound the poet is certain, and his spirit rises to wheel in happiness with the wheeling music of the bird. This sensation of joyful movement repeats and renews the poet's youthful experiences of home. What happens to him at Laverna is a refreshening of his spirit, a new baptizing of his imagination through a raising of his instincts for pleasure. He is able to bid the bird farewell without anxiety, because he knows that the bird has awakened a quality in himself which will not disappear with the disappearance of the bird. Nature is still an occasion for self-knowledge, though it is not the knowledge itself. Wordsworth's real and enduring identification is made through human companionship, through relationships he best understands as sublimations of instincts stirred as by the music of this Cuckoo at Laverna.

THE "AUTOBIOGRAPHICAL MEMORANDA" he dictated to his nephew Christopher in November 1847 is a brief set of notes which focus upon his mother, her death, and the sad consequences to Wordsworth. He describes how he could remember his mother "in only some few situations": when she sent him off to say his catechism, when she chastised him for his having expected a reward after he observed "a woman doing penance in the church in a white sheet," and when she fell ill just before her death. These memories constitute a nagging unhealed wound in his conscious life. To the end he could not forgive her for her death. Nor could he forgive himself for being a "naughty" child. He expresses bitterness toward a certain friend for having put his mother up in London "in what used to be called 'a best bedroom.'" Here he blames this friend for causing his mother's mortal illness. Then he curtly explains that his father "never recovered his usual cheerfulness of mind after this loss, and died when I was in my fourteenth year." The conjunction of the two events, his mother's death and his father's depression leading unto his own death, although separated by some five-to-six years, is psychologically held in a cause-effect relationship by Wordsworth.

There are some curious things about his memories that hint at more curious feelings in his unconscious mind, such as the particular experience for which his mother reprimanded him. Observing "a woman doing penance in the church in a white sheet" could very well serve as a vehicle for his reconstructed feelings toward his mother herself. She perhaps should have done penance for her "sin" of early death and maybe even for having brought such a naughty child as Wordsworth into the world. The memory suggests that Wordsworth has projected upon a displaced image of his mother his own guilt feelings of desire for her. Apart from these unconscious feelings in this particular memory, his conscious memories are more expansive when he describes himself as a child for whom his mother had expressed some anxiety. She had once said that "the only one of her five children about whose future life she was anxious, was William; and he, she said, would be remarkable either for good or evil."

These are words which Wordsworth obviously has nursed throughout his long, and mainly successful, life—although probably not successful enough to satisfy his harsh super-ego that still punishes him with those words supposedly spoken by his mother long ago. That he had to agree with his mother's assessment is the main point of his next memories: while living with his maternal grandparents, he suffered in ways that adults find difficult to appreciate, and he suffered the indignities of "poor relations." Upon one such occasion, "some indignity having been put upon" him, he rushed to the attic where he intended to destroy himself, but, he says, "my heart failed." He was, he admits, "of a stiff, moody, and violent temper," having given his poor mother good reason to fear for his future. On another occasion, he challenged his brother to use their whips to "strike through that old lady's petticoat," referring to the portrait of a woman hanging on a wall of his grandfather's house.

These memories of guilt, violence against himself and violence against others (especially parental authority), are confessions of feelings that Wordsworth has always been free to make in his poetry, but not always so clearly associated with his parents and their deaths. He explains that his happy times were days spent reading: they were days when he felt most free of guilt and anger. "They were very happy ones, chiefly because I was left at liberty, then and in the vacations, to read whatever book I liked." He identifies his reading as an escape, and as an experience of fulfillment after so much "real" frustration. In *The Prelude* he says that he sought out nature as his consolation after the death of his mother, but to that he should have added, as he does in these autobiographical comments, that he also sought out the companionship of books. The books he found most to his taste were books of heroic travel and books of satire: "Fielding's works, Don Quixote, Gil Blas, and any part of Swift. . . . Gulliver's travels, and the Tale of the Tub, being both much to my taste." Any one of these works could have satisfied a young man's desire for using literature as a tool and a weapon, to make and to attack. His own art became more and more such a tool, and Wordsworth grew more willing to consider it a conscious tool of mental adaptation.

Art so used might become poetry as propaganda and preaching. In the years between 1839 and 1841 he composed a queer sonnet sequence, *Sonnets Upon the Punish-*

*ment of Death*. These fourteen sonnets make an argument for retaining the death penalty. They go over points quite familiar to anyone who has given this matter serious consideration. They call for sympathy from all readers, liberal and conservative alike, to consider not only the religious and moral arguments, but also the civil and political ones. These sonnets do not succeed at their argumentative task more than they could as prose, if their only function is to persuade readers to support laws that justify capital punishment. Even when they picture the moral misery of beings condemned to die, or to linger in wretched prisons, or even those marked as victims by criminals, the sonnets are not particularly effective as rhetoric. One of Wordsworth's favorite novelists, Fielding, could have done a better job— and did.

The *Sonnets Upon the Punishment of Death* are like a dream, nightmarish, and irrational, in their visual effects: strangely laden with the mysteries of God and death, powerful in their fascination with death and the punishment of death. The most startling event in the sonnets is an announcement at the end, in the opening lines of the last sonnet, that the poet himself is in chains: "The formal World relaxes her cold chain / For One who speaks in numbers." He is a prisoner along with those whose misery he has been describing. His life has been a labor that "beats / Against all barriers." He has come as a prisoner in chains down the same painful road which led to the Weeping Hill of the first sonnet.

There are not only a few special criminals who deserve the punishment of death. The speaker himself is such a criminal and, by implication, so is all humankind. All are brought to the special "spot" that opens the sequence, where they look toward the prison rising up "as if to lord over air." Here they stand, "blinded as tears fell in showers / Shed on their chains." Not only criminals under man's law must be punished; so must criminals under

God's law as well. The "brood of conscience" haunt and drive all people in a "restless walk" down the road where the State "plants well-measured terrors." Every being must walk this road, until each is "condemned alone within his cell" where "remorse / Stings to the quick." In this condition, the criminal in every mind calls out for the punishment it deserves, which is finally the only punishment that means very much—death itself. All other punishments have been merely preparations for this one. All life has been a practice in separations, to deal with the final separation which must come to all in the end, just as it came to all in the beginning. Because it must come to all, it must be just.

In these sonnets Wordsworth recognizes that the need for punishment by death is connected with feelings for parents, particularly for the father. He points to the Roman Consul who "doomed his sons to die." This man had plumbed the depths of political necessity and psychological reality; he knew that the "duty" he performed in the name of his nation's security was but the "surface" of a deeper reality: "Upon the surface of humanity, / He rested not; its depths his mind explored." The father's agony was obvious, but not so obvious was his pleasure masked as duty. Wordsworth concludes this sonnet with a strange observation that some who kill "pass sentence on themselves" and end by soliciting their own deaths as punishment. This is strange because the Roman father had ordered his sons' deaths, and so he was one of these who "by wilful act" took human life, leaving the reader to conclude that he therefore did "pass sentence on himself." If so, his sentence was in the murder of his own sons—a self-punishment (hence, his "agony").

Later Wordsworth describes the "wise Legislator" who copies "with awe the one Paternal mind," who is, "when most severe, oft most kind." Laws of punishment, as expressions of the Paternal mind, give "eternal life" to conscience, as the ninth sonnet explains. Capital punishment is the operation of conscience. It controls the will, the disobedient ego, of the body politic as the super-ego does the body of the individual. The state is to its citizens as the father is to his child. In this capacity, the law intends "to preclude or quell the strife / Of individual will, to elevate / The grovelling mind." Finally the obedient child, or the guilty ego, will love the punishment meted out by "Wisdom's heavenly Father."

The opening sonnet, to which the final one returns the reader, recreates a scene long familiar from Wordsworth's early poetry. It creates once again the bleak and dreary landscapes of Salisbury Plain, the lonely moor in *The Borderers,* and the strange "spots of time" from *The Prelude (s).* Here once again is a "bare eminence," a fear that binds, a menacing form that rises up to threaten and admonish the viewer. Wordsworth finds in yet another "Spot" a place of imaginative power, which paradoxically "might soothe in human breasts the sense of ill." If it can also "charm it out of memory," then it can do so without permanent effect, like the continuing need for analysis; the magic of the place is mainly in its power to chastise with the punishment of death, the only permanent cure for guilt and anxiety. Wordsworth can thus, looking into the face of death, dare to deal with inevitable punishment in terms that are psychologically and morally meaningful: if death must come, it must be deserved. When he asks in the fourth sonnet if it is possible that death is "the thing that ought / To be *most* dreaded?" he is also asking if *not* to be punished is even more to be dreaded. In a sonnet of 1828, about a son's care for his father's "last work on earth," Wordsworth speaks for all sons and fathers:

> Thence has it, with the Son, so strong a hold
> Upon his Father's memory, that his hands,
> Through reverence, touch it only to repair
> Its waste.

# BIBLIOGRAPHIES

## I

Unless otherwise indicated in the text, quotations from Wordsworth's writings are from *The Poetical Works of William Wordsworth,* ed. E. De Selincourt, in five volumes. Oxford: At The Clarendon Press. Vol. I, 1940; Vol. II, 1944; Vol. III, 2nd edition, with Helen Darbishire, 1954; Vol. IV, with Helen Darbishire, 1947; and Vol. V, with Helen Darbishire, 1949. *The Prose Works of William Wordsworth,* ed. W.J.B. Owen and Jane Worthington Smyser. 3 vols. Oxford: At The Clarendon Press, 1974.

Texts published in "The Cornell Wordsworth," General Editor, Stephen Parrish, are cited in appropriate bibliographies under names of their editors.

## II

### General Reference

Bateson, F.W. *Wordsworth: A Re-Interpretation.* London: Longman's Green, and Co., 1954.

Brisman, Leslie. *Milton's Poetry of Choice and Its Romantic Heirs.* Ithaca and London: Cornell University Press, 1973.

_____. *Romantic Origins.* Ithaca and London: Cornell University Press, 1978.

Brown, Norman O. *Life Against Death: The Psychoanalytic Meaning of History.* Middletown, Connecticut: Wesleyan University Press, 1959.

_____. *Love's Body*. New York: Random House, 1966.

Cooke, Michael G. *Acts of Inclusion: Studies Bearing on an Elementary Theory of Romanticism*. New Haven and London: Yale University Press, 1979.

Curtis, Jared. ed. *Poems, in Two Volumes, and Other Poems 1800-1807*. Ithaca and London: Cornell University Press, 1985.

Ellis, David. *Wordsworth, Freud and The Spots of Time: Interpretation in The Prelude*. Cambridge: Cambridge University Press, 1985.

Erikson, Erik. *Insight and Responsibility: Lectures on the Ethical Implications of Psychoanalytic Insight*. New York: W.W. Norton & Company, Inc., 1964.

Erikson, Erik. *Toys and Reasons: Stages In The Ritualization of Experience*. New York: W.W. Norton & Company, Inc., 1977.

_____. *Young Man Luther: A Study In Psychoanalysis and History*. New York: W.W. Norton & Company, Inc., 1958.

Freud, Anna. *The Ego and The Mechanisms of Defence*. London: The Hogarth Press, 1968. Originally published in German in 1936; English translation by Cecil Baines in 1937. Revised ed. First published in 1966.

Freud, Sigmund. *Beyond The Pleasure Principle* (1920). *The Complete Psychological Works of Sigmund Freud*. Standard Edition. Translated from the German under the General Editorship of James Strachey, In Collaboration with Anna Freud, Assisted by Alix Strachey and Alan Tyson. Vol. 18 (London: The Hogarth Press and The Institute of Psycho-Analysis), 7-64.

_____. *Civilization And Its Discontents* (1930). Standard Edition, Vol. 21, pp. 59-145.

_____. *The Ego and The Id* (1923). Standard Edition, Vol. 19, pp. 3-66.

_____. *Group Psychology and The Analysis of The Ego* (1921). Standard Edition, Vol. 18, pp. 67-143.

_____. *Inhibitions, Symptoms and Anxiety* (1926). Standard Edition, Vol. 20, pp. 75-174.

_____. *Introductory Lectures on Psychoanalysis* (1915-1917). Standard Edition, Vol. 15, 16.

_____. "Mourning and Melancholia" (1917). Standard Edition, Vol. 14, pp. 239-58.

_____. "On Narcissism" (1914). Standard Edition, Vol. 14, pp. 69-102.

_____. *The Question of Lay Analysis* (1926). Standard Edition, Vol. 20, pp. 179-258.

_____. *Totem and Taboo* (1913). Standard Edition, Vol. 13, pp. 1-161.

Friedman, Michael H. *The Making of a Tory Humanist: William Wordsworth and The Idea of Community*. New York: Columbia University Press,

1979.

Gill, Stephen. "'Affinities Preserved': Poetic Self-Reference in Wordsworth," *Studies in Romanticism,* 24 (Winter 1985), 531-49.

Hartman, Geoffrey H. *The Unremarkable Wordsworth.* Foreword by Donald G. Marshall. Theory and History of Literature, Vol. 34. Minneapolis: University of Minnesota Press, 1987.

Hartman, Geoffrey H. *Wordsworth's Poetry 1787-1814.* New Haven and London: Yale University Press, 1964 and 1971.

Johnston, Kenneth R. *Wordsworth and The Recluse.* New Haven and London: Yale University Press, 1984.

Jones, John. *The Egotistical Sublime: A History of Wordsworth's Imagination.* London: Chatto and Windus, 1954.

Knight, G. Wilson. *The Starlit Dome: Studies in The Poetry of Vision.* London: Oxford University Press, 1941.

Kris, Ernst. *Psychoanalytic Explorations in Art.* New York: International Universities Press, Inc., 1952.

Langbaum, Robert. "Wordsworth's Lyrical Characterizations," *Studies in Romanticism,* 21 (Fall 1982), 319-339.

Marcuse, Herbert. *Eros and Civilization: A Philosophical Inquiry Into Freud.* New York: Vintage Books, A Division of Random House, 1962. Originally published by The Beacon Press, 1955.

Onorato, Richard J. *The Character of The Poet: Wordsworth in The Prelude.* Princeton, N.J.: Princeton University Press, 1971.

Rieff, Philip. *Freud: The Mind of the Moralist.* Anchor Books. Garden City, New York: Doubleday & Company, Inc., 1959, 1961.

Sherry, Charles. "Wordsworth's Metaphors for Eternity: Appearance and Representation," *Studies in Romanticism,* 17 (Spring 1978), 193-213.

Trilling, Lionel. "The Fate of Pleasure: Wordsworth to Dostoevsky," *Romanticism Reconsidered,* ed. Northrop Frye. New York and London: Columbia University Press, 1963, pp. 73-106.

_____. *Freud and The Crisis of Our Culture.* Boston: The Beacon Press, 1955.

Ward, J.P. "Wordsworth and the Sociological Idea," *The Critical Quarterly,* 16 (Winter 1974), 331-55.

Wilson, Douglas B. "Wordsworth and the Uncanny: 'The Time is Always Present,'" *The Wordsworth Circle,* 16 (Spring 1985), 92-97.

Wordsworth, Jonathan. *William Wordsworth: The Borders of Vision.* Oxford: Clarendon Press, 1982.

III

*Special Reference*

Preface

Erlich, Avi. *Hamlet's Absent Father*. Princeton, New Jersey: Princeton University Press, 1977.

Hartman, Geoffrey H. "A Touching Compulsion," Ch. 2 in *The Unremarkable Wordsworth*, pp. 18-30. Originally published in *The Georgia Review*, 21 (Summer 1977).

Holland, Norman N. *Poems In Persons: An Introduction to The Psychoanalysis of Literature*. New York: W.W. Norton & Company, Inc., 1973.

_____. *Psychoanalysis and Shakespeare*. New York: McGraw-Hill Book Company, 1964, 1966.

McFarland, Thomas. "Wordsworth on Man, on Nature, and on Human Life," *Studies in Romanticism*, 21 (Winter 1982), 601-18.

Skura, Meredith Ann. *The Literary Use of the Psychoanalytic Process*. New Haven and London: Yale University Press, 1981.

CHAPTER ONE:
My Father's House:  Introduction

Bloom, Harold. *The Anxiety of Influence: A Theory of Poetry*. London, Oxford, New York: Oxford University Press, 1973.

_____. *Poetry and Repression: Revisionism From Blake to Stevens*. New Haven: Yale University Press, 1976.

_____. *The Visionary Company: A Reading of English Romantic Poetry*. Revised and enlarged edition. Ithaca & London: Cornell University Press, 1971.

DeMan, Paul. *Blindness and Insight: Essays in the Rhetoric of Contemporary Criticism*. New York: Oxford University Press, 1971.

Fenichel, Otto. *The Psychoanalytical Theory of Neurosis*. New York: W.W. Norton & Company, Inc., 1945.

Ferry, David. *Limits of Mortality: An Essay On Wordsworth's Major Poems*. Middletown: Wesleyan University Press, 1959.

Grob, Alan. "Wordsworth's *Nutting*," *Journal of English and Germanic Philology*, 61 (1962), 826-32.

Groom, Bernard. *The Unity of Wordsworth's Poetry*. New York: St. Martin's Press, 1966.

Hertz, Neil. *The End of the Line: Essays on Psychoanalysis and the Sublime*. New York: Columbia University Press, 1985.

Jackson, Geoffrey. "Nominal and Actual Audiences: Some Strategies of Communication in Wordsworth's Poetry," *The Wordsworth Circle*, 12 (Autumn 1981), 226-31.

Miller, J. Hillis. "Wordsworth," Chapter Two in *The Linguistic Moment: From Wordsworth To Stevens*. Princeton, N.J.: Princeton University Press, 1985.

Moorman, Mary. *William Wordsworth: A Biography*. Vol. One. *The Early Years, 1770-1803*. Oxford: Clarendon Press, 1957. Vol. Two. *The Later Years, 1803-1850*. Oxford: Clarendon Press, 1965.

Perkins, David. *Wordsworth and The Poetry of Sincerity*, especially Chapter VI, "Wordsworth and His Audience." Cambridge, Massachusetts: The Belknap Press of Harvard University Press, 1964.

Rieff, Philip. *The Triumph of the Therapeutic: Uses of Faith After Freud*. New York: Harper & Row, 1966.

Thomson, Douglass H., "Wordsworth's Lucy of 'Nutting,'" *Studies in Romanticism*, 18 (Summer 1979), 287-98.

## CHAPTER TWO:
## A Guilty Thing Surprised, 1791-1799

Bewell, Alan, "Introduction: *The Borderers*, A Forum," with Michael G. Cooke, *Studies in Romanticism*, 27 (Fall, 1988), 353-54.

Biggs, Murray, "Staging *The Borderers*: Dragging Romantic Drama Out of the Closet," *Studies in Romanticism*, 27 (Fall, 1988), 411-17.

Campbell, Oscar James, and Mueschke, Paul. "'Guilt and Sorrow': A Study in the Genesis of Wordsworth's Aesthetic," *Modern Philology*, 23 (1926), 293-306.

Carlson, Julie, "A New Stage For Romantic Drama," *Studies in Romanticism*, 27 (Fall, 1988), 419-27.

Cooke, Michael G., "Romanticism and the Paradox of Wholeness," *Studies in Romanticism*, 23 (Winter 1984), 435-453.

Douglas, Wallace W. *Wordsworth: The Construction of a Personality*. Kent, Ohio: Kent State University Press, 1968.

Freud, Sigmund. "Contributions to the Psychology of Love" (1910, 1912).

Standard Edition, Vol. 11, pp. 164-175, 179-190.

Gill, Stephen, ed. *The Salisbury Plain Poems of William Wordsworth*. The Cornell Wordsworth. Ithaca, New York: Cornell University Press, 1975.

Jewett, William, "Action in *The Borderers*," *Studies in Romanticism*, 27 (Fall 1988), 399-410.

Marshall, David. "The Eye-Witnesses of *The Borderers*," *Studies in Romanticism*, 27(Fall 1988), 391-98.

McFarland, Thomas. *Romanticism and the Forms of Ruin: Wordsworth, Coleridge, and Modalities of Fragmentation*. Princeton, New Jersey: Princeton University Press, 1981.

Osborn, Robert, ed. *The Borderers*. Includes "Fragment of the *Gothic Tale*" and "Argument for Suicide." The Cornell Wordsworth. Ithaca and London: Cornell University Press, 1982.

Parker, Reeve. "'In some sort seeing with my proper eyes': Wordsworth and the Spectacles of Paris," *Studies in Romanticism*, 27 (Fall 1988), 369-90.

Sperry, Willard L. *Wordsworth's Anti-Climax*. New York: Russell & Russell, 1966; reprinted from Harvard University Press, 1935.

Storch, R.F. "Wordsworth's *The Borderers*: The Poet as Anthropologist," *Journal of English Literary History*, 36 (June 1969), 340-60.

Trilling, Lionel. "Wordsworth and the Rabbis," *The Opposing Self: Nine Essays In Criticism*. New York: The Viking Press, 1955. pp. 118-150.

Whitaker, Thomas R. "Reading the Unreadable, Acting the Unactable," *Studies in Romanticism*, 27(Fall 1988), 355-67.

Woodman, Ross. "Milton's Satan in Wordsworth's 'Vale of Soul-making,'" *Studies in Romanticism*, 23 (Spring 1984), 3-30.

# CHAPTER THREE:
## Those First Affections, 1787-1800/1806

Averill, James, ed. *An Evening Walk*. The Cornell Wordsworth. Ithaca and London: Cornell University Press, 1982.

Birdsall, Eric, ed., with the assistance of Paul M. Zall. *Descriptive Sketches*. The Cornell Wordsworth. Ithaca and London: Cornell University Press, 1984.

Clarke, Bruce. "Wordsworth's Departed Swans: Sublimation and Sublimity in *Home at Grasmere*," *Studies in Romanticism*, 19 (Fall 1980), 355-74.

Dangerfield, Anthony. "'The Faded Plain': Memory and Experience in Wordsworth's *An Evening Walk*," *The Wordsworth Circle*, 17 (Summer 1986), 164-186.

Darlington, Beth, ed. *Home at Grasmere*. The Cornell Wordsworth. Ithaca and London: Cornell University Press, 1977.

Ferenczi, Sandor. *Thalassa: A Theory of Genitality*, trans. Henry Alden Bunker. New York: W.W. Norton & Company, 1968; first published in 1938.

Foster, Mark. "'Tintern Abbey' and Wordsworth's Scene of Writing," *Studies in Romanticism*, 25 (Spring 1986), 75-95.

Freud, Sigmund. "Formulations Regarding the Two Principles of Mental Functioning" (1911). Standard Edition, Vol. 12.

____. "Instincts and their Vicissitudes" (1915). Standard edition, Vol. 14, pp. 111-40.

Jump, Harriet. "'That Other Eye': Wordsworth's 1794 Revisions of *An Evening Walk*," *The Wordsworth Circle*, 17 (Summer 1986), 156-63.

Kroeber, Karl. "'Home at Grasmere': Ecological Holiness," PMLA, 89 (January 1974), 132-41.

Larkin, Peter. "The Secondary Wordsworth's First of Homes: *Home at Grasmere*," *The Wordsworth Circle*, 16 (Spring 1985), 106-13.

Matlak, Richard E. "Classical Argument and Romantic Persuasion in 'Tintern Abbey.'" *Studies in Romanticism*, 25 (Spring 1986), 97-129.

Nichols, Aston. "Towards 'Spots of Time': Visionary Dreariness in 'An Evening Walk,'" *The Wordsworth Circle*, 14 (Autumn 1983), 233-237.

Ramsey, Jonathan. "Seeing and Perceiving in Wordsworth's *An Evening Walk*," *Modern Language Quarterly*, 36 (December 1975), 376-89.

Sampson, David. "Wordsworth and the Poor: The Poetry of Survival," *Studies in Romanticism*, 23 (Spring 1984), 31-59.

Spector, Stephen J. "Wordsworth's Mirror Imagery and the Picturesque Tradition," *Journal of English Literary History*, 44 (Spring 1977), 85-107.

# CHAPTER FOUR:
## Indisputable Shapes, 1798-1804

Brownwich, David. "Wordsworth, Frost, Stevens and the Poetic Vocation," *Studies in Romanticism*, 21 (Spring 1982), 87-100.

Bushnell, John P. "'Where is the Lamb for a Burnt Offering?': Michael's Covenant and Sacrifice," *The Wordsworth Circle*, 12 (Autumn 1981), 246-52.

Freud, Sigmund. *New Introductory Lectures on Psycho-Analysis* (1933). Standard Edition, Vol. 22, pp. 3-182.

____. *The Psychopathology of Everyday Life* (1901). Standard Edition, Vol. 6.

Grob, Alan. "Process and Permanence in 'Resolution and Independence,'" *Journal of English Literary History*, 18 (1961), 89-100.

Halper, Sheldon. "*Michael:* Wordsworth's Pastoral of Common Man," *Notre Dame English Journal*, 8 (1982), 22-33.

Hartman, Geoffrey H. "Timely Utterance Once More," Ch. 10 in *The Unremarkable Wordsworth*, pp. 152-160.

Hinchliffe, Keith. "Wordsworth and the Kinds of Metaphor," *Studies in Romanticism*, 23 (Spring 1984), 81-100.

Manning, Peter J. "'My former thoughts returned': Wordsworth's *Resolution and Independence*," *The Wordsworth Circle*, 9 (Autumn 1978), 398-405.

_____. "Placing Poor Susan: Wordsworth and the New Historicism," *Studies in Romanticism*, 25 (Fall 1986), 351-69.

Matlak, Richard E. "Wordsworth's Lucy Poems in Psychobiographical Context," PMLA, 93 (January 1978), 46-65.

Perkins, David. *The Quest for Permanence: The Symbolism of Wordsworth, Shelley and Keats*. Cambridge, Massachusetts: Harvard University Press, 1959.

Robinson, Jeffrey C. "The Immortality Ode: Lionel Trilling and Helen Vendler," *The Wordsworth Circle*, 12 (Winter 1981), 64-70.

Trilling, Lionel. "Art and Neurosis," *The Liberal Imagination: Essays on Literature and Society*. Garden City, New York: Doubleday & Company, Inc., 1953. pp. 155-75. First published in 1945.

_____. "Freud and Literature," *The Liberal Imagination*, pp. 32-54. First published in 1940.

_____. "The Immortality Ode," *The Liberal Imagination*, pp. 125-54. First published in 1942.

Vendler, Helen. "Lionel Trilling and the *Immortality Ode*," *Salmagundi*, 41 (Spring 1978), 66-86.

Wiliams, Anne. "The *Intimations Ode:* Wordsworth's Fortunate Fall," *Romanticism Past and Present*, 5 (1981), 1-13.

# CHAPTER FIVE:
## The Child is Father, 1798-1806

Altieri, Charles. "Wordsworth's Wavering Balance: The Thematic Rhythm of *The Prelude*," *The Wordsworth Circle*, 4 (Autumn 1973), 226-40.

Bahti, Timothy. "Figures of Interpretation, the Interpretation of Figures: A Reading of Wordsworth's 'Dream of the Arab,'" *Studies in Romanticism*, 18 (Winter 1979), 601-27.

Bartlett, Brian. "'Inscrutable Workmanship': Music and Metaphors of Music in

*The Prelude* and *The Excursion,"* *The Wordsworth Circle,* 17 (Summer 1986), 175-80.

Bate, Walter Jackson. *John Keats.* Cambridge, Massachusetts: The Belknap Press of Harvard University Press, 1964.

Bernhardt-Kabisch, Ernest. "The Stone and the Shell: Wordsworth, Cataclysm, and the Myth of Glaucus," *Studies in Romanticism* 23 (Winter 1984), 455-90.

Brennan, Matthew C. "The 'ghastly figure moving at my side': The Discharged Soldier as Wordsworth's Shadow," *The Wordsworth Circle,* 18 (Winter 1987), 19-23.

_____. "The Light of Wordsworth's Desire for Darkness in *The Prelude,"* *Romanticism Past and Present,* 7 (Summer 1983), 27-40.

Chase, Cynthia. "The Accidents of Disfiguration: Limits to Literal and Rhetorical Reading in Book V of *The Prelude,"* *Studies in Romanticism,* 18 (Winter 1979), 547-65.

DeSelincourt, Ernest, ed. *The Prelude or Growth of a Poet's Mind.* 2nd ed. rev. by Helen Darbishire. Oxford: At The Clarendon Press, 1959.

Freud, Sigmund. "Family Romances" (1908). Standard Edition, Vol. 9, pp. 236-41.

_____. "Negation" (1925). Standard Edition, Vol. 19, 234-239.

Frosch, Thomas R. "Wordsworth's 'Beggars' and a Brief Instance of 'Writer's Block,'" *Studies in Romanticism,* 21 (Winter 1982), 619-36.

Fry, Paul H. "The Possession of the Sublime," *Studies in Romanticism,* 26 (Summer 1987), 187-207.

Galperin, William H. "'Desynonymizing' the Self in Wordsworth and Coleridge," *Studies in Romanticism,* 26 (Winter 1987), 513-26.

Haney, David P. "The Emergence of the Autobiographical Figure in *The Prelude,* Book I," *Studies in Romanticism,* 20 (Spring 1981), 33-63.

Hartman, Geoffrey H. "The Poetics of Prophecy," Ch. 11 in *The Unremarkable Wordsworth,* pp. 163-181. Originally published in *High Romantic Argument: Essays For M.H. Abrams,* ed. Lawrence Lipking (1981), pp. 15-40.

Havens, Raymond Dexter. *The Mind of a Poet: A Study of Wordsworth's Thought.* Baltimore: Johns Hopkins, 1941.

Heffernan, James A.W. "The Presence of the Absent Mother in Wordsworth's *Prelude,"* *Studies in Romanticism,* 27 (Summer 1988), 253-72.

Hertz, Neil. "The Notion of Blockage in the Literature of the Sublime," *Psychoanalysis And The Question of the Text: Selected Papers from the English Institute, 1976-1977.* Ed. Geoffrey H. Hartman. New Series, No. 2. Baltimore and London: The Johns Hopkins University Press, 1978. pp. 62-85. Reprinted in *The End of the Line,* pp. 40-60.

Keats, John. *Letters of John Keats,* ed. Robert Gittings. London: Oxford

University Press, 1970.

Kelley, Theresa M. "The Economics of the Heart: Wordsworth's Sublime and Beautiful," *Romanticism Past and Present*, 5 (1981), 15-32.

Kishel, Joseph F. "The 'Analogy Passage' from Wordsworth's Five-Book *Prelude*," *Studies in Romanticism*, 18 (Summer 1979), 271-85.

Lindenberger, Herbert. *On Wordsworth's Prelude*. Princeton, New Jersey: Princeton University Press, 1963.

Manning, Peter J. "Reading Wordsworth's Revisions: Othello and The Drowned Man," *Studies in Romanticism*, 22 (Spring 1983), 3-28.

Matlak, Richard E. "The Men in Wordsworth's Life," *The Wordsworth Circle*, 9 (Autumn 1978), 391-97.

McConnell, Frank D. *The Confessional Imagination: A Reading of Wordsworth's Prelude*. Baltimore and London: The John Hopkins University Press, 1974.

McGavran, James Holt, J. "The '*Creative* Soul' of *The Prelude* and the 'Sad Incompetence of Human Speech,'" *Studies in Romanticism*, 16 (Winter 1977), 35-49.

McGhee, Richard D. "'In The Countenance of All Science': The Lessons of *The Prelude*," *Bulletin of the Kansas Association of Teachers of English* (February 1972), 11-17.

Parrish, Stephen, ed. *The Prelude, 1798-1799*. The Cornell Wordsworth. Ithaca, New York: Cornell University Press, 1977.

Proffitt, Edward. "Book V in *The Prelude*: A Developmental Reading," *Romanticism Past and Present*, 8 (Winter 1984), 1-13.

Stelzig, Eugene L. "Presence, Absence, and the Difference: Wordsworth's Autobiographical Construction of the Romantic Ego," *The Wordsworth Circle*, 16 (Summer 1985), 142-45.

Stoddard, Eve Walsh. "Flashes of the Invisible World: Reading *The Prelude* in the Context of the Kantian Sublime," *The Wordsworthian Circle*, 16 (Winter 1985), 32-37.

_____. "The Spots of Time: Wordsworth's Semiology of the Self," *Romanticism Past and Present*, 9 (Summer 1985), 1-24.

"Waiting for the Palfreys: The Great *Prelude* Debate," in a special issue of *The Wordsworth Circle*, 17 (Winter 1986), 1-38.

Weiskel, Thomas. *The Romantic Sublime: Studies in the Structure and Psychology of Transference*. Baltimore and London: The Johns Hopkins University Press, 1976.

Wordsworth, Jonathan, Abrams, M.H., and Gill, Stephen, eds. *The Prelude, 1799, 1805, 1850*. New York: Norton, 1979.

## CHAPTER SIX:
## Desires Corrected, 1805-1809

Beer, John. "Nature and Liberty: The Linking of Unstable Concepts," *The Wordsworth Circle*, 14 (Autumn 1983), 201-13.

Christensen, Jerome. "'Thoughts That Do Often Lie Too Deep for Tears': Toward a Romantic Concept of Lyrical Drama," *The Wordsworth Circle*, 12 (Winter 1981), 52-64.

Freud, Sigmund. "Creative Writers and Day-Dreaming" (1908). Standard Edition, Vol. 9.

_____. "Leonardo da Vinci" (1910). Standard Edition, Vol. 11, pp. 59-137.

_____. *An Outline of Psycho-Analysis* (1940). Standard Edition, Vol. 23, pp. 141-207.

La Bossiére, Camille R. "'As a Body': Unity and Creed in Wordsworth's Epic Sequence of 1807-1811," *Interpretations: A Journal of Idea, Analysis, and Criticism*, 14 (Fall 1982), 25-32.

Pulos, C.E. "The Unity of Wordsworth's Immortality Ode," *Studies in Romanticism*, 13 (Summer 1974), 179-88.

Thomas, Gordon K. "Wordsworth's Iberian Sonnets: Turncoat's Creed?" *The Wordsworth Circle*, 13 (Winter 1982), 31-34.

Stelzig, Eugene L. "Coleridge in *The Prelude:* Wordsworth's Fiction of Alterity," *The Wordsworth Circle*, 18 (Winter 1987), 23-27.


## CHAPTER SEVEN:
## Blind Thoughts, 1802-1808

Betz, Paul F. *Benjamin The Waggoner*. The Cornell Wordsworth. Ithaca and London: Cornell University Press, 1981.

Comparetti, Alice Pattee, ed. *The White Doe of Rylstone, by William Wordsworth: A Critical Edition*. Ithaca: Cornell, 1940. Cornell Studies in English, No. 29.

Freud, Sigmund. "Dostoevsky and Parricide" (1928). Standard Edition, Vol. 21, pp. 175-96.

_____. "Dynamics of Transference" (1912). Standard Edition, Vol. 12.

_____. "The 'Uncanny'" (1919). Standard Edition, Vol. 17.

Gates, Barbara. "Wordsworth's Symbolic White Doe: The Power of History in the Mind," *Criticism*, 17 (Summer 1975), 234-245.

Heffernan, James A.W. *Wordsworth's Theory of Poetry: The Transforming Imagination*. Ithaca and London: Cornell University Press, 1969. Especially Chapter 6, "The Making of Emblems."

Rudy, John G.  "Structure and Unity in *The White Doe of Rylstone*," *Aeolian Harps: Essays In Literature In Honor of Maurice Browning Cramer*, ed. Donna G. Fricke and Douglas C. Fricke.  Bowling Green, Ohio: Bowling Green University Press, 1976.  pp. 133-48.

## CHAPTER EIGHT:
## Bound by Natural Piety, 1797-1814

Butler, James, ed.  *The Ruined Cottage and The Pedlar.*  The Cornell Wordsworth. Ithaca, New York: Cornell University Press, 1979.

Freud, Sigmund.  *The Future of An Illusion* (1927).  Standard Edition, Vol., 21, pp. 3-56.

Hazlitt, William.  "Observations on Mr. Wordsworth's Poem The Excursion," *The Complete Works of William Hazlitt*, ed. P.P. Howe.  Vol. 4.  London and Toronto: J.M. Dent and Sons, Ltd., 1930.

Johnston, Kenneth R.  "Wordsworth's Reckless Recluse:  The Solitary," *The Wordsworth Circle*, 9 (Spring 1978), 131-44.  Incorporated into *Wordsworth and The Recluse* (1984).

Kramer, Lawrence.  "Ocean and Vision:  Imaginative Dilemma in Wordsworth, Whitman, and Stevens," *Journal of English and Germanic Philology*, 79 (April 1980), 210-30.

Lyon, Judson Stanley.  *The Excursion: A Study.*  New Haven: Yale, 1950.  Yale Studies in English, Vol. 114.

Manning, Peter J.  "Wordsworth, Margaret, and The Pedlar," *Studies in Romanticism*, 154 (Spring 1976), 195-220.

McInerney, Peter F.  "Natural Wisdom in Wordsworth's *The Excursion*," *The Wordsworth Circle*, 9 (Spring 1978), 188-99.

Noyes, Russell.  "Why Read *The Excursion*?"  *The Wordsworth Circle*, 4 (Spring 1973), 139-51.

Parker, Reeve.  "'Finer Distance':  The Narrative Art of Wordsworth's 'The Wanderer,'" *Journal of English Literary History*, 39 (March 1972), 87-111.

Piper, H.W.  *The Active Universe: Pantheism and the Concept of the Imagination in The English Romantic Poets.*  London:  Athlone (University of London), 1962.

Smith, David Q.  "The Wanderer's Silence:  A Strange Reticence in Book IX of *The Excursion*," *The Wordsworth Circle*, 9 (Spring 1978), 162-72.

Stelzig, Eugene L. "Mutability, Ageing, and Permanence in Wordsworth's Later Poetry," *Studies in English Literature*, 19 (Autumn 1979), 623-44.

Thomas, Gordon K. "A Guide to Wordsworth's Guides," *The Wordsworth Circle*, 18 (Winter 1987), 28-32.
Worthington, Jane (later Smyser). *Wordsworth's Reading of Roman Prose*. New Haven: Yale, 1946. Yale Studies in English, Vol. 102.

## CHAPTER NINE:
## Worlds Not Realised, 1787-1814

Durrant, Geoffrey. "The Elegiac Poetry of *The Excursion*," *The Wordsworth Circle*, 9 (Spring 1978), 155-61.
Freud, Sigmund. "Analysis Terminable and Interminable" (1937). Standard Edition, Vol. 23, pp. 211-53.
_____. "Notes Upon a Case of Obsessional Neurosis [Rat Man]" (1909). Standard Edition, Vol. 10, pp. 153-249.
_____. "Notes on . . . A Case of Paranoia [The Case of Schreber]: (1911). Standard Edition, Vol. 12, pp. 9-82.
Howard, William. "Narrative Irony in *The Excursion*," *Studies in Romanticism*, 24 Winter 1985), 511-30.
Patterson, Charles I. "The Still Sad Music of Humanity in *The Excursion:* Wordsworth's Tragic View of Man," *Milton and The Romantics*, 4 1980), 32-41.

## CHAPTER TEN:
## Thanks to the Human Heart, 1814

Freud, Sigmund. *Interpretation of Dreams* (1900). Standard Edition, Vols. 4, 5.
_____. "Recommendations for Physicians Practising Psycho-Analysis" (1912). Standard Edition, Vol. 12.
Hay, Samuel H. "Wordsworth's Solitary: The Struggle with Despondency," *TheWordsworth Circle*, 14 (Autumn 1983), 243-45.
Patterson, Annabel. "Wordsworth's Georgic: Genre and Structure in *The Excursion*," *The Wordsworth Circle*, 9 (Spring 1978), 145-54.
Radcliffe, Evan. "'In Dreams Begins Responsibility': Wordsworth's Ruined Cottage Story," *Studies in Romanticism*, 23 (Spring 1984), 101-19.

## CHAPTER ELEVEN:
## High Instincts, 1816-1828

Batho, Edith.  *The Later Wordsworth*.  New York:  Russell & Russell, 1963.  Originally published 1933.

Erikson, Erik.  *Childhood and Society*.  2nd ed. rev.  New York:  W.W. Norton & Company, Inc., 1963.

Freud, Sigmund.  "The Resistances to Psycho-Analysis" (1924).  Standard Edition, Vol. 19, pp. 212-24.

————. "Why War?" (1933).  Standard Edition, Vol. 22, pp. 197-215.

George, Diana Hume.  *Blake and Freud*.  Ithaca and London:  Cornell University Press, 1980.

Hartman, Geoffrey H.  "Blessing the Torrent:  On Wordsworth's Later Syle,"  PMLA, 93 (March 1978), 196-204.  Reprinted as Ch. 6 in *The Unremarkable Wordsworth*, pp. 75-89.

————. "Words and Wounds," in *Medicine and Literature*, ed. Enid Rhodes Peschel. New York:  Neale Watson Academic Publications, Inc., 1980. pp. 178-88.

Klein, Melanie.  *Envy and Gratitude & Other Works, 1946-1963*. Delacorte Press/ Seymour Lawrence, 1975.

————. *Love, Guilt and Reparation & Other Works, 1921-1945*. Delacorte Press/ Seymour Lawrence, 1975.

Parsons, Talcott.  "The Father Symbol:  An Appraisal in the Light of Psychoanalytic and Sociological Theory," *Social Structure and Personality*. London:  The Free Press, Collier-Macmillan Ltd., 1964.

Roazen, Paul.  *Freud:  Political and Social Thought*. New York:  Alfred A. Knopf, 1970.

Spiegelman, Willard.  "Wordsworth's *Aeneid*," *Comparative Literature*, 26 (Spring 1974), 97-109.

Sulloway, Frank J.  *Freud, Biologist of the Mind: Beyond the Psychoanalytic Legend*. New York:  Basic Books, Inc., 1979.

## CHAPTER TWELVE:
## More Habitual Sway, 1814-1822

Freud, Sigmund.  *Moses and Monotheism* (1939).  Standard Edition, Vol. 23, pp. 3-137.

Gates, Barbar T.  "Wordsworth's Mirror of Morality:  Distortions of Church History," *The Wordsworth Circle*, 12 (Spring 1981), 129-32.

Hartman, Geoffrey H.  "Words, Wish, Worth," as Ch. 7 in *The Unremarkable*

*Wordsworth,* pp. 90-119. Originally published in *Deconstruction and Criticism,* by Harold Bloom, et al.

Jones, Ernest. *The Life and Work of Sigmund Freud.* Volume 3: *The Last Phase 1919-1939.* New York: Basic Books, Inc., 1957.

Larkin, Peter. "Wordsworth's 'After-Sojourn': Revision and Unself-Rivalry in the Later Poetry," *Studies in Romanticism,* 20 (Winter 1981), 409-36.

McGhee, Richard D. "'Conversant With Infinity': Form and Meaning in Wordsworth's 'Laodamia,'" *Studies in Philology,* 68 (July 1971), 357-69.

_____. "'And Earth and Stars Composed a Universal Heaven': A View of Wordsworth's Later Poetry," *Studies in English Literature,* 11 (Autumn 1971), 641-57.

Palumbo, Linda J. "The Later Wordsworth and the Romantic Ego: Bede and the Recreant Soul" *The Wordsworth Circle,* 17 (Summer 1986), 181-84.

Potts, Abbie Findlay. "Introduction," *The Ecclesiastical Sonnets of William Wordsworth: A Critical Edition.* Cornell Studies in English, No. 7. New Haven, Conn.: Yale University Press, 1922.

Tillich, Paul. *Systematic Theology.* Chicago, Ill.: The University of Chicago Press, 1967. Three Volumes in One. I (originally published 1951); II (originally published 1957).

Wilcox, Stewart C. "Wordsworth's River Duddon Sonnets," PMLA, 69 (March 1954), 131-41.

# CHAPTER THIRTEEN:
## A Sober Coloring, 1819-1931

Freud, Sigmund. "Constructions in Analysis" (1937). Standard Edition, Vol. 23, pp. 256-69.

Hartman, Geoffrey H. "The Morality of Style," *Yale Review,* 64 (March 1975), 418-22.

McGhee, Richard D. "Resistance and Revision in Wordsworth's *Prelude,*" *Literature and Psychology,* 32 (1986), 37-52.

# CHAPTER FOURTEEN:
## Father of the Man, 1832-1841

Hartman, Geoffrey H. "Wordsworth Revisited," Ch. 1 in *The Unremarkable*

*Wordsworth,* pp. 3-17.  Originally published as "Wordsworth,"  *The Yale Review,* 57 (Summer 1969).

Jarvis, Robin.  "Shades of Milton: Wordsworth at Vallombrosa,"  *Studies in Romanticism,* 25 (Winter 1986), 483-504.

Leyda, Seraphia D.  "Wordsworth's *Sonnets Upon the Punishment of Death,*" *The Wordsworth Circle,* 14 (Winter 1983), 48-52.

McFarland, Thomas.  "Wordsworth:  Prophet of the Past," *The Wordsworth Circle,* 14 (Autumn 1983), 251-55

Schliefer, Ronald.  "Wordsworth's Yarrow and the Poetics of Repetition," *Modern Language Quarterly,* 38 (December 1977), 348-66.

# INDEX

Moon/Moonlight, 21, 38, 42, 94, 128-9, 177-9, 296.
"Morning Exercise, A," 316, 319.
"Mourning and Melancholia," 105-6.
"Musings Near Aquapendente," 317, 319-21.

Napoleon, 126, 141-2, 146, 193, 231, 232, 239, 240, 242, 276, 303.
*National Independence and Liberty, Poems Dedicated To*, 126-8, 141-3.
*Night on Salisbury Plain, A*, 19, 20-25, 28, 66, 76, 149, 177-8, 181, 263, 327.
"Not Love, Not War," 255-256.
"November, 1813," 147.
"Nutting," 3-6, 65.

"Ode, Composed on May Morning," 253.
"Ode to Duty," 76, 78-80, 139-41, 143, 233, 237.
"Ode to Lycoris, May, 1817," 248-9, 252.
"Ode 1815 ('Imagination-ne'er before content')," 233, 238.
"Ode: Intimations of Immortality," 76, 80-83, 129-34, 144, 145, 162, 163, 168, 184, 312, 313.
Oedipal Project, The, 92, 114, 155-6, 168-9, 175, 203-4, 267, 323.
"On The Power of Sound," 227-29.

*Paradise Lost*, 205-7.
"Pass of Kirkstone, The," 224-5.
Parricide/Patricide, 17, 28-29, 31-32, 67, 97, 105, 107, 110, 113, 139, 155-6, 167-9, 179-80, 186, 235, 270, 294, 326-7.
*Pedlar, The*, 166-8, 212.
*Peter Bell*, 63-70, 72.
"Pillar of Trajan, The," 230-1.
*Postscript* (1835), 303-4, 306.
"Power of Music, The," 148-9.
"Prayer for My Daughter, A," (Yeats), 128.
Preface to the Edition of 1815, 14, 223, 231.
Preface to *Lyrical Ballads* (1800), 2-3, 55, 56, 119-21, 151.
*Prelude, The*, 8-10, 12, 13, 17, 26, 42, 46, 50, 52, 65, 85-110, 111-19, 123, 125, 129, 131, 137, 150-1, 158, 165, 178, 180, 209, 217-18, 226, 227, 263, 273-81, 293, 312, 219, 327.
"Presentiments," 312-14.
Primal Scene, 5, 28, 32, 85, 88, 179.
"Primrose of the Rock, The," 310-11.
"Processions," 260-2.
*Psychopathology of Everyday Life*, 64.

William Wordsworth at Age 74
by Henry Inman

*from* the Collection of Art,
The University of Pennsylvania
by permission